Preface

This workbook is a basic introduction to the main "Work Bench" functions CATIA V5 has to offer. The work benches covered in this workbook are Sketcher, Product Structure, Part Design, Drafting, Assembly Design, Generative Shape Design, DMU Navigator and Rendering.

This workbook is not meant to be a CATIA V5 reference guide. It is meant to be an organized, planned process to learn CATIA V5. The CATIA V5 Help Menu is a great reference and The CATIA Companion makes a good supplement to this workbook. The contents of this workbook are a combination of materials gathered and adapted from CATIA V4 basic training conducted by Metalcraft Technologies, Inc. for its engineering personnel. The material was adapted to CATIA V5 Release 1 for Southern Utah University during the spring semester 1999. The material has evolved from CATIA V5 Release 1 to Release 7 since that time. The workbook has continued to evolve with each CATIA V5 release. This manual was the first CATIA V5 classroom curriculum developed.

Workbook Revisions

The first edition of this workbook was developed on CATIA V5 Release 3 during the summer of 2000. The second edition of this workbook was developed on Release 5 in December of 2000.

This is the **Third Edition** of the CATIA V5 Workbook developed on CATIA V5 R6. Although this edition was developed on Release 6, the workbook can be used for Release 7. Release 7 has added additional work benches, tools and options to existing tools. The processes, steps and tools remain the same for this work book.

This release has incorporated many of the additional functions included in CATIA V5 Releases 6. Each lesson has been expanded to use additional tools. Lessons 1, 5 and 9 have been expanded the most. Lesson 10, the Rendering Work Bench, has been added.

Schroff Development Corporation and I are dedicated to keeping this workbook current and accurate to the latest CATIA V5 release level. For workbook updates, additional information and sample models log on to www.schroff1.com .

Acknowledgments

The concept of this book was derived from my attempt to create classroom curriculum for Southern Utah University's Basic CATIA V5 class. It was Stephen Schroff at Schroff Development Corporation that encouraged me to make it available to the CATIA V5 world.

I want to acknowledge Tracy Garrett for her excellent work in testing and checking the quality of the lessons, reviews and exercises. I want to acknowledge Brandon Griffiths for his contributions in developing the graphics for this workbook. For the long hours spent on this workbook, Thank You.

I also want to acknowledge and thank my good friend Virgil Seaman, Ph.D. at California State University, Los Angeles for contributing the material for Lesson 9 and 10. Daniel Ochoa, a student at CSULA designed the SuperMileage Assembly used in Lesson 9.

I want to thank my wife, for her support and suggestions. I also want to thank my four boys for putting up with me being gone so much while developing this workbook.

Download Site

****

To access and download workbook CATParts, CATProducts, CATdrawings, updates, additional information and sample models, as well as the model required for Lesson 9, log on to www.schroff1.com.

CATIA is a registered trademark of Dassault Systemes.

TABLE OF CONTENTS

Introduction To CATIA V5

Lesson 1   Sketcher Work Bench

Lesson 2   Part Design Work Bench

Lesson 3   Drafting Work Bench

Lesson 4   Drafting Work Bench

Lesson 5   Complex & Multiple Sketch Parts

Lesson 6   Assembly Design Work Bench

Lesson 7   Generative Shape Design Work Bench

Lesson 8   Generative Shape Design Work Bench

Lesson 9   DMU Navigator

Lesson 10   Rendering Work Bench

Terms And Definitions

NOTES:

Introduction To CATIA V5

CATIA is one of the worlds leading high-end CAD/CAM/CAE software packages. CATIA V5 takes the power of an industry and technology-leading legacy CAD/CAM/CAE program and updates the programming (a total rewrite) to take advantage of the new Windows technology. CATIA V5 programming also allows you the flexibility of using sketched and parametric based design. CATIA V5 is the power you expect from CATIA with a greatly reduced learning curve. CATIA V5 makes a lot of processes practically automatic. You, the user, define the variables and CATIA V5 creates it for you. If it isn't exactly what you wanted, you adjust your variables and CATIA V5 will update the creation. CATIA V5 functionality is growing with each release; it will be the program that does it all. It is the leading edge technology starting with its product concept, through design, assembly, testing, manufacturing and modeling, to its rendering capabilities. For more detail on CATIA V5, refer to the CATIA V5 Home page on the Internet. The address is: http://www.catia.com

Workbook Objectives

The objective of this workbook is to instruct anyone who wants to learn CATIA V5 through organized, graphically rich, step-by step instructions on the basic processes and tools CATIA V5 has to offer.

Although most of the steps are detailed for the beginner, the steps and processes are numbered and bolded so the more experienced user can go directly to the subject and/or area of interest.

All of the lessons follow the same format:

    a.) A basic **Introduction** to the work bench being covered.

    b.) A list of **Lesson Objectives**.

    c.) The Work Bench Tool Tar (icons) with the tool titles and a brief definition.

    d.) A brief introduction to what you are expected to create and learn while completing the lesson.

    e.) Step-by-step instruction on how to use the tools and to successfully create a part. There are **Note's**, **Hints** and **Comments** along with links to all of the graphics for visual explanations.

f.) A **Lesson Summary** brings everything you have learned together.

g.) The **Lesson Review** consists of 20 questions taken from the lesson. The purpose of the review is to help solidify the concepts and tools taught in the lesson.

h.) The last section of each lesson is the **Practice Exercises**. Being able to answer questions is one thing, being able to create it is another! The **Practice Exercises** are practice problems that require the use of the tools and processes covered in the lesson. Some of the **Practice Exercises** have helpful hints on how to create the part.

The workbook tells you what you are about to learn. The workbook then tells you and shows you (graphically) how and what you are supposed to accomplish. The workbook then follows up by giving you the opportunity to explain what you just learned with the **Lesson Review** questions. The workbook then gives you the opportunity to solidify your newfound knowledge by completing the **Practice Exercises**.

To get the most out of each lesson, it is suggested that you preview the entire lesson so you get an idea of what you are going to be learning. This preview will also give you an idea of what it will take to complete the lesson. Read through the **Lesson Review** questions before you begin, this way you can be searching for the answers as you go through the lesson. Preview the **Practice Exercises**, as you go through the lesson you can be looking for the tools and processes required to complete the **Practice Exercises**.

Overview of Workbook Lessons

Introduction,
CATIA Standard Menus and Tools

This section is critical, because it gives you the foundation to start building your CATIA V5 knowledge of general screen layout, standard tools and mouse functions.

Lesson 1,
Introduction To The Sketcher Work Bench

How to start CATIA V5; selecting work benches; brief explanation to the **Sketcher Work Bench** screen layout, tools and tool bars; customizing and setting standards; creating a new part; create sketcher geometry such as lines, arcs etc.; constraining the sketcher geometry; exiting sketcher; extruding a profile; saving the newly created file and exiting CATIA V5; **Lesson 1 Review** and **Lesson 1 Practice Exercises**.

Lesson 2,
Introduction To The Part Design Work Bench

Review of Lesson 1; pulling up an existing file; brief explanation to the **Part Design Work Bench** screen layout, tools and tool bars; customizing and setting standards; review extruding a profile; creating fillets, chamfers, holes and patterns, translating, rotating, symmetry, mirror, scaling; adding constraints; applying material to a solid; modifying constraints and properties; managing the **Specification Tree**; review saving and exiting CATIA V5; **Lesson 2 Review** and **Lesson 2 Practice Exercises**.

Lesson 3,
Introduction To The Drafting Work Bench, Creating Sheets & Views

Brief explanation to the **Drafting Work Bench** screen layout, tools and tool bars; creating sheets and views; creating sheet and view layouts using an existing **CATPart**; customizing default values; creating new sheets; creating detail views, section views and auxiliary views; saving the new drawing file; **Lesson 3 Review** and **Lesson 3 Practice Exercises**.

Lesson 4,
Introduction To The Drafting Work Bench, Creating Text & Dimensions

A continuation of Lesson 3; review screen layout, tools and tool bars; creating text and dimensions; creating and modifying text; creating and modifying leaders; creating borders; importing picture files; printing the drawing; **Lesson 4 Review** and **Lesson 4 Practice Exercises**.

Lesson 5,
Introduction To Creating Complex & Multiple Sketch Parts

Review the **Drafting** and **Part Design Work Bench** screen layout, tools and tool bars; brief explanation of multiple sketch and **Boolean Geometry**; explain the process of creating parts that require multiple sketches; creating parts that require **Boolean Geometry**; **Lesson 5 Review** and **Lesson 5 Practice Exercises**.

Lesson 6,
Introduction To The Assembly Design Work Bench, Creating An Assembly

Brief introduction to the **Assembly Design Work Bench** screen layout, tools and tool bars; opening the **Assembly Design Work Bench**; setting the standards; inserting components into the assembly; moving parts in the assembly; assembling parts; constraining the assembly; assembly analysis; **Lesson 6 Review** and **Lesson 6 Practice Exercises**.

Lesson 7,
Introduction To The Generative Shape Design Work Bench, Creating Wireframe & Surface Geometry

Brief introduction to the **Generative Shape Design Work Bench** screen layout, tools and tool screen layout, tools and tool bars; creating a local axis; creating points; creating lines; creating corners; creating surfaces; filleting surfaces; splitting/trimming surfaces; creating a solid from a surface; **Hide/Show** the wireframe; **Lesson 7 Review** and **Lesson 7 Practice Exercises**.

Lesson 8,
Introduction To The Generative Shape Design Work Bench, Creating Surfaces

A continuation of Lesson 7, using additional tools; creating surfaces using sweeps; joining surfaces; splitting surfaces, creating a surface offset, extruding a surface, closing a surface; creating a solid from a closed surface; **Hide/Show** a surface; **Lesson 8 Review** and **Lesson 8 Practice Exercises**.

Lesson 9,
Introduction To The DMU Navigator Work Bench, Using The Fly Mode

A brief introduction to the **DMU Navigator Work Bench**; screen layout; tools and tool screen layout, tools and tool bars; downloading the **SuperMileage.CATProduct**; navigating the assembly; inserting objects; **Lesson 9 Review** and **Lesson 9 Practice Exercises**.

Lesson 10
Introduction The Rendering Work Bench

A brief introduction to the **Rendering Work Bench**; **Rendering**ools and tool bars; loading models into the **Rendering Work Bench**; creating an **Environment**; defining a light; adding images to the walls; creating a **Camera** and a **Shooting; Lesson 10 Review** and **Lesson 10 Practice Exercises**

Workbook/CATIA V5 Terms and Definition

This is another critical section, because it adds to your CATIA V5 foundation of knowledge. This section will also help you navigate and understand the terms used in this workbook.

CATIA V5 Running On Windows NT

This book was developed with CATIA V5 running on **Microsoft Windows 2000**. CATIA V5 running on UNIX is almost identical. The biggest difference is UNIX will not have all of the **Windows NT** functionality. The **Windows NT** functionality gives the user the flexibility of having several options in completing almost any task. For example, you have the **Cut/Copy** and **Paste** tools in the **Windows NT** pull down menu, you have the quick keys that accomplish the same thing (**Ctrl c** and **Ctrl v**) or you could use the CATIA V5 **Cut** and **Paste** tool found in the CATIA V5 **Standard** tool bar. Another example is you have the choice to highlight an entity then select the tool to apply or you can reverse the choices and select the tool, then select the entity. Some of these options are not available on the UNIX operating system. This workbook assumes you have at minimum a basic knowledge of the different **Windows 2000/NT** functions.

CATIA V5 Standard Menus And Tools

The following graphic shows you where on the CATIA V5 standard screen layout the different tools and tool bars are located. The numbers coordinate with the following page where the tool label is bolded and underlined. The tool label is followed by a brief explanation and in some cases, steps on how to use and/or access the tool.

The following is not meant to be a comprehensive definition of every tool on the standard CATIA V5 screen. The purpose is a quick reference and explanation only. If more detailed information is needed and/or required, refer to the CATIA V5 **Help** menu and/or Internet homepage.

—— 6.1
—— 6.2
—— 6.3
—— 6.4
—— 6.5
—— 6.6
—— 6.7
—— 6.8
—— 6.9
—— 6.10
—— 6.11
—— 6.12

—— 7.1
—— 7.2
—— 7.3

—— 8.1
—— 8.2
—— 8.3
—— 8.4
—— 8.5
—— 8.6
—— 8.7
—— 8.8
—— 8.9
—— 8.10
—— 8.11

—— 10.1
—— 10.2
—— 10.3
—— 10.2
—— 10.3

—— 11.1
—— 11.2
—— 11.3

—— 12.1
—— 12.2

1   **The Start Menu**: The **Start** pull down menu gives you access to all of the CATIA V5 work benches. Lesson 1 explains how to select a specific work bench. This workbook only covers the **Sketcher**, **Part Design**, **Drafting**, **Assembly Design**, **Generative Shape Design** and **DMU Navigator Work Benches**.

2   **The Specification Tree**: The **Specification Tree** contains the history of tools and processes used to create a part. For example, you can look at a completed part and see that there were fillets and holes applied to it. At what point in the part creation were the fillets and holes added? Are there redundant processes and extra elements? Can the process for part creation be improved? Looking at the resultant part will not answer any of these questions. The **Specification Tree** on the other hand has all of this information. The **Specification Tree** contains the entire history of the part creation. For a complex part, the **Specification Tree** could get large. Select the **Tools**, **Options**, **General** and **Tree** option to specify what you want the **Specification Tree** to show and how you want it to appear. The branches of the **Specification Tree** can be expanded and contracted by selecting the – and + symbols located on each branch. You can **Zoom In** and **Pan** the **Specification Tree** the same way you would a part. You must double click on a **Specification Tree** branch to make the part go under intensified. Once the part is under intensified, all of the screen manipulation tools will apply to the **Specification Tree**. Double clicking a **Specification Tree** branch will bring the part back to normal. The [F3] key will hide the **Specification Tree** from view. CATIA V5 allows you to make modifications to the part by using the part its self and/or by using the **Specification Tree**. The **Specification Tree** is used in all nine lessons, but at a basic level. The **Specification Tree** is a very powerful tool, but you must know how to use it to your advantage. This brief explanation is not nearly enough information to fully appreciate its potential uses. For more detailed information, reference the **Help** menu.

3   **The Standard Windows NT Tool Bar**: This tool bar contains your standard **Windows NT** pull down menus. There are specific CATIA V5 tools found in the different pull down menus. The tools you will be required to use in this workbook will be defined in the lesson that they are used in.

4   <u>**The Active Work Bench Icon**</u>: The work bench icon shown in this location signifies which work bench is active. This is especially critical when you have several windows open with different work benches. If you have them displayed on a split screen, the active window will be the one with the blue border. This work bench icon can also be selected to bring up the "**Welcome To CATIA V5**" window. This window allows you to select a new work bench. The selected work bench icon will become the active work bench. Notice, as you select a different work bench, the tools and tool bars on the right side of the screen change with the work bench. Particular branches on the **Specification Tree** will also be added depending on what work bench you enter. For example, the **PartBody** branch is added when entering the **Part Design Work Bench** and the **Open_Body** branch is added when the **Generative Shape Design Work Bench** is entered.

5   <u>**The Part Select Tool Bar**</u>: Selecting this tool allows you to select entities in the workspace. The default selector is the **Select Arrow**, which allows single point and left click selections. If you select the small arrow to the right of the icon, it will reveal the other selection tools, they are:

   5.1   **Selection Trap**: This allows you to draw a box around the entities that you want to select. The box is exclusive to entities that intersect with the selection box. This is a quick and easy multi-select tool.

   5.2   **Intersecting Trap**: This allows you to draw a box around the entities, but will also select the entities that are intersected with the box. The selection box is inclusive.

   5.3   **Polygon Trap**: This selection is similar to the box selection trap, but allows you to sketch a more defined area of inclusion and exclusion of entities. This selection tool is quick, but allows you to be more exclusive in the multi-selection process.

   5.4   **Paint Stroke Selection**: This selection tool allows you to paint a line across the screen and any entity that the paint stroke crosses is selected.

6   <u>**The CATIA V5 Standard Tool Bar**</u>: This tool bar has twelve tools in it, some offer an alternative method of accomplishing a similar task found in the **Standard Windows NT** tool bar. Some tools are for more advanced users and will not be used in this workbook. The tools are listed below, with some definition, if it applies to this workbook.

   6.1   **New**: Creates a new file (document).

6.2 **Open**: Opens an existing file (document).

6.3 **Save**: Saves the active file (document).

6.4 **Quick Print**: Prints the active file (document).

6.5 **Cut**: Deletes the selected element and/or elements. This tool has the **Windows NT** functionality of select, drag and drop.

6.6 **Copy**: Another method of copying a selected element and/or elements. The tool places the copied element and/or elements onto the **Windows NT** clipboard.

6.7 **Paste**: Another method of pasting an element and/or elements from the **Windows NT** clip board.

6.8 **Undo**: The greatest OOPS tool developed since the invention of the computer! This tool allows you to step backwards one mistake (function) at a time!

6.9 **Redo**: Make that a double OOPS! This tool allows you to undo your undo! If your last operations weren't so bad and you don't remember all of the parameters you entered, this tool is for you.

7 **Knowledge Tool Bar**: This tool bar allows you to use formulas and spread sheets to parameterize your sketches, parts and assemblies.

7.1 **Formula**: This tool allows you to use a formulas to drive parameters.

7.2 **Design Table**: This tool allows you to use data from an existing spread sheet to drive assigned parameters within a design.

7.3 **Knowledge Inspector**: This tool allows you to preview a design change prior to committing to the change. This is an advanced tool.

8 **The View Tool Bar**: The **View** tool bar contains CATIA V5 specific functions. This workbook will have you use most of them in one lesson or another. Hopefully you will use the tool on your own once you learn how to use it. Most of the tools apply to all of the work benches.

8.1 **Sets the Fly mode**: This is a very powerful and fun tool. Reference Lesson 9 on how to use this tool.

8.2 **Fit All In**: This is similar to other graphics programs. This tool will show the extent of all the graphics currently on the screen. It is a quick way to see what elements are on the screen and where they are in relationship to one another.

8.3 **Pan**: This is similar to other graphics programs. It allows you to move the part around on the screen. The part does not change its location in the XYZ coordinate system, only in relationship to the screen. Every time you want to **Pan** the part you must select this tool first, unless you have a three-button mouse. **Quick Key**: With a three-button mouse you can press the middle mouse button down and drag the part to the desired location on the screen.

8.4 **Rotate**: This tool allows you to rotate the part in three-dimensional space and in real time. It will place a representation of a space ball (sphere) in the center of the screen. There is a three-dimensional X on the space ball, you drag the X to where you want on the space ball and the part will rotate accordingly. This tool is critical to part manipulation. It is important that you get the hang of rotating the part to the orientation you want. This tool must be selected every time you want to rotate the part. **Quick Key:** A quicker method is using the mouse. Press the middle mouse button first, while holding the middle button down, press the left mouse button and drag the mouse around on the sphere. This brings up the space ball (sphere). This process is explained and shown step-by-step in Lesson 2, Step 7.

8.5 **Zoom In**: This is similar to other graphics programs. This allows you to get a closer look at finer detail. **Quick Key**: Press the middle mouse button, hold it down as you press the left mouse button and release it. Now drag the mouse up the screen and the part will **Zoom In**. Another method is to press the CTRL key while pressing the middle mouse button and dragging the mouse up the screen. Using the mouse to **Zoom In** is a much smoother zooming method; you have more control.

8.6 **Zoom Out**: This is similar to other graphics programs. This allows you to get the big picture, making the part smaller. **Quick Key**: Press the middle mouse button, hold it down as you press the left mouse button and release it. Now drag the mouse down the screen and the part will **Zoom Out**. Another method is to press the CTRL key while pressing the middle mouse button and dragging the mouse down the screen.

8.7 **Normal View**: This tool allows you to view a particular plane/surface in a true length view. You specify the plane/surface and CATIA V5 will rotate the plane/surface 90 degrees to your screen view. This will make the geometry on that plane/surface true length. This is a very useful tool. You could try to rotate a plane using the space ball so it is normal to your point of view, but you could only get it "close". This tool gets it "exact". This tool can also be used to flip the direction in which you view a sketch. If in any of the lessons you go into the **Sketcher Work Bench** and your view is from the wrong direction use this tool to flip your view 180 degrees. It will switch your point of view from looking down on a part, to looking up from the bottom.

8.8 **Quick View**: This tool icon has the arrow to the bottom right of it, as explained in tool bar 5. The tool options are all of the orthographic view options: **Iso, Front**, **Back, Left, Right, Top** and **Bottom**. You select one of the view options and CATIA V5 will automatically display your part in that view.

8.9 **View Mode**: This tool icon has the arrow to the bottom right of it, as explained in tool bar 5. There are six different options associated with this tool; they are listed below.

    8.9.1 **Wireframe (NHR)**: This shows the part as a wireframe, no solid, no shading. The (NHR) means "No Hidden Line Removal". With no hidden line removed, all edges of the part will be visible at all times. This can be confusing at times; you could lose track of what is the front side and what is the back side of a part.

    8.9.2 **Hidden Line Removal (HLR)**: This is similar to the **Wireframe (NHR)** in that there is no solid or shading representation. It is different in the fact that the lines that would be hidden or not visible are not shown. This way you cannot confuse the back edges of the part with the front, only the front would be visible.

    8.9.3 **Dynamic Hidden Line Removal**: This is very similar to the **Hidden Line Removal** tool except as you rotate the part, the hidden line removal is real time, where as the **Hidden Line Removal** tool will only update the hidden line removal after the rotating process is complete.

    8.9.4 **Shading (SHD)**: This tool shows the solid shaded without any edge line representation.

8.9.5　**Shading With Edges**: This tool allows you to control how your part is going to be represented, how it looks on the screen. This tool shows the solid shaded and with the edge line representation. The majority of the graphics in this workbook are represented in this format.

8.9.6　**Applies customized view parameters**: This tool will bring up a "**Custom View Mode**" window that gives you many different parameters to choose from. If you apply material to your solid you will not see the material represented unless you select the material option in the "**Custom View Mode**" window.

8.10　**Hide/Show**: This tool allows you to select any entity or multiple entities and place them in "no show space". This removes the selected entity/entities from the "working space". Sometimes there are entities that you want to keep for future references but do not want them visually in the way. You can pull the entities back into the "working space" when you are ready for them.

8.11　**Swap visible space**: This tool works hand in hand with the **Hide/Show** tool. Selecting this tool will take you out of the "working space" window and into the "no show space". To pull an element from the "no show space" you would select the **Swap Visible** tool icon. This would show the "no show space". You could select the entity you want back in the "working space", and then select the **Hide/Show** tool icon. This would take the entity back to the "working space". You would then need to select the **Swap Visible** tool icon to get back to the "working space". This can be confusing; try bringing a part back and forth until you get control of the two tools.

9　**The Apply Material Tool Bar**: This tool allows you to apply a material to your solid. Applying a material will give it the properties of the material such as the density so CATIA V5 can calculate weight, volume and other part analysis information. Applying material also gives the solid the texture and color of the selected material. CATIA V5 has a library of material. The use of this tool is covered in Lesson 2. Remember, to see the material applied to the solid, you must select **Apply Material** in the **Applies Customized View Parameters** (tool 7.10.6)

10 **The Tools Tool Bar**: This tool bar changes depending on what work bench you are in. The three tools that are consistently in this tool bar are listed below.

    10.1 **Update All**: This tool will be under intensified unless there is an entity in the file that requires updating. If the tool is colored (not under intensified) it is signifying that some entity requires updating. Selecting the tool will update all of the entities. This tool is used most when revisions/changes are made to existing constraints whether it is part design changes and/or assembly changes. If you make a change and the part/assembly does not reflect the change, check this tool, it may require you to select it to force an update.

    10.2 **Axis System**: This tool allows you to create multiple local axis systems. Lesson 7 gives detailed instructions on how to create and orient new axis systems.

    10.3 **Mean Dimension**: This tool only works if you have previously defined a tolerance to the entity. When tolerances have been applied this tool will compute the actual dimension of the entity being reviewed.

    10.4 **Create Datum**: This tool deactivates the history mode. The entities used to create it will not be linked. The tool, is a toggle tool, if you select it you must unselect it to turn it off.

    10.5 **Open catalog**: This tool allows access to the user-defined catalog. Reference the **Help** menu for detailed instruction and application.

11 **The Measure Tool Bar**: There are three analysis type tools; they are listed below.

    11.1 **Measure Between**: This tool allows you to measure the distance between two different entities. You can measure the distance between surfaces, planes, lines, points etc. Select the **Measure Between** tool and then the two entities. This will bring up the **Measure Between** window. This window has more information than most designers would want. In most cases, the dimension created between the two selected entities is enough information.

    11.2 **Measure**: This tool is very similar to the **Measure Between** tool except that it measures the length of an individual entity. Select the **Measure Item** tool and then select the item to be measured. This will bring up the **Measure Item** window. As in 10.1, in most cases, the dimension created on the selected entity is all that is needed.

11.3 **Measure Inertia**: This measures the physical attributes of the selected solid such as volume, mass, centroid, etc. Reference Lesson 6 on how this tool is used.

12 **The Analysis Tool Bar**: This is another tool bar that is dependant on the active work bench. 11.1 and 11.2 are the most common tools.

12.1 **Draft Analysis**: This tool allows you to analyze draft angles and distances. This tool is particularly helpful when the angles and distances are tool small to visually inspect.

12.2 **Curvature Analysis**: This tool allows you to analyze the curvature of surface. This is particularly helpful when you have a max and min curvature radius.

13 **The Compass Tool**: This allows you modify the location and orientation of a part relative to the **XYZ** coordinates and/or relative to the other parts if they are in an assembly. The application of this tool is described in Lessons 2 and 6.

14 **The Current Work Bench Tools**: This side bar will be filled with tool bars and tools associated with the current work bench. As you select a different work bench you will notice the tool bars and tools will change. Each lesson covers the specific tools and tool bars found in the work bench being covered by that lesson.

15 **The Prompt Zone**: This is a very helpful area. When CATIA V5 is waiting on input from you, the user, there are usually some helpful prompts found in this area. It will let you know what type of entity it is looking for. In this workbook the prompts are bolded.

16 **The Power Input Mode**: This input window is for more advanced uses. You will notice as you select a tool, the tool command will appear in this window. In advanced uses, this window can be used similarly to quick keys and scripting. For detailed information, reference the**Help** menu. This tool is not used in this workbook.

17 **CATIA User Interface Style**: This states the current CATIA Style (P1 or P2). You can change this by going to **Tools**, **Options**, selecting **General** option in the box on the left and then the **General** tab in box on the right. For more detailed information, reference the CATIA V5 Help menu.

18 **Arrows:** When the work bench tool bars show these arrows at the bottom or end of the tool bar, it signifies there are additional tools belonging to that particular work bench. Selecting the bottom tool bar and dragging it up on the screen can access the additional tools. The tool bars can be tore off and placed anywhere on the screen. Lesson 2 covers this process in detail. If you are looking for a tool that is supposed to belong to a particular work bench, it's probably there, just not yet placed in view.

19 **Additional Tools**: The additional tools are not shown in this Introduction. There are other tools that appear depending on the current work bench. The **Drafting Work Bench** and the **Sketcher Work Bench** are the only work benches that have tools that are not shown in this section, but are used in this workbook.

19.1 **Sketcher Grid**: This is for two-dimensional geometry creation. The **Sketcher Grid** tool is a toggle tool, you turn it on and off by selecting it.

19.2 **Snap To Point**: This tool is also a toggle tool. Its function is obvious; it turns the snap on and off.

19.3 **Show Constraint**: This is another toggle tool. It allows you to show or not to show the constraints.

19.4 **Create Detected Constraint**: This is another toggle tool. It allows CATIA V5 to create a constraint automatically if it is detected.

19.5 **Construction/Standard Elements**: Construction elements are for construction only, similar to being reference only. Construction elements are dashed and under intensified elements. They are created in the **Sketcher Work Bench** and are not carried over into the **Part Design Work Bench**. They can be selected and switched from standard elements to construction elements and visa versa.

19.6 **Geometrical Constraints**: This is a toggle tool that turns the **Geometrical Constraints** tool on and off. Examples of **Geometrical Constraints** are; parallelism, perpendicular and cylindrical. This tool is more for information and conformation.

19.7 **Dimensional Constraints**: This is another toggle tool. **Dimensional Constraints** are actual measurable constraints, anything that is controlled by a dimension. This tool is critical in creating a parametric sketch.

NOTES:

Introduction To The Sketcher Work Bench

This lesson will take you through each step in creating a simple sketch and ending with a part that will be referred to as the "**L Shaped Extrusion**". Later in this lesson you will be asked to save this part (file) as the "**L Shaped Extrusion.CATPart**". The completed "**L Shaped Extrusion**" is illustrated in Figure 1.1. In some cases, optional processes will be explained. Referenced illustrations will be used to help explain certain processes and to compare results. It is important that you complete and understand every step in this lesson; otherwise, you will have difficulties in future lessons where much of the basic instruction will not be covered (it will be assumed that you know it). The concepts taught in these steps will give you the tools to navigate through the basics of the **Sketcher Work Bench**. Following the step-by-step instructions, there are twenty questions to help you review the major concepts covered in this lesson. There are practice exercises at the end of this lesson. The practice exercises will help you strengthen and test your newfound CATIA V5 knowledge. This lesson covers the most commonly used tools in the **Sketcher Work Bench**. The less common and/or advanced tools will be covered in later lessons and/or in the Advanced Workbook. It is not the intent of this book to be a comprehensive reference manual, but provide basic instructions for the most common tools and functions in CATIA V5. CATIA V5 in the **Windows NT** environment allows multiple methods of accomplishing the same task. You are encouraged to explore all of the different options.

Figure 1.1

Lesson 1 Objectives

This Lesson will show you how to do the following:

- Start CATIA V5
- Select a working plane
- Enter the **Sketcher Work Bench**
- Customize the **Sketcher Work Bench**
- Create a sketch using the standard sketch tools
- Apply **Constraints** to the sketch
- Modify existing **Constraints**
- Exit the **Sketcher Work Bench**
- Create a **Pad** in the **Part Design Work Bench**
- **Save** the newly create file
- **Exit** CATIA V5

Sketcher Work Bench Tool Bars

There are four standard tool bars found in the **Sketcher Work Bench**. The four tool bars are shown below. The individual tools found in each of the four tool bars are labeled to the right of the tool icon.

Some tools have an arrow located at the bottom right of the tool icon. The arrow ▼ is an indication that there is more than one variation of that particular type of tool. The tools that have more than one option are listed to the right of the default tool. To display the other tool options (as shown in Figure 1.2) you must select and hold the left mouse button on the arrow. This will display the optional tools window. Move your mouse to the desired tool and release the mouse button. The desired tool now becomes the default tool, shown on the tool bar. All you have to do to select the new default tool is to double click on it. Selecting the bar as shown in Figure 1.2 also allows you to tear off the tool bar and relocate it anywhere else on the screen. This is done by holding the right mouse button down, dragging it to the desired location and releasing the mouse button. Relocating the bar will display the name of the tool bar as shown in Figure 1.3. If you use several of the tools on one particular tool bar more than others you might want to expand and relocate the tool bar so you don't have to select through the different tool icons every time.

Figure 1.2

select arrow to expand tool options

select bar to relocate bar

additional tools

Figure 1.3

The **Operation** Tool Bar

Tool Bar	Tool Name (default)	Tool Type Options

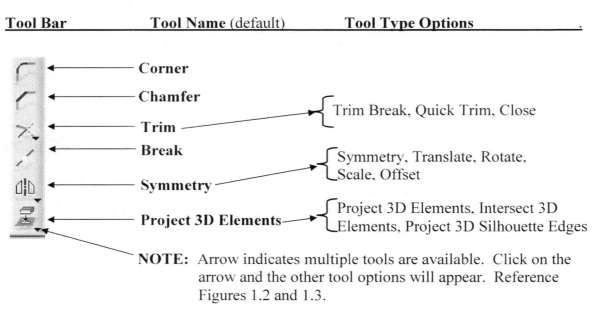

Corner

Chamfer

Trim ——— { Trim Break, Quick Trim, Close

Break

Symmetry ——— { Symmetry, Translate, Rotate, Scale, Offset

Project 3D Elements ——— { Project 3D Elements, Intersect 3D Elements, Project 3D Silhouette Edges

NOTE: Arrow indicates multiple tools are available. Click on the arrow and the other tool options will appear. Reference Figures 1.2 and 1.3.

Tools covered in this lesson: **Corner**, **Chamfer**, **Trim** and **Break**.

The **Profile** Tool Bar

Tool Bar	Tool Name (default)	Tool Type Options

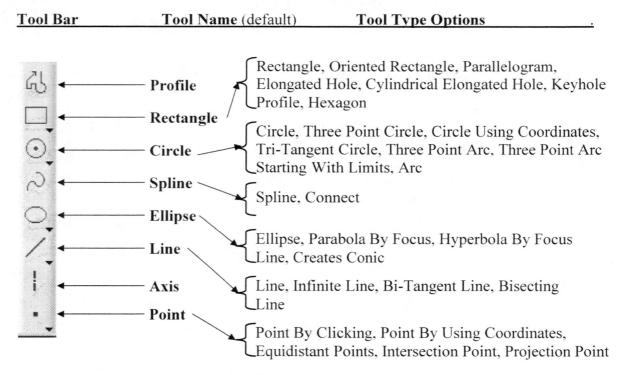

Profile ——— { Rectangle, Oriented Rectangle, Parallelogram, Elongated Hole, Cylindrical Elongated Hole, Keyhole Profile, Hexagon

Rectangle

Circle ——— { Circle, Three Point Circle, Circle Using Coordinates, Tri-Tangent Circle, Three Point Arc, Three Point Arc Starting With Limits, Arc

Spline ——— { Spline, Connect

Ellipse ——— { Ellipse, Parabola By Focus, Hyperbola By Focus Line, Creates Conic

Line

Axis ——— { Line, Infinite Line, Bi-Tangent Line, Bisecting Line

Point ——— { Point By Clicking, Point By Using Coordinates, Equidistant Points, Intersection Point, Projection Point

Tools covered in this lesson: **Profile**, **Rectangle**, **Circle**, **Line** and **Point**.

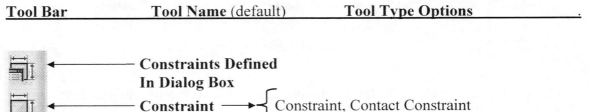

The **Constraints** Tool Bar

Tool Bar	Tool Name (default)	Tool Type Options

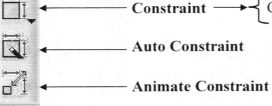

Constraints Defined In Dialog Box

Constraint ⟶ Constraint, Contact Constraint

Auto Constraint

Animate Constraint

All of the constraint tools are covered in this lesson.

The **Sketcher Tool** Tool Bar

Tool Bar	Tool Name (default)	Tool Type Options

Snap To Point

Construction/Standard Element

Geometrical Constraints

Dimensional Constraints

This tool bar only appears when you are in the **Sketcher Work Bench**. The four tools found in this tool bar are toggle tools (when they are highlighted, they are on). The **Construction** tool is for the creation of elements required to build the profile but will not be extruded into a solid. **Construction Elements** are **Sketcher Work Bench** elements only.

This particular tool bar changes depending on what other **Sketcher Work Bench** tool is currently selected. For example, if you select the **Rectangle** tool from the **Profile** tool bar you will notice the **Tools** tool bar will change to what is shown in Figure 1.4. The tool bar allows you to type in specific values for the element you are creating. Figure 1.4 is prompting for the **Horizontal** and **Vertical** location of the first corner of the **Rectangle**. Select some of the other **Profile** tools and observe what different options the **Tools** tool bar prompts you for.

Figure 1.4

The **Tools** tool bar with the **Rectangle** tool selected from the **Profile** tool bar

When you are in the **Sketcher Work Bench**, the first three tool bars (**Operation**, **Profile** and **Constraints**) are located by default on the right side of the screen. The fourth tool bar (the **Tools** tool bar) by default will appear in the upper left hand corner of the screen. The four tool bars contain too many tools to show all of them in one lesson. To view and have access to all of the tools, you can select the shaded tab located at the top of each tool bar and drag it anywhere on the screen. This is important, because when you get to Step 12, by the default setup, you will not be able to visually locate the **Operation** tool bar. You will have to select and drag the **Operation** tool bar from the bottom right side of the screen to the location you select.

CATIA V5 allows you an additional method of selecting all of the **Sketcher Work Bench** tools. To select the **Sketcher Work Bench** tools, select **Insert** from the **Standard NT Window** tool bar. **Insert** contains the three **Sketcher** tool bars. This method displays the names with the tools. Figure 1.5 shows the same selection as shown in Figure 1.2 using this method.

Figure 1.5

Steps To Creating A Simple Part Using The Sketcher Work Bench

You are now going to use the tools just introduced to you to create an "**L Shaped Extrusion**". The part is referred to as an "**L Shaped Extrusion**" because its profile or shape is similar to an upper case letter L. When you complete all of the steps in this lesson, the result should look similar to the part shown in Figure 1.1.

If you are not able to finish all of the steps in this lesson in one session, you can jump to Steps 23 & 24, which covers saving and exiting CATIA V5. This will allow you to save your work for your next session.

1 Start CATIA V5 CATIA V5R6

From the **NT Desktop**, double click on the **CATIA V5R5** icon. Be patient, it may take a few moments to bring up the CATIA V5 start logo and the actual CATIA V5 working window. CATIA V5 by default will start in **Product Structure Work Bench** as shown in Figure 1.6.

Figure 1.6   **Product Structure Work Bench**

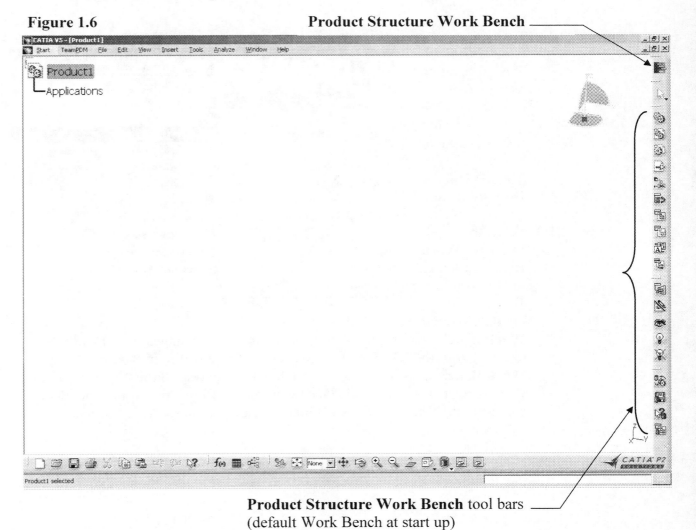

Product Structure Work Bench tool bars
(default Work Bench at start up)

2 Select The Sketcher Work Bench.

How your CATIA V5 screen looks at start up will depend on how it was setup and/or customized. This step will cover most of the options you could encounter. The CATIA V5 screen will appear as it does in Figure 1.6. The default work bench is the **Product Structure Work Bench**. For this lesson, you will need to select the **Sketcher Work Bench**.

There are two possible methods to selecting the **Sketcher Work Bench**.

2.1   The first method of selecting a work bench is using the **Start** menu located in the **Standard Windows** tool bar. If you have not previously set up your favorite work benches this step will only display the work benches under the CATIA V5 Functions. Step 2.3 explains how to create your favorite work benches.

    2.1.1   Select the **Start** tool in the top left side of the screen, reference Figure 1.7. This will bring up a pull down menu that includes all of the CATIA V5 Functions and their work benches, such as **Infrastructure**, **Mechanical Design**, **Shape** etc.

    2.1.2   Select the **Mechanical Design** function as shown in Figure 1.7. This will display all the work benches in the **Mechanical Design** function.

Figure 1.7

    2.1.3   Select the **Sketcher Work Bench** as shown in Figure 1.7. This will bring up the **Part Design Work Bench**. Notice that the **Specification Tree** changes from **Product1** to **Part1** with the **XY**, **YZ** and **ZX Planes**. Once you're in the **Part Design Work Bench** all you have to do is define the working **Plane**; the plane you want to create the sketch on. Once you select a **Plane**, the work bench will change to the **Sketcher Work Bench**. Selecting the working **Plane** is explained in Step 3.

    2.1.4   To start creating the "**L Shaped Extrusion**", continue to Step 3. To learn the other methods of selecting work benches continue to Step 2.2.

2.2   The work benches that appear in the **Welcome To CATIA V5** window depend on how CATIA V5 was installed. To find out which work benches were added to the **Welcome To CATIA V5** window complete the following steps.

2.2.1   Select the **Product Structure Work Bench** in the top right of your screen, reference Figure 1.9. Selecting the current work bench will activate the **Welcome To CATIA V5** window.

2.2.2   If there are no work benches displayed in the **Welcome To CAITA V5** window then nothing was added at installation. Figure 1.9 shows three work benches. Step 2.3 shows you how to customize this window.

2.3   To add your favorite work benches to the **Welcome To CATIA V5** window complete the following steps.

2.3.1   From **Standard Windows** tool bar select **Tools**.

2.3.2   Select **Customize**. This brings up the **Customize** window as shown in Figure 1.8.

Figure 1.8

2.3.3   Select the **Start Menu** tab. This brings up two boxes. The first box is labeled **Available**. It contains all of the work benches that are licensed to the computer. The second box is labeled **Favorites**. This is the box where you will place the work benches you want to use most often.

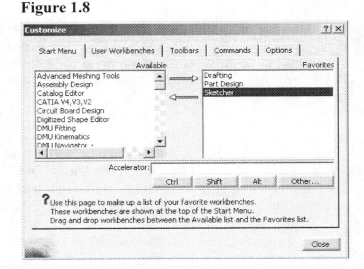

2.3.4   From the **Available** box select the **Sketcher, Part Design** and **Drafting Work Benches.** Use the **Windows** multi-select by holding down the **Ctrl** key.

2.3.1   Select the arrow pointing to the **Favorite** box. This will place the selected work benches in the **Favorite** box.

2.3.2   You can create an **Accelerator** (quick key) by selecting the
particular work bench and typing in the chosen **Accelerator** keys in
the **Accelerator** box. The keys must be separated by the "+" key.
For this step, create an **Accelerator** key for the **Sketcher Work
Bench** by completing the following steps.

2.3.2.1   Highlight the work bench in the **Favorites** box that you are
going to create the **Accelerator** key for.

2.3.2.2   With the correct work bench highlighted, place the cursor
in the **Accelerator** box.

2.3.2.3   Select the Ctrl key.

2.3.2.4   Type in the character "+" with no spaces between the Ctrl.

2.3.2.5   Type in the small letter "**k**", again with no spaces between
the characters.

2.3.2.6   Hit Enter. The **Accelerator** key is now created.

If you attempt to use **Accelerator** keys already assigned, a pop-up
window will warn you that it has already been assigned to a
particular function. This step has given you one more method of
selecting the **Sketcher Work Bench**.

2.3.3   Select the **Close** button. The **Customize** window will disappear.

2.3.4   Select the current work bench as shown in Figure 1.9. This will
bring up the **Welcome To CATIA V5** window. This time the
Sketcher, Part Design and **Drafting Work Benches** will be in the
Welcome To CATIA V5 window as shown in Figure 1.9.

2.3.5   You can also select the **Start** tool as shown in Step 2.1.1 and Figure
1.7. This time the three work benches added to the **Welcome To
CATIA V5** window will appear in the **CATIA Functions**. The
work benches can be selected from this menu also.

2.4   Select the **Sketcher Work Bench** from the **Start** tool bar or the **Welcome To
CATIA V5** window. This will bring up the **Part Design Work Bench** and all
of the **Part Design** tools. The reason it brings up the **Part Design Work
Bench** instead of going directly into the **Sketcher Work Bench** is that you the
user must specify the working plane before entering the **Sketcher Work
Bench**. The **Sketcher Work Bench** is a tool used to create two-dimensional
profiles for use in the **Part Design Work Bench**. You could think of the
Sketcher Work Bench as a required step to using the **Part Design Work**

Bench. Step 3 will show you how to define the working plane and how to actually enter the **Sketcher Work Bench**.

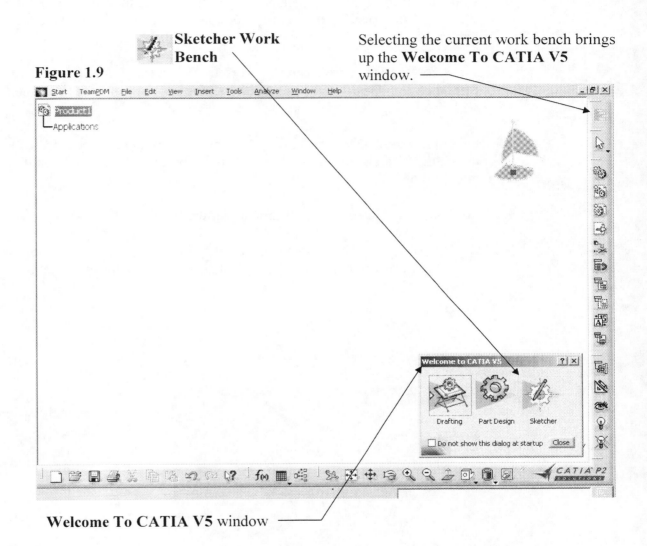

Sketcher Work Bench

Selecting the current work bench brings up the **Welcome To CATIA V5** window.

Figure 1.9

Welcome To CATIA V5 window

3   Specify A Working Plane

The next step is to create a two-dimensional profile of the part. The **Sketcher Work Bench** is a two-dimensional (planar) work area. To use the **Sketcher Work Bench** you must specify which **Plane** the profile is to be created on. Specifying the **Plane** can be done several different ways.

3.1 Select (highlight) the desired **Plane** from the graphical representation in the center of the screen as shown in Figure 1.10. Notice, as a particular **Plane** is selected, the equivalent **Plane** in the **Specification Tree** is highlighted. If the **Specification Tree** isn't showing the branches with the **Plane** it will need to be expanded. To do this, select the **Plus** symbol ✤ to the left of the **Specification Tree** or double click on the branch you want expanded.

3.2 The step described above can be reversed. Select the **Plane** in the **Specification Tree** and the coordinating plane in the center of the screen will also be highlighted.

3.3 Other planes, surfaces and/or other planner objects can also be selected to define the **Sketcher Plane**. This option will be covered in more detail later in the book.

3.4 For this lesson select the **ZX Plane** as shown in Figure 1.10.

NOTE: The background color may vary from figure to figure. The lessons do not require you make the changes. The variation is for presentation only.

Figure 1.10

ZX plane

Specification Tree

4 Entering the Sketcher Work Bench

Once a **Plane** is selected the screen will animate rotating until the selected **Plane** is parallel to the computer screen (perpendicular to you, true size). The default grid will also appear. You are now officially in the **Sketcher Work Bench**, but before you create the planar profile of the "**L Shaped Extrusion**" you need to customize the grid.

5 Customizing The Grid

Figure 1.11   select

Tools   Window   Help

$f(x)$ Formula...

Image

Macro

Parent/Children...

Customize...

Visualization Filters...

Options...

Search Order...

Conferencing

5.1   Go to the top tool bar in the pull down menu and click on **Tools**, **Options** as shown in Figure 1.11. This brings up the **Options** window as shown in Figure 1.12. For Steps 5.1 through 5.6, reference Figure 1.12.

5.2   Select the **Mechanical Design** branch to expand it if it is not already expanded.

5.3   Select the **Sketcher** branch under the **Mechanical Design** branch.

5.4   The **Sketcher** tab is the only tab available; therefore, you are not required to select a tab. It will be important for you to remember where these selections are located, as you may want to customize your set up in later lessons.

5.5   The first section under the **Sketcher** tab is the **Grid** section. The first option in the **Grid** section is **Display**. For this particular exercise check the **Display** option, this will display the grid when in the **Sketcher Work Bench**. The **Tools** tool bar allows you to quickly toggle this tool on/off.

5.6   The second option in the **Grid** section is **Snap To Point** option. For this particular exercise check the **Snap To Point** option. You guessed it; this toggles the **Snap To Point** option to **ON**. The **Tools** tool bar allows you to quickly toggle this tool on/off.

5.7   The third option that you need to know about is **Primary Spacing**. The user can set the desired spacing. If the default measurement is in metric, the spacing will be in mm. To change this default reference Figure 1.13 and complete the following steps.

5.7.1   In the **Options** window and under the **General** branch select the **Parameters** branch.   To get the **Options** window select the **Tools**, **Options** as described in Step 5.1 above.

5.7.2   Select the **Units** tab. The **Options** window on the screen should now look similar to what is shown in Figure 1.13.

Figure 1.12   5.4   5.5   5.6   5.7   5.8

5.7.3   The **Units** box inside the **Options** window allows you to select any type of measurement CATIA V5 recognizes. The scroll bar to the far right of the box allows you to scroll through the many options. For this particular step select the **Length** option.

5.7.4 The **Length** option will appear at the bottom of the window as shown in Figure 1.13. Selecting the arrow at the far right will display all the different types of measurements of length that CATIA V5 allows you to work in. For this particular step select the **Inch (in)**.

5.7.5 Now go back to the **Sketcher** options by selecting the **Sketcher** branch under the **Mechanical Design** branch. Notice the **Primary Spacing** option is now showing in inches, reference Figure 1.12.

NOTE: If you select the **OK** button right after completing Step 5.7.4 you will have to re-select the **Tools**, **Options** tools to get back to the **Sketcher** options.

Figure 1.13

5.8   The fourth option you need to know about under the **Grid** section is **Graduations**. This option divides the **Primary Spacing** into divisions, defined by you. Reference Figure 1.12. As an example, if the **Primary Spacing** is 1" and the **Graduations** is 1 (division), the grid will remain in 1in grids. If the **Primary Spacing** is 1" and the **Graduations** is set to 2 (divisions), the grid will be a .5in grid. To change the **Primary Spacing** and the **Graduations**, select the value in the window and type in the new value. When entering the values for the **Primary Spacing**, it is not necessary to enter the measurement type. The lowest value allowed for **Graduations** is 1 (zero will not be accepted). For this exercise enter **1** for the **Primary Spacing** and enter **10** for the **Graduations**. Select the **OK** button to apply the **Primary Spacing** and the **Graduations** values. The **Primary Spacing** is represented in the **Sketcher Work Bench** with a solid line while the **Graduations** is a dotted line as shown in Figure 1.14. It is important to remember that the zoomed view on the screen will dictate how the **Primary Spacing** and **Graduations** are represented. If you are zoomed out the **Graduations** and **Primary Spacing** could look very similar to each other, not distinguishable. If you find yourself in this situation use the **Zoom** tool on the tool bar at the bottom of the screen (Figure 1.15). Continue to zoom in until the **Primary Spacing** and **Graduations** are distinguishable.

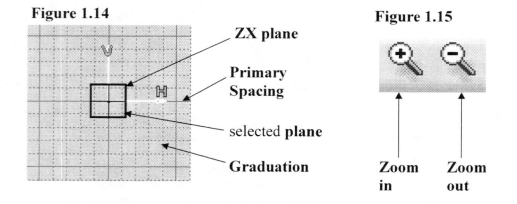

Figure 1.14

ZX plane

Primary Spacing

selected **plane**

Graduation

Figure 1.15

Zoom in   **Zoom out**

6   Creating Geometry Using The Profile Tools

You are now ready to create the profile (periphery) of the "**L Shaped Extrusion**". The first tool you will use from the **Profile** tool bar is the **Point by Clicking** tool ▪, covered in Step 7. The second tool is the **Line** tool ╱, covered in Steps 8, 9 and 10. The third tool is the **Profile** tool ⌂, covered in Step 11. On the **Tools** tool bar, at the bottom right of the screen, make sure the **Snap To Point** ▦ is **On**, the **Geometrical Constraints** ✺ is **On** and the **Dimensional Constraints** ⤵ is **On**. If the tools are highlighted in red they are on. The tools in the **Tools** tool bar can be toggled **On** and **Off** by selecting them. The **Tools** tool bar is shown in Figure 1.19. Now you are ready to create some sketch geometry!

7   The Starting Point ▪

The (0,0) point in the **Sketcher Work Bench** is the intersection of the **Horizontal (H)** and **Vertical (V)** axis. It can also be described as the intersection of the three planes (**XY**, **ZX** and **YZ**). Reference Figures 1.10, 1.14 and 1.17. The starting point for your profile will be (1,1). You should be able to locate the (1,1) location using the **Primary Spacing** and **Graduations**. To visually verify the location and to **Anchor** your first two lines to the (1,1) location, create a point at the (1,1) coordinate location. To create a point, complete the following steps.

7.1   Select the **Point By Clicking** icon found in the **Profile** tool bar on the right side of the screen. After selecting the **Point By Clicking** icon the mouse will be accompanied by a **Target Selector** ╬. This tool allows you to select and snap to a location on the screen. As Figure 1.16 shows, the target selector also gives you the current location of the **Target Selector**. CATIA V5 will prompt you (in the **Prompt Zone**) to "**Click To Create The Point**". Another way of specifying the location of the point is to type the location in the **Point Coordinates: H:** and **V:** boxes. The **H:** is for horizontal and **V:** is for vertical coordinates. Reference Figure 1.16. **Point By Clicking** allows you to create the point by selecting a location or by typing the **H** and **V** values.

Target Selector location (1,1) ——
Figure 1.16   Target Selector ——

point (0,0) ——

7.2   For this step, create the point at the 1,1 location. You could create the
      point by snapping to the location as shown in Figure 1.16, but for this
      particular step you need to create the point by typing the value in the
      Tools tool bar input window as shown in Figure 1.16. To type in the
      values complete the following.

      7.2.1   Type in **1in** for the **Horizontal** coordinate.

      7.2.2   Hit the $\boxed{\text{Tab}}$ key to move the cursor over to the **Vertical**
              coordinate.

      7.2.3   Enter **1in** for the **Vertical** coordinate.

      7.2.4   Hit the $\boxed{\text{Enter}}$ key to have CATIA V5 create the new point.

      This method will create constraints that will lock down the location of the
      point. Figure 1.18 shows what the **Constraint** looks like, similar to green
      dimensions, locating the newly created point. If you want to create points
      by coordinates only, select the "**Point By Using Coordinates**" tool,
      the second **Point** tool option. This will bring up the **Point Definition**
      widow as shown in Figure 1.17. Notice you are given the opportunity to
      create the point using a **Cartesian** coordinate or **Polar** coordinate system.

7.3   A **Point** (+) will appear at the (1,1) coordinate. It will remain highlighted
      until you make another selection. Notice a **Point.1** has been added to the
      Specification Tree, reference Figure 1.18. Remember, you may have to
      expand the **Specification Tree** to see all of the entities. **Point.1** is under
      the **Geometry** branch under the **Sketch.1** branch.

Figure 1.17

Figure 1.18

Dimensional Constraint Toggle (toggle on)

New point, "**Point.1**" (1,1)
Dimensional Constraints

8 Creating Line 1

Remember, the grid you set up is 1in **Primary Spacing** with 10 **Graduations**. This means the dotted lines represent .1 of an inch. Complete the following steps to create **Line.1**.

8.1 Select the **Line** tool from the **Profile** tool bar. The **Tools** tool bar will be modified to display the line variables; **Start Point**, **End Point**, **Length** and **Angle** as shown in Figure 1.19. You will be prompted to "**Select A Point Or Click To Locate The Start Point**". After selecting a **Start Point** you will be prompted to select an **End Point**. The mouse will be accompanied by a **Target Selector** and current the location same as when you created the point. Notice that the **Line** tool bar is similar to the **Point** tool bar.

Figure 1.19

8.2   The starting point for **Line.1** will be **Point.1** that was created in Step 7. Using your mouse, select **Point.1**. You will now be prompted to "**Select A Point Or Click To Locate The End Point**". The **Tools** tool bar window will also update to prompt for the **End Point**.

8.3   The end point for **Line.1** is (1,2). If you can use the grid to locate the correct location, do so. Move your **Target Selector** up one full grid line, but don't move it to the right or left (0 in the horizontal direction). Click on the grid line intersection (1,2). If you have any doubt where (1,2) is, type in the values using the **Tools** pop-up window. Type in **1** for the **H:** box and **2** for the **V:** box.

8.4   The first line is now created. **Line.1** should look similar to the one shown in Figure 1.21.

Figure 1.20

NOTE: Connecting one entity to another is safer and easier when the **Snap To Point** tool ▦ is on. When the **Snap To Point** tool is off you must be careful when connecting one entity to another. Both entities must share the same common point. For example, for two connected lines, the end point for the first line must be the same exact starting point for the second line. The lack of a shared point will make the entities unlinked. This broken link will cause problems when moving and/or modifying your profile. The entities will not move together. Another problem with a broken link is that it creates an unclosed profile. Unclosed profiles will be covered later in this lesson. CATIA V5 does supply a visual tool to help you know exactly when the point being selected is shared with another entity. The symbol is shown in Figure 1.20. The blue circle filled with a blue dot signifies the point being selected is the end point of another entity. This will link the two entities together. This is a helpful tool, especially when the **Snap To Grid** tool is off.

NOTE: The **Tools** tool bar gives you more options than the ones covered in Steps 8.1 thru 8.3. If you are typing in the information to create a line, you have the option of giving **Polar Coordinate** information, reference Figure 1.19. You enter a **Start Point**, **L:** (length of line) and **A:** (for angle). Though this lesson does not require you to use this option, it could be helpful in the future.

9   Creating Line 2

To create the second line, double click on the **Line** tool. Double clicking on the **Line** tool will allow you to create multiple lines without being required to repeatedly select the **Line** tool. With the **Line** tool double clicked, create **Line 2 [Start Point** (1,1), **End Point** (2,1)]. (Double clicking on the **Line** tool still requires you to select a **Start Point** and an **End Point** every time, but you will not have select the **Line** tool for every line.)

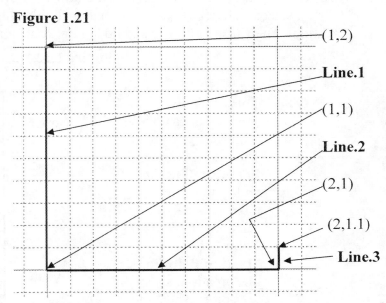

Figure 1.21

This will create the bottom horizontal line as shown in Figure 1.21.

10 Creating Line 3

To create the third line, just select your **Start Point** and **End Point** since the **Line** tool is still active. Create **Line 3 [Start Point** (2,1), **End Point** (2,1.1)]. Double click on the **End Point** of the last line you want to create, thus disengaging the **Line** tool.

> **NOTE:** If you make a mistake when creating one of the lines you can use the **Undo** tool. The **Undo** tool is located at the bottom of the screen. The **Undo** tool allows you to undo multiple steps. Another option for removing a mistake is deleting it. This can be done using the **Cut** tool also located at the bottom of the screen. Highlight the entity to be deleted then select the **Cut** tool.

11 Creating Line 4, 5, And 6 Using The Profile Tool

The 4th, 5th and 6th line will be created using the **Profile** tool. The **Profile** tool allows true successive line creation. The **End Point** for one line and the **Start Point** for the next line require only one selection. The connected lines will continue to be created with every point selected until you double click. Double clicking the **Ending Point** will end the **Profile** command. The lines created are separate entities, but the command that created them is recognized as one, so if you select the **Undo** command all of the lines created in one **Profile** operation will be undone.

With this tool added to your toolbox of knowledge, finish the "**L Shaped Extrusion**". Create **Lines 4**, **5** and **6** by selecting the following coordinates in succession: select (2,1.1), select (1.1, 1.1), select (1.1,2) and double click on (.6, 2) to end the line creation. The finished profile should similar to the one shown in Figure 1.22.

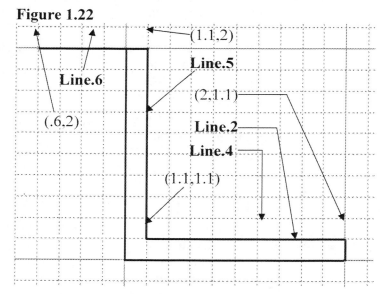

Figure 1.22

NOTE: This particular exercise does not require any features with radii, but the **Profile** tool has the ability to create them. Instead of selecting an **End Point** and a **Starting Point** for line creation, select the point (where the arc is to begin), hold down the left mouse button and drag it away from the starting point, then release the mouse button. You will notice as you drag the mouse button around, the arc radius and location change. Move the mouse around until you get the radius you want then select that point on the screen.

Steps 12 through 16 give instruction on how to use additional tools to modify the sketch entities you have created.

12 Breaking Line 6

Step 11 purposely instructed you to create **Line 6** longer than required. In this step you will learn how to **Break** a line. Step 14 will instruct you on how to trim **Line 6** back to **Line 1**. To break **Line 6** simply select the **Break** tool from the **Operation** tool bar. Select **Line 6** as shown in Figure 1.23. The line will highlight then select a location on the line where you want the line broken. For the purpose of this lesson select approximately three **Graduation** lines from the left end point (Figure 1.23). The line is now broken. The easiest way to verify this is to select the broken line; only one of the two line segments will highlight. You could also select the **Measure** tool found at the bottom of the screen (Figure 1.24). Select the **Measure** tool then select (apply to) the line you want to measure. This will tell you how long the selected (broken) line is.

Figure 1.23 (trimming **Line 6**)

Line.6

break here

Figure 1.24 (**Measure** tool)

13 Deleting The Broken Line

This is another easy step, but one that should be remembered. Select the left line fragment of the former line known as **Line 6**; it will highlight. Now select the **Cut** tool (scissors) located at the bottom left of the screen. The highlighted line will be deleted (Figure 1.25). You could also select the **Cut** command from the top pull down menu (under **Edit**) or hit the Delete key. This deleting (erase) process is similar in all windows functions and applies to any entity you want to delete (as long as it is selectable).

Figure 1.25

select here

14 Completing The Profile Using The Trim Tool

The profile of the "**L Shaped Extrusion**" is now complete, or is it? Extending **Line.6** past **Line.1** does not close the profile properly. If you were to exit **Sketcher Work Bench** at this point and try to extrude the profile you would get an error, because **Line.6** is over running **Line.1**. To fix this problem select the **Trim** tool and select **Line.6** on the right side of **Line.1**. Now select **Line.1**. **Line.6** is automatically trimmed to the second line selected. Reference Figure 1.26 for line selection and Figure 1.27 for final result after **Trim**.

Figure 1.26   **Figure 1.27** (**Line.6** after trim)

15 Modifying The Profile Using The Corner Tool

The **Corner** tool is located in the **Operations** tool bar. This tool modifies existing entities; in this case, it will put a specified radius in the place of a square corner. The following instructions take you through the process of creating **Corners** (fillets).

15.1 Select the **Corner** tool.

15.2 The command prompt at the bottom left hand of the screen will prompt you with the following: "**Select the first curve, or a common point**".

15.3 For this exercise select **Line.4**. Reference Figure 1.22.

15.4 The next command prompt will ask you to "**Select the second curve**".

15.5 For this exercise select **Line.5**. Reference Figure 1.22.

15.6 Now move your mouse around; the radius of the corner you just created will grow and shrink according to the location of your mouse. The command prompt will prompt you to "**Click to locate the corner**"; in other words, move the mouse until the radius of the **Corner** is where you want it and click.

15.7 You now have a radius for that **Corner**. Your part should now look similar to the part shown in Figure 1.28. If your radius dimension does not match the one shown below it is ok, it will be modified later.

Figure 1.28 (sketch with **Corner** added)

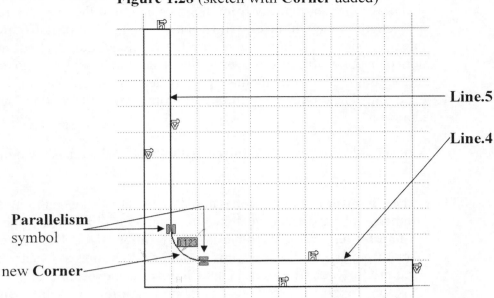

Parallelism symbol

new **Corner**

Line.5

Line.4

NOTE: The **Corner** will have a green dimension with a value attached to it. The value is the radius of the **Corner** you just created. Step 19 (modifying constraints) will supply us with the tools to make this radius exact. Lesson 2 will explain a method of creating a corner (radius) on a solid in the **Part Design Work Bench**.

16 Modifying The Profile Using The Chamfer Tool

The **Chamfer** tool is also located in the **Operations** tool bar. This procedure assumes you know what a **Chamfer** is. The steps required to create a **Chamfer** are almost identical to creating a **Corner**.

Figure 1.29

Line.6

Line.5

16.1   Select the **Chamfer** tool.

16.2   The command prompt at the bottom left hand of the screen will prompt you with the following: "**Select the first curve, or a common point**".

16.3   For this exercise select **Line.5**. Reference Figure 1.29.

16.4   The next command prompt will ask you to "**Select the second curve**".

16.5   For this exercise select **Line.6**. Reference Figure 1.29.

16.6 Now move your mouse around, the length of the **Chamfer** will grow as you move the mouse away from the intersection of the two selected lines. The length of the **Chamfer** will shrink as you move it back towards the intersection. If you move the mouse to the top left quadrant you will notice the **Chamfer** also moves to that quadrant. CATIA V5 gives you the option of all four quadrants. For this lesson use the bottom left quadrant. The command prompt will prompt you to "**Click to locate the chamfer**".

16.7 You should now have a **Chamfer** that looks like the one shown in Figure 1.29.

NOTE: The **Chamfer** has two green colored dimensions attached to it. Both dimensions have values attached to them. One dimension is the **Chamfer** length and the other is the **Chamfer** angle. Reference Step 19 (modifying constraints) on how to modify the values to exactly what you require for your **Chamfer**. This **Chamfer** is a two-dimensional entity. Lesson 2 explains a method of creating **Chamfer**s for solids using a **Part Design Work Bench**.

17 Anchoring The Profile Using The Anchor Tool ⚓

Select **Line.6**. As you select the line hold the mouse button down. Now drag the mouse up. Notice that the entire profile expands and contracts as you drag the mouse button around. **Lines 1** and **2** can be modified in length, but the location can't change. All of the other lines can be modified in position, length and angle. You cannot modify the location of **Lines 1** and **2** because they are linked to **Point.1** and **Point.1** is constrained to the location (1,1). The green dimension lines that were created with **Point.1** are constraints. It is the constraint values that tie **Point.1**, **Line.1** and **Line.2** to their current positions. To move the point and/or either line you have to modify the constraint. This will be covered in Step 19.

If there is a particular entity you don't want to move in relationship to another entity, you can constrain it. Constraints are restrictions on one entity to another entity. The **Anchor** tool restricts the entities movement in relationship to the coordinate location only. **Lines 1** and **2** are not truly anchored because the constraint has tied their relationship to **Point.1.** The effect is the same; **Lines 1** and **2** cannot be moved. If you want to constrain the location of an entity without constraining any other entity, the **Anchor** tool is a good option. For example, you may want to modify the "**L Shaped Extrusion**", but you know you don't want **Line.6** to move at all. You can restrict **Line.6** by **Anchoring** it. Elements can be **Anchored** by completing the following steps.

17.1 Select the entity that you want to **Anchor**. For this lesson select **Line 6**.

17.2 Select the **Constraints Defined In Dialog Box** tool . This will bring up the **Constraint Definition** window. Reference Figure 1.30.

17.3 The **Constraint Definition** window gives you a lot of options as far as selecting a constraint. For this lesson select the **Fix** constraint.

17.4 Select the **OK** button to apply the **Fix** constraint. Notice that **Line.6** will turn green, meaning that it is constrained, and the **Anchor** tool also shows up on the line. This signifies what kind of constraint is applied as shown in Figure 1.31.

Figure 1.30   select

Allowing quick modification to a sketch can be a powerful tool, especially in the beginning stages of a design. As the design nears completion, the ideas are being locked down and there are fewer variables. This is where CATIA V5 constraints come to the aid of the designer. As variables become known constants you can constrain them.

The purpose of this step was to give you a brief introduction to how CATIA V5 allows you to move and modify the sketched entities. It also introduced you to how to constrain the entities. The only way to fully understand all of the tools available to you is to test them yourself. Step 18 covers constraints in more detail.

Figure 1.31

18 Constraining The Profile

There are several reasons why you would want to constrain your profile. One reason is that you or any one else could accidentally select a line and move it out of position as you experienced in Step 17. **Constraints** help to keep the required relationships between the **Sketcher** entities that make up the profile. There are multiple ways of constraining a part in CATIA V5. The nice thing about CATIA V5 is that constraining is optional, not required. Hopefully, this step will convince you that **Constraints** can be a powerful tool.

18.1 **Constraint**

This tool allows you to create individual constraints one at time. You have already applied a **Constraint** and may not even know it. The **Anchor** tool in Step 17 is a **Constraint**. The values attached to the **Chamfer** and **Corner** are **Constraints**. To apply **Dimensional Constraints** complete the following steps.

18.1.1 Select the **Constraint** tool.

18.1.2 Select the line and/or **Sketcher** element to be constrained.

18.1.3 The **Sketcher** element will turn green (**Constraint** symbol) along with the appropriate dimension and box with the value in it.

18.1.4 To relocate the **Constraint** value, select the value box and drag the mouse to the desired location.

18.1.5 If the initial location of the **Constraint** is not satisfactory reselect the dimension and drag and drop it at a new location.

18.1.6 To edit the value of the **Constraint** double click on the value box. This will bring up the **Constraint Definition** window shown in Figure 1.32. This window shows the existing value for the **Sketcher** element. This value can be

Figure 1.32

edited by typing the new value over the existing value. Then select **OK** or hit the **Enter** key. The entity linked to the **Constraint** will automatically be updated to the new value.

If the **Constraint** is between two different entities, such as lines, select the first line and then the second line. CATIA V5 will constrain the distance between the two entities. The **Constraint** value will appear near the constraint. To move the **Constraint** value, follow Steps 18.1.4 and 18.1.5. For this lesson constrain your "**L Shaped Extrusion**" similar to the one shown in Figure 1.33.

Figure 1.33

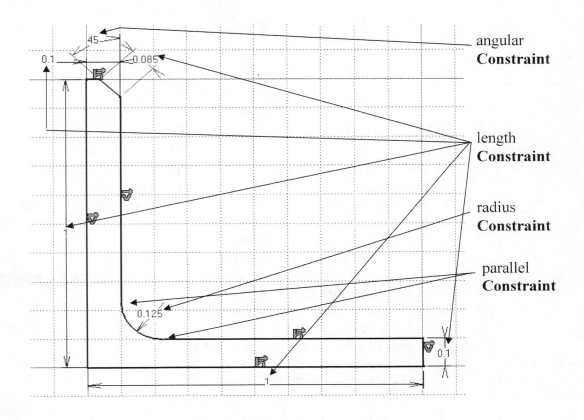

angular **Constraint**

length **Constraint**

radius **Constraint**

parallel **Constraint**

18.2 **Auto Constraining The Profile**

This method accomplishes the same task as the **Constraint** tool just explained except that **Auto Constrain** can be much quicker (automatic). Once you select the **Auto Constraint** tool CATIA V5 will bring up the **Auto Constraint** window prompting you to select which entities you want to constrain. Figure 1.34 shows what the **Auto Constraint** window looks like. You can select one entity at a time, multi-select or select only a few specific entities that you want constrained. After making your selection select **OK** located at the bottom of the **Auto Constraint** window. The entities selected will show up in green with the **Constraint** value box. Getting complete control of this tool will take some practice and patience. If you feel brave, use this tool to constrain your "**L Shaped Extrusion**" and see if you get the same results shown in Figure 1.33.

Figure 1.34

18.3   **Constraint Defined In Dialog Box**

To use this tool you have to select one or more entities and then select the **Constraint Definition In a Dialog Box** tool. This will bring up the **Constraint Definition** window as shown in Figure 1.35. The window will contain all the possible **Constraints**, but not all will be selectable. The only selectable **Constraints** are the ones that apply to the entities selected. For example, if you selected a line you could apply the **Length**, **Fix** and **Horizontality Constraints**; all of the other **Constraints** will be dimmed (meaning they are not selectable). CATIA V5 will not allow you to select the **Radius/Diameter** constraint because it does not apply to lines. Relationships between entities can also be established using this tool. For example, if you wanted **Parallelism** and **Horizontality Constraints** between the top profile line and the bottom profile line on the base leg of the "**L Shaped Extrusion**", you would do the following.

Figure 1.35

Constraint Definition	? X
☐ Distance	☐ Fix
☐ Length	☐ Coincidence
☐ Angle	☐ Concentricity
☐ Radius / Diameter	☐ Tangency
☐ Semimajor axis	☑ Parallelism
☐ Semiminor axis	☐ Perpendicularity
☐ Symmetry	☑ Horizontality
☐ Middle point	☐ Verticality
☐ Equidistant point	
	OK Cancel

18.3.1 Select both the bottom and top lines of the base leg of the "**L Shaped Extrusion**" (**Lines 2** and **4** shown in Figure 1.36). This is a windows multi-select task, which is accomplished by holding down the **CTRL** key while selecting both lines. Both lines will highlight.

18.3.2 Select the **Constraints Defined In Dialog Box** tool.

18.3.3 The **Constraint Definition** window will pop up as shown in Figure 1.35.

18.3.4 Select the **Parallelism** box and the **Horizontality** box.

18.3.5 Select **OK**.

NOTE: The **Constraints** that appear on the sketch are: the **Parallelism** and **Horizontality** symbols, reference Figure 1.36.

Figure 1.36

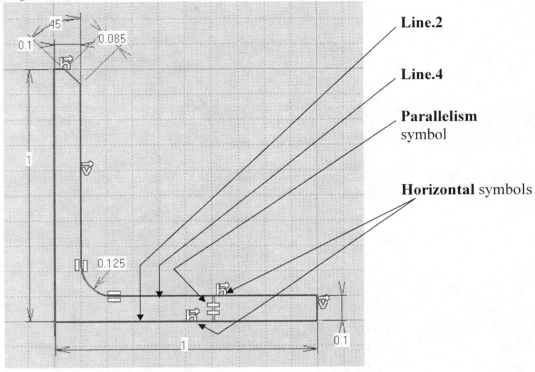

Line.2

Line.4

Parallelism symbol

Horizontal symbols

The only way to really get complete control of this tool is to use it, experience it and don't be afraid to make a few mistakes (that's why there is an **Undo** button).

18.4 Animate Constraint

The **Animate Constraint** tool allows you to visualize the effect one **Constraint** has on the entire profile. This is a very helpful tool, but be aware, you may not always end up with what you started with. Remember, entities will not always stay attached as other entity values change. CATIA V5 will remember the relationships the different entities have with each other, if they were created with a relationship. For example, just because the end point of one line is the same as the start point of another line it does not mean there is any relationship between the two lines. To use this tool follow the steps listed below.

18.4.1 Select one existing **Constraint**. Only one **Constraint** can be animated at a time.

18.4.2 Select the **Animate Constraint** tool.

18.4.3 The **Animate Constraint** window will pop up as shown in Figure 1.37.

18.4.4 Modify the parameters as desired/required and/or accept the default values.

18.4.5 Select the **Play** button. This will start the animation from the starting limit to the ending limit.

18.4.6 Watch the profile change as the selected entity animates from the first value to the last value. The **Animate Constraint** window has other options that you can test.

NOTE: If your profile has entities created without relationship to other entities, the **Rewind** button could result in a different profile than what you started with. Be careful.

Figure 1.37

Rewind button

Stop button   **Play** button

19 Modifying The Constraints

This process was previously described in Step 18. The ability to modify **Constraints** in CATIA V5 is essential, so the following steps are for your review.

19.1 Select the value box of the **Constraint** you want to modify. The value box is the green dimension line with an attached value.

19.2 The **Constraint Definition** window will pop up as shown in Figure 1.38. This window shows the existing value for the **Sketcher** element.

19.3 Edit the value by typing over the existing value.

19.4 Apply the new value by selecting the **OK** button or pushing the Enter key.

19.5 The entity linked to the **Constraint** will automatically be updated to the new value. Your profile also updates automatically.

Figure 1.38

If you want to know more information about a particular **Constraint**, double click on it and the **Constraint Definition** window will pop up. Select the **More** button to get detailed **Constraint** information. Figure 1.39 shows how the **Constraint Definition** window looks when the **More** button is selected. To get back to the default **Constraint Definition** window select the **Less** button.

Figure 1.39 (**Constraint Definition** window with the **More** button selected)

See what you can learn about one of the **Constraints** on the **"L Shaped Extrusion"**. Double click on the **Constraint** on the bottom line of the base leg. From the **Constraint Definition** window, select the **More** button. The pop-up window gives you information on other entities the selected **Constraint** is connected (linked) to. It also gives you the opportunity to change the name of the **Constraint** that shows up on the **Specification Tree**.

20 Over Constraining The Profile... Not A Good Thing!

It is possible to over constrain a profile in **Sketcher Work Bench**. When you over constrain the profile CATIA V5 will inform you that you have a problem. The CATIA V5 definition of over constraining is putting two different **Constraints** on one or more entities. The two **Constraints** can be correct individually, but collectively have conflicting values. When an over constrained condition exists CATIA V5 will turn all of the affected constraining values purple. **Purple is the default color for over constrained sketches!** Remember, an over **Constraint** condition is not a good thing. CATIA V5 will not allow you to extrude an over constrained profile. The easiest way to get out of the over constrained condition is to **Undo** or **Cut** the last **Constraint** created, the **Constraint** that caused the over constrained condition. You must reconsider which **Constraints** are necessary to accomplish what you want. In the case of the "**L Shaped Extrusion**" you are creating the **Constraints** that are used to maintain the specified dimensions. If your profile is not over constrained, you are ready to move on to the next step. If the instructions were followed an over constrained condition should not exist.

21 Exiting The Sketcher Work Bench

If your "**L Shaped Extrusion**" is similar to the one shown in Figure 1.33, you are ready to move the profile into the 3D world, the **Part Design Work Bench**. As a reminder, the following conditions will not allow you to successfully extrude your profile once out of the **Sketcher Work Bench**.

21.1 An unclosed profile as shown in Figure 1.40a. Notice the profile has a gap in it.

21.2 A profile with floating entities as shown in Figure 1.40b. Notice there is a line not attached to any other entity, it is floating.

21.3 Multiple profiles in one sketch as shown in Figure 1.40c. Notice both profiles are closed profiles, but there are two of them. CATIA V5 allows only one profile per sketch. Lesson 5 covers designs requiring multiple sketches.

21.4 An over constrained profile as shown in Figure 1.40d. Notice this example shows that one line is being dimensioned two different ways.

Figure 1.40 Profiles that cannot be extruded

a Unclosed Profile   **b** Floating Entities   **c** Multiple Profiles   **d** Over Constraint

You can exit the **Sketcher Work Bench** with your profile in any of the above conditions, but CATIA V5 will not extrude the profile into a three-dimensional (solid) part.

If you are ready to exit the **Sketcher Work Bench**, select the **Exit** tool . The **Exit** tool is located at the top right of the **Sketcher Work Bench**.

> **NOTE:** The profile rotates back to the original three-dimensional view with your newly created profile of the "**L Shaped Extrusion**". The **Sketcher Work Bench** grid disappears. The tools on the right hand tool bar will change as shown in Figure 1.41. The only tools available for your use at this time are **Pad**, **Shaft**, **Rib** and **Loft**. The **Pad** tool is covered in Step 22 and Lesson 2. The next step will tell you how to use the **PAD** tool.

If your screen looks similar to Figure 1.41, you are now in the **Part Design Work Bench** and ready to go to Step 22.

Figure 1.41

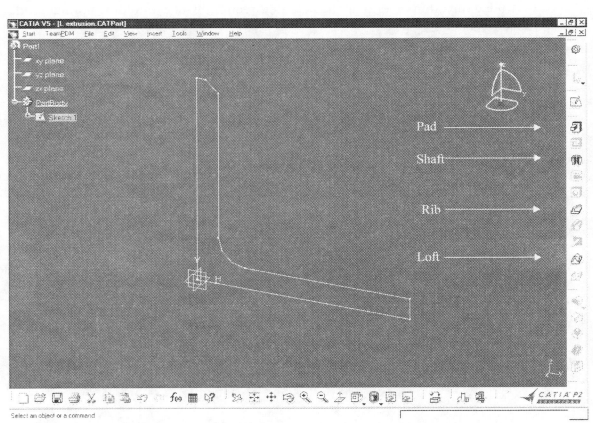

22 Extruding The Newly Created Profile Using The Pad Tool

This step will put your newly created profile of the "**L Shaped Extrusion**" to the test. This is where you find out if there are any problems with your profile sketch created in the **Sketcher Work Bench**.

If you haven't selected anything in the work area since exiting the **Sketcher Work Bench**, your profile should still be highlighted. If it is not still highlighted, select the profile or select the **Sketch** branch from the **Specification Tree**. When the profile is highlighted you can select the **Pad** tool. This will bring the **Pad Definition** window up as shown in Figure 1.42 and 1.43. As the **Pad Definition** window pops up you should notice your profile becomes three-dimensional. The **Specification Tree** just added another branch, the **Pad.1** branch. At this point you can specify how long to extrude the profile. You can type it in or select the up arrow and watch the part grow. Select the down arrow and watch it shrink. You can reverse the direction and/or mirror the extruded length. If these are not enough options you can select the **More** button in the **Pad Definition** window (Figure 1.43). The **More** button will let you specify the start location, **First Limit,** and the ending plane **Second Limit** of the profile being extruded. The **Reverse Direction** button will allow you to select an extruded direction other than the default direction, which would be normal to the sketch plane.

Figure 1.42

new branch
added

Figure 1.43 (**Pad Definition** window with **More** selected)

Type options available

These options are the same in the first and second limit boxes

Once you have the **Pad Definition** window set up the way you want it select the **Apply** button, this will give you a preview of what you just created. If you are not satisfied with the result select the **Cancel** button. If you are satisfied select the **Ok** button. The **Ok** button will create a three-dimensional part (solid) from your sketch. For the "**L Shaped Extrusion**" extrude the profile 12 inches. Your "**L Shaped Extrusion**" should look similar to what is shown in Figure 1.44.

23 Saving The Newly Created "L Shaped Extrusion"

You can stop what you are doing at any time and save the file you are working on. CATIA V5 also allows the user to set the time period for the automatic save. Before saving and exiting make sure you have finished all operations you have started. If you save and/or exit in the middle of an operation, the operation will not be saved. CATIA V5 allows you to name the file as you wish. The file extension will be named "*.CATPart". All of the files created in the **Sketcher Work Bench** and finished in the **Part Design Work Benches** will have a "*.CATAPart" extension. To **Save** a CATIA V5 file complete the following steps.

Figure 1.44

23.1 Verify that all operations are complete and the part (**CATPart**) is the way you want it to be saved.

23.2 Select **File** from the top tool bar (Figure 1.45).

23.3 Select **Save As** (Figure 1.45).

Figure 1.45

23.4 In the **Save As** window, select the directory you want the **CATPart** to be **Saved in** as shown in Figure 1.46.

23.5 In the same window, type in the **File name**. For this lesson save the file as "**L Shaped Extrusion**".

23.6 Notice CATIA V5 will automatically give the file the extension "***.CATPart**".

23.7 If everything is the way you want it in the **File**, **Save As** window select the **Save** button.

Figure 1.46

NOTE: Remember the file name and the directory you saved it to, you will need it for Lesson 2.

24 Exiting CATIA V5

To exit CATIA V5, complete the following steps.

24.1 Make sure you saved the **CATPart** (if you wanted it saved). If you have made any changes to the **CATPart** and not saved CATIA V5 will prompt you to save when exiting.

Figure 1.47

24.2 Select **File** from the top pull down tool bar as shown in Figure 1.47.

24.3 Select **Exit**.

24.4 If the **CATPart** was previously saved CATIA V5 will shut down and your computer will go back to the NT Desktop. As described above, if some changes were made to the **CATPart** without being saved CATIA V5 will prompt you to "**Save**" before allowing you to exit to the NT Desktop.

Lesson 1 Summary

If you are not use to the concepts of a sketch tool and parameterized entities this can be a difficult lesson, a lot of people struggle with it. It is not difficult it is just different! It is critical that you get comfortable with these two concepts before moving on to the next lesson. After you spend enough time using this process you will learn to appreciate the power these concepts possess.

Lesson 1 Review

After completing this lesson you should be able to answer the questions and explain the concepts listed below.

1. What is the definition of a **Constraint**?
2. Does CATIA V5 require **Constraints** to create a profile in the **Sketcher Work Bench**?
3. What is meant by an unclosed profile?
4. **T** or **F** Unclosed profiles can be extruded using the **Pad** tool.
5. **T** or **F** There is more than one way to select the XY plane when defining the XY plane as a sketch plane.
6. **T** or **F** **Over Constraining** a profile is a good thing!
7. Explain your answer to question 6.
8. What does **Anchoring** the profile do in the **Sketcher Work Bench**?
9. Explain how you would change the **Sketcher** units of measurements from mm to inches.
10. The **Sketcher Grid** is made up of two different entities, one is the **Primary Spacing**, name the other.
11. What is the advantage of **Constraining** a profile in the **Sketcher Work Bench**?
12. How do you modify a **Constraint**?
13. What icon do you use to exit the **Sketcher Work Bench** and enter the **Part Design Work Bench**?
14. How can you view all of the default tool bars in the **Sketcher Work Bench**?
15. What tool in the **Part Design Work Bench** is used to extrude a profile created in the **Sketcher Work Bench**?
16. The actual process of extruding a profile adds what branch to the **Specification Tree**?
17. List all four of the **Constraints** tools.
18. Can one **Sketch** have more than one profile?
19. While in the **Sketcher Work Bench** and using the mouse, how would you move (pan) the profile around the screen?
20. When you are connecting one end point of a line to another, how does CATIA V5 let you know you are **Snapping** to the existing end point and not just getting close?

Lesson 1 Practice Exercises

Now that your CATIA V5 tool box has some tools in it, put them to use on the following practice exercises. The shapes are simple and can be completed in one **Sketch**. The dimensions represent the **Constraints** you are to use in the **Sketcher Work Bench**. The first practice exercise has suggested steps to complete the task along with some helpful hints. Each subsequent practice exercise contains less suggested steps and helpful hints. By the last practice exercise you will be on your own!

Each practice exercise has a name to use when saving the exercise. It is critical that you use the suggested name so you can find the correct CATPart if it is used in a later lesson. Good Luck!

1. Using the **Sketcher Work Bench** and the other tools covered in Lesson 1, create the following profile and extrude to the dimensions shown below. When completed save as "**Lesson 1 Exercise 1.CATPart**".

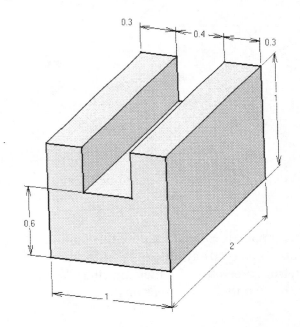

Suggested Steps:

1. Select the XY plane (the plane the profile will be sketched on). Reference Step 3 for information on selecting planes.
2. Enter the **Sketcher Work Bench**. Reference Step 4.
3. Sketch the profile of the part.
   Hint: use the **Profile** tool.
4. Anchor the lower left hand corner of the sketch. Reference Step 17 for anchoring a profile.
5. Constrain the profile to match the dimensions shown above. Reference Step 18 for constraining a profile.

6. Exit the **Sketcher Work Bench**, return to the **Part Design Work Bench** (the 3D environment). Reference Step 21 for exiting the **Sketcher Work Bench** and entering the **Part Design Work Bench**.
7. Once in the **Part Design Work Bench**, extrude the profile to the dimension shown (2"). Reference Step 22 for extruding a profile.
8. Save the part as "**Lesson 1 Exercise 1.CATPart**". Reference Step 23 for saving a file.

2. This part (profile) should be straightforward. This would be a good exercise to try different methods of constraining and testing the results. Save the shape as "**Lesson 1 Exercise 2.CATPart**".

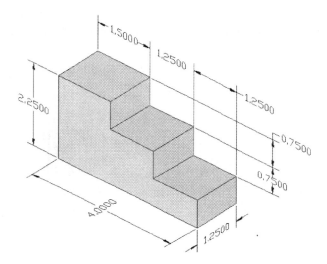

HINT: To help make it easier to sketch this part, set the grid **Primary Spacing** to 1 and the **Graduations** to 4. This will put the grid lines in the **Sketcher** screen to a .25 inch spacing. With that spacing, all you have to do is snap to the intersections of the grid to sketch the part.

3. This practice exercise should challenge you. For this part, use radius values, not angles. Save this CATPart as "**Lesson 1 Exercise 3.CATPart**".

HINT: This part can be done using the radius option in the profile command. Before starting, set the grid **Primary Spacing** to 1 and the **Graduations** to 4.

Sketching with the Profile icon (radius option)

1. Start at the bottom left corner of the part.

2. Select the **Profile** icon from the right menu bar.
3. Sketch the vertical 1.50 inch line that defines the left edge of the part.
4. Now sketch the first arc along the top of the part. To do this, hold down the left mouse button and drag it in the direction you want the arc to go then release the mouse button. The arc will appear and allow you to drag and place it where you want. Place it on the grid intersection 2 inches above the bottom of the part and a half-inch to the right. This will only create half of the arc needed, so the process will have to be repeated to sketch the other half of the arc.
5. Finish sketching the rest of the part. When you reach the inside .25 radius repeat Step 4.
6. When the sketch is done constrain it to double check that all of the dimensions match the part shown above. Make changes if necessary.

4. This will give you more practice with the **Line** and **Profile** icons in the
    Sketcher Work Bench. When you are done save the part as "**Lesson 1
    Exercise 4.CATPart**".

5. This exercise will give you some practice using the **Corner** and **Line** icons.
    When you are done save the CATPart as "**Lesson 1 Exercise 5.CATPart**".

6. This will give you more practice using the **Line** and **Corner** icons. Save this
    CATPart as "**Lesson 1 Exercise 6.CATPart**".

Part is .50 thk

HINT: Use the **Line** or **Profile** icon first to sketch the profile using sharp corners (no radius). Once it is constrained to the dimensions above go back and add in the radii using the **Corner** icon.

7. This practice exercise is a little bit more challenging; see what you can do with it. Save this CATPart as "**Lesson 1 Exercise 7.CATPart**".

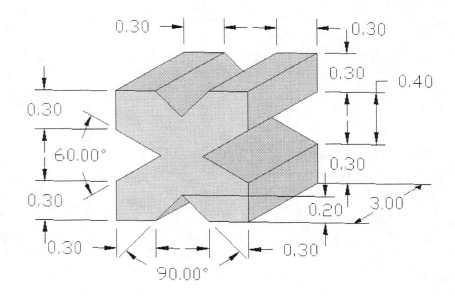

HINT: It is not as complicated as it looks. If your grid **Graduations** are set to 10, just snap to the intersections for the beginning and ending points of your lines. To set the constraint for the angles select the angled lines and the angle constraint will appear. Reference Step 19 for modifying the angle value. If the profile gets over constrained, delete the **Parallel** constraint. Save the file as "**Lesson 1 Exercise 7.CATPart**".

Lesson 2

Introduction To the Part Design Work Bench

This lesson uses the "**L Shaped Extrusion.CATPart**" created in Lesson 1. The first part of this lesson introduces you to all the default tool bars found in the **Part Design Work Bench**. The following section covers specific tools found in the five different tool bars. The object of this lesson is to complete the "**L Shaped Extrusion**" started in Lesson 1. When you complete this lesson the "**L Shaped Extrusion**" will be a "**T Shaped Extrusion**" and look similar to what is shown in Figure 2.1. The steps to complete the part are described in detail. Not all of the tools will be used to complete the part. This lesson is basic; therefore, there will be some overlap from Lesson 1.

Figure 2.1 The completed "**T Shaped Extrusion.CATPart**"

Lesson 2 Objectives

This lesson will show you how to do the following:

- Select the **Part Design Work Bench**
- Open the "**L Shaped Extrusion.CATPart**"
- Review **Pad** creation.
- Create several different **Fillets**
- Create a **Chamfer**
- Create and placing **Holes**
- Create **Patterns**
- Modify the existing "**L Shaped Extrusion**"
- **Translate** entities

- **Rotate** entities
- Use the **Symmetry** tool
- **Mirror** entities
- **Scale** entities
- Create **Part Design Constraints**
- **Apply Material** to entities
- Manage the **Specification Tree**
- Customize the **Specification Tree**
- Replay the design process
- **Save** the file
- **Exit** CATIA V5 (review)

Part Design Work Bench Tool Bars

There are seven standard tool bars found in the **Part Design Work Bench**. The seven tool bars are shown below. The individual tools found in each of the seven tool bars are labeled to the right of the tool icon.

Tools that have multiple options have an arrow at the bottom right of the tool icon. Reference the Lesson 1 section titled "**Sketcher Work Bench Tool Bars**" for information on how to change the default tool and on tools that have multiple options.

The **Sketcher** Tool Bar (Access The **Sketcher Work Bench**)

Tool Bar	Tool Name (default)	Tool Type Options
	Sketcher	

The **Transformation Features** Tool Bar

Tool Bar	Tool Name (default)	Tool Type Options
	Translation	Translation, Rotation, Symmetry
	Mirror	
	Rectangular Pattern	Rectangular Pattern, Circular Pattern, User Pattern
	Scaling	

The **Dress-Up Features** Tool Bar

Tool Bar	Tool Name (default)	Tool Type Options
	Fillet	Edge Fillet, Variable Radius Fillet, Tritangent Fillet, Face-Face Fillet
	Chamfer	
	Draft Angle	Draft Reflect Line
	Shell	
	Thickness	
	Thread /Tap	

The **Annotations** Tool Bar

Tool Bar	Tool Name (default)	Tool Type Options
	Text With Leader	
	Flag Note With Leader	

The **Sketch-Based Features** Tool Bar

Tool Bar	Tool Name (default)	Tool Type Options
	Pad	**Drafted Filleted Pad**
	Pocket	**Drafted Fillet Pocket**
	Shaft	
	Groove	
	Hole	
	Rib	
	Slot	
	Stiffener	
	Loft	
	Removed Loft	

The **Constraints Features** Tool Bar

Tool Bar	Tool Name (default)	Tool Type Options
	Constraints Defined In Dialog Box	
	Constraints	

The **Surface-Based Features** Tool Bar

Tool Bar	Tool Name (default)	Tool Type Options
	Split	
	Surface Thickness	
	Close Surface	
	Sew Surface	

Figure 2.2

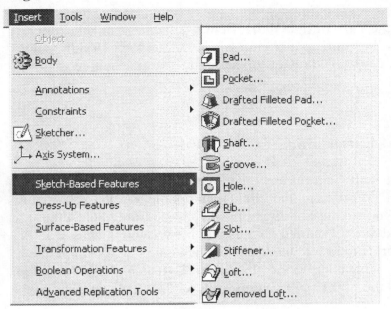

All of the tools listed above in the individual tool bars can also be accessed from the **Insert** pull down menu. This method of tool selection is helpful to the new user because all of the tool names are visible. This method also displays some additional tools as Figure 2.2 shows. The additional tools will not be used in this lesson, but it is important for you to know for future reference.

Steps To Extrude A Profile Using The Part Design Work Bench

The following steps will give detailed step-by-step instructions on taking the profile of the "**L Shaped Extrusion**" created in Lesson 1 and extruding it into a completed three-dimensional part. For every step covered, there are multiple methods that could be used. This lesson, for the most part, will show you one method. You are encouraged to follow the steps and then explore other options on your own.

CATIA V5R6

1   Start CATIA V5

This was covered in Lesson 1. If you need to review this step, refer to Lesson 1 Step 1. Lesson 1 shows the screen you should see when you first enter CATIA V5.

2   Select The Part Design Workbench

The method of selecting the **Part Design Work Bench** is the same as selecting the **Sketcher Work Bench** in Lesson 1. Make sure you select the **Part Design** tool and not the **Sketcher** tool. For a detailed review on selecting a workbench, refer to Lesson 1 Step 2.

3   Open The "L Shaped Extrusion.CATPart" File

Opening a CATIA V5 file is the same as any other Windows and/or Windows NT program. From the top menu bar select the **File, Open** options. A pop-up window will appear, which gives you a choice of directories to choose from. Select the directory where you saved the **"L Shaped Extrusion"** file created in Lesson 1. All of the CATIA V5 CATPart files should be displayed including the **"L Shaped Extrusion.CATPart"**. Double click on the **"L Shaped Extrusion.CATPart"** file. CATIA V5 will now load the **"L Shaped Extrusion.CATPart"** as you last saved it.

4   Review The "L Shaped Extrusion.CATPart"

Before continuing to the next step, review the "**L Shaped Extrusion.CATpart**" CATAI V5 loaded. Verify that everything is the way you expected it to be. If you completed every step in Lesson 1, your "**L Shaped Extrusion.CATPart**" is already extruded into a three-dimensional part and you can skip to Step 6.

5   Extruding The Sketcher Profile Using The Pad Tool

This step was covered in detail in Lesson 1, even though the **Pad** tool is a **Part Design Work Bench** tool. This is a critical step, so you want to make sure that if this process was not completed in Lesson 1, it is not missed before proceeding to Step 6. If you have not completed this step, refer to Lesson 1 Step 22 for detailed instructions on how to use the **Pad** Tool. Lesson 1 is a good representation of what your part should look like after completing Step 22 from Lesson 1.

> **NOTE**: It is critical that your "**L Shaped Extrusion.CATPart**" part look similar to what is shown in Figure 1.44 before proceeding!

6 Creating A Fillet

A **Fillet** is a rounded corner on an outside or inside edge of a part. It can also be defined as a radial transition between two adjacent surfaces. CATIA V5 has several **Filleting** options to choose from. These options are the **Edge Fillet, Variable Radius Fillet, Face-Face Fillet** and the **Tritangent Fillet**. These options can be seen by holding down the left mouse button on the arrow next to the default **Fillet** tool. The most commonly used **Fillet** command is the **Edge Fillet**. The following steps will take you step-by-step through the process of creating an **Edge Fillet** on your "L Shaped Extrusion.CATPart".

6.1　Make sure the **Units** are set to inches (for a review on how to do this, refer back to Lesson 1 Step 5).

6.2　Select the right edge of the part as shown in Figure 2.3. The line will turn red indicating it has been selected.

6.3　Select the **Edge Fillet** tool from the **Dress Up Feature** tool bar.

6.4　The **Edge Fillet Definition** window will appear on the screen, reference Figure 2.4.

Figure 2.3

select

6.5　For the **Radius** type in **.50** then tab. This will set the **Fillet** radius to .50 of an inch. The radius and the dimension now appear on the part. CATIA V5 will preview the fillet before it actually creates it.

6.6　The **Object(s) to fillet** box should indicate that one edge has been selected as shown in Figure 2.4.

6.7　Leave the **Propagation** box set to **Tangency** as shown in Figure 2.4.

6.8　If you are satisfied with the preview and the options are typed in as shown in Figure 2.4, select the **OK** button and the **Fillet** will be created.

select here

The part should now look like the one shown in Figure 2.5.

Figure 2.5

> **NOTE:** The **Fillet** was added to the **Specification Tree** as **EdgeFillet.1** (Figure 2.6).

Figure 2.6

new **Fillet** added ⟶ EdgeFillet.1

6.9 Follow Steps 6.3 through 6.8 to put a **Fillet** on the other end of the part. The results should look similar to the one shown in Figure 2.7. The new **Fillet** will also show up on the **Specification Tree**.

Figure 2.7

.5" Fillet

7 Creating A Fillet On The Back Edge Of The "L Shaped Extrusion"

7.1 To select the back edge of the extrusion, you will need to rotate the part until the line that defines the edge is visible. To do this, select the **Rotate** tool from the bottom of the screen. Then select an area in the middle of the screen and drag the mouse in the direction you want the part to be rotated. A dotted sphere will appear on the screen showing the axis of rotation (Figure 2.8).

Figure 2.8

center of rotation

select this edge
to be filleted

7.2   Once the part is rotated so that the back edge of the extrusion is visible, select the line as shown in Figure 2.8.

7.3   Select the **Edge Fillet** tool.

Figure 2.9

7.4   When the **Edge Fillet Definition** pop-up window appears, change the value in the **Radius** box to **.225"** as shown in Figure 2.9.

7.5   Your "**L Shaped Extrusion**" should now look similar to the one shown below in Figure 2.10.

Figure 2.10

Filleted edge

7.6   Save the revised "**L Shaped Extrusion.CATPart**". Select **File**, **Save** and **Yes** replace existing file. For a review on saving a **CATPart** see Lesson 1 Step 23.

8 Creating A Chamfer

Chamfers are used quite often on three-dimensional objects. The main purpose of a chamfer is to break a sharp edge on a part or to add a taper to an edge. You will now add a chamfer to your "**L Shaped Extrusion**"

8.1   This step will show you how to create a chamfer on the back edge of the part. Since Step 7 had you create a fillet on the back edge, you will have to remove it before replacing it with the chamfer. To remove the fillet created in Step 7, complete the following steps.

8.1.1   Highlight the **Edge Fillet 3** from the **Specification Tree** in the upper left hand corner of the screen (Figure 2.11). If you followed the steps exactly, the **Specification Tree** should label the fillet on the back edge of the part as **Edge Fillet.3**. If you have been exploring on your own, your fillet may be labeled another number. You can verify that you selected the correct fillet by checking which fillet is hightlighted on your "**L Shaped Extrusion**". If the highlighted **Fillet** is the same as shown in Figure 2.11, you have selected the correct fillet and may continue.

Figure 2.11

select here

8.1.2   Select the **Cut** tool ✂ at the bottom of the screen or hit the **Delete** key on the key board. The **EdgeFillet.3** should dissappear from the tree and the corresponding **Fillet** on the "**L Shaped Extrusion**" should also dissappear. The back edge of the part should be a square edge. Your part should now look like the one in Figure 2.7.

8.2   This step is almost identical to what you did in Step 7. Rotate the view to where the back edge is in view. Select the line that defines the back edge of the "**L Shaped Extrusion**". See Figure 2.8 to see which line to select. Once the line is highlighted, select the **Chamfer** tool.

8.3   The **Chamfer Definition** window will appear as shown in Figure 2.12. The first option given is the **Mode** box. You specify the chamfer by determining the length and the angle (**Length1/Angle**) or by determining the length of both sides of the chamfer (**Length1/Length2**). For this lesson, select the **Length1/Angle** option.

Figure 2.12

different mode options:

8.4   Enter **.125in** value in for the **Length 1** box and **45deg** in for the **Angle** box. If your **Chamfer Definition** window looks like the one in Figure 2.12, select **OK**.

8.5   Your part should look similar to the one shown in Figure 2.13. Notice that **Chamfer.1** has also been added to the **Specification Tree**.

Figure 2.13

8.6   It would be a good idea to save your current **CATPart** before continuing.

9   Creating Holes

The following steps will take you through the process of creating and locating holes.

9.1   Make sure you have the "**L Shaped Extrusion**" with the radii and chamfer up on your screen as shown in Figure 2.14. As a double check, verify that your default units are set to inches.

9.2   The first hole will be created on the left side of the standing leg. Before the hole can be created, two edges need to be selected. The two edges are required to correctly and accurately locate the holes. The surface the hole is located on will also have to be selected. The two lines (edges) and the surface can be selected at the same time by holding down the Ctrl key as you select the lines and surface. Select the lines and surface as shown in Figure 2.14.

NOTE: If you select the surface first, the edges of the surface will highlight. You will still have to select the edges individually when prompted. When an edge has been selected twice, once for the surface and a second time for the edge, the second highlight color is a deeper red color.

Figure 2.14

select this
surface

edge 1

edge 2

Figure 2.15

9.3   Select the **Hole** tool from
       the **Sketch-Based Features**
       tool bar located on the right
       side of the screen. The lines
       and surface selected in Step 9.2
       must still be highlighted.

9.4   The **Hole Definition** window
       will appear on the screen as
       shown in Figure 2.15. A
       highlighted outline of the hole
       will appear on the part with the
       constraints that show the
       distance from the two edges
       selected in Step 9.2.

9.5   You now need to accurately position the hole in the correct location. To
       do this you will use the **Constraints** created in Step 9.4. The **Constraints**
       you created in Step 9.4 will most likely be crowded together, in fact, you
       may not even be able to read the **Constraint** values. This can be fixed by
       zooming up on the **Constraints**, selecting one of the **Constraints** and
       dragging it away from the collection of **Constraints**. Then select another
       Constraint, dragging and dropping it far enough away from the other
       constraints that it can be read and selected. The **Constraint** values can be
       modified by double clicking on the **Constraint**. Double clicking on the
       Constraint brings up the **Constraint Definition** window as shown in
       Lesson 1. This **Constraint Definition** box allows you to type in the
       Constraint Value. For this step, change the **Value** of the vertical
       Constraint to **.35in** and the horizontal **Constraint** to **1in** as shown in
       Figure 2.16.

9.6   You now need to specify the type   **Figure 2.16**   depth dim.
       of hole you want to create.
       CATIA V5 has several different types
       of holes to choose from. The
       different hole types can be accessed
       by selecting the **Type** tab at the top of
       the **Hole Definition** window as
       shown in Figure 2.17. The box on the
       right hand side of the window will
       display a visual picture of the hole
       currently highlighted. These different
       pictures are shown in Figure 2.18.
       For this step select the "**Simple**"
       option as shown in Figure 2.17.

horizontal dim.   diameter dim.

vertical dim.

Figure 2.17 (Types of holes)

Figure 2.18
Simple   Taper   Counter   Counter   Counter
                          bored   sunk   drilled

9.7   The **Hole Limit** will need to be selected next. The limit will specify how deep the hole will go. CATIA V5 has several different options available in **Hole Limits**. To specify a limit type, select the **Extension** tab located next to the **Type** tab (Figure 2.15). The first box in the **Extension** tab is an **Options** Box. By selecting the down arrow at the right side of the box, you will see the different options you have to choose from. The options are shown in Figure 2.20. For this step, select the **Up To Last** option as shown in Figure 2.19.

Figure 2.19   **Figure 2.20**   Up To   Up To   Up To   Up To
                         Blind   Next   Last   Plane   Surface

9.8   The last constraint not yet specified is the **Diameter** of the hole. Type in **.25in** for the diameter value as shown in Figure 2.15.

9.9   If your **Hole Definition** window looks like the one in Figure 2.15, select **OK**. You now have a hole in the standing leg of your "**L Shaped Extrusion**". Reference Figure 2.21. Notice that a new branch was added to the **Specification Tree**. The branch is labeled **Hole.1**.

Figure 2.21

9.10 Now to test the knowledge you have gained. Add a second hole on the other end of the "**L Shaped Extrusion**". Use the same hole to edge dimensions used for the first hole. When you are done, your part should look like the one shown in Figure 2.22.

Figure 2.22

10 Creating A Pattern Of Holes

Creating patterns are easy and fast using the CATIA V5 **Pattern** tool. The following steps will show you how to create a pattern of holes in your "**L Shaped Extrusion**".

10.1 Before you get started, make sure the part on your screen looks like the one in Figure 2.22 and that the **Units** are set to **Inches**.

10.2 The hole pattern will be created on the standing leg of the "**L Shaped Extrusion**". The first hole created in Step 9 will be used as the strating hole.

10.3 Select **Hole.1** from the **Specification Tree** or by selecting the actual hole. The selected hole should be highlighted, signifying it has been selected. The corresponding hole on the part should also be highlighted (Figure 2.23).

Figure 2.23

Part1
- xy plane
- yz plane
- zx plane
- PartBody
  - Pad.1
    - Sketch.1
  - EdgeFillet.1
  - EdgeFillet.2
  - Chamfer.1
  - Hole.1
    - Sketch.4
  - Hole.2
    - Sketch.6

select (hole 1)

10.4 Select the **Rectangular Pattern** tool from the **Transformation Feature** tool bar located on the right side of the screen. If the tool icon is not visible on the right side of the screen, it

Figure 2.24 (lower right hand corner of screen)

arrows indicating hidden toolbars

CATIA P2 SOLUTIONS

may be hidden below the screen. If there is a tool bar hidden on the bottom of the screen, there will be two little arrows on the end of the last tool bar as shown in Figure 2.24. You can view them by clicking on the arrows with the left mouse button and dragging the hidden tool bar up into view. You can use the windows drag and drop method of placement. If you drag one tool bar up and the arrows are still there that means there are still more hidden tool bars. Drag and drop the tool bars until you find the **Transformation Features** tool bar. The **Rectangular Pattern** tool is located on this tool bar.

10.5 The **Rectangular Pattern Definition** window will appear on the screen as shown in Figure 2.25. Notice that there is a **First Direction** and **Second Direction** tab at the top of the window. CATIA V5 allows you to specify the hole pattern in two directions. For your "**L Shaped Extrusion**", we will only be using the **First Direction** tab.

Figure 2.25

10.6 The first box in the **First Direction** tab is the **Parameters** box. CATIA V5 gives you several options to choose from. Select the **Instance(s) & Spacing** option (Figure 2.25). This will allow you to specify the number of holes you want and the spacing between each hole.

10.7 The **Instances** box specifies how many times the hole is going to be copied in the specified direction. For this step, type "**4**" in the **Instances** box. It is important to know that the value entered in the **Instances** box will count the existing hole as one of the entered value. For example, you just entered the value of **4** in the **Instances** box. A total of 4 holes will be created, one you selected to pattern after and three additional holes.

10.8 For the **Spacing** value type in **1.25in** This will place the holes 1.25 inches apart from each other.

10.9 The **Length** box will display the total length of the hole pattern from the center of the first hole to the center of the last hole. The **Length** box will be dimmed, which means the value can not be changed.

10.10 You now need to specify the direction of the hole pattern. You can specify the direction by selecting the **Reference Element** box. The box will turn blue indicating it is selected.

10.11 Select the top edge of the "**L Shaped Extrusion**" as shown in Figure 2.26.
       The top edge will highlight signifing it has been selected. At this point
       CATIA V5 will preview the hole pattern in the part. This highlighted
       preview allows you to verify that the pattern is what you want. If the hole
       pattern is previewed in the wrong direction, you can select the **Reverse**
       button located just below the **Reference Element** box. This reverses the
       direction of the hole pattern. If your part looks similar the the one in
       Figure 2.27, select the **OK** button. Notice that **RectPattern.1** branch has
       been added to the **Specification Tree**.

Figure 2.26

select this edge to
specify direction

distance dim.

Figure 2.27

10.12   Now use what you have learned to create the same hole pattern on the other side of the part. Use **Hole.2** to start the hole pattern. Figure 2.28 shows what your part should look like when your second hole pattern is complete. Notice that the **Specification Tree** has added another hole pattern below the **Hole.2** branch.

Figure 2.28

11 Modifying The Width Of The Base Leg

In the past, design modification has been a very time consuming process. Most designs go through mulitple modifications prior to being manufactured. CATIA V5 has made design modification much quicker and easier. To demonstrate CATIA V5's ability to modify parts, this step will take you through the process of adjusting the width of the base leg of the "**L Shaped Extrusion**".

11.1   Before you get started, make sure the **Units** are set to **Inches**. Make sure the part on your screen looks similar to the one shown in Figure 2.28.

11.2   In order to adjust the base leg of the "**L Shaped Extrusion**", you need to go back to where you specified its current width. This was specified when you created the sketch in the **Sketcher Work Bench** (Lesson 1). You can bring that sketch back and modify the constraint that controls the base leg width. There are several methods to bring up the sketch. For this step use the **Specification Tree**. The **Sketch.1** branch must be visible. If the

Sketch.1 branch is not visible, select the plus ⊞ to the side of the **Pad.1** branch. The ⊞ expands the **Specification Tree.** The ⊟ contracts the **Specification Tree.**

Figure 2.29

11.3   With the **Sketch.1** branch visible, double click on it. Reference Figure 2.29. The screen will change from the **Part Design Work Bench** (3D environment) to the **Sketcher Work Bench** (2D sketch environment). As the screen changes from the **Part Design Work Bench** to the **Sketcher Work Bench,** the "**L Shaped Extrusion**" will rotate to where the plane selected in Lesson 1 will be normal (perpendicular) to the screen.

This is the plane **Sketch.1** was created in. **Sketch.1** is linked to this plane. Your screen should look similar to the one shown in Figure 2.30. You are now ready to modify the width of the base leg.

Figure 2.30

Figure 2.31

double click here

11.4 Double click on the **Constraint** that specifies the width of the base leg.
As shown in Figure 2.30, the constraint is currently 1".

11.5 The **Constraint Definition** window will appear with the 1" value
highlighted in the **Value** box. Change the 1" value to 2" as shown in
Figure 2.31.

11.6 Select the **OK** button at the bottom of the **Constraint Definition** window.
Notice that the sketch automatically modifies the base leg from 1" to 2".
Figure 2.32 shows the modified sketch.

Figure 2.32

new constraint

11.7 You have completed the sketch modification in the **Sketcher Work Bench**. It is time to continue this lesson in the **Part Design Work Bench**. To exit the **Sketcher Work Bench,** select the **Exit** ⊏ᴸ᷒ tool from the upper right hand corner of the screen. This will take you out of the **Sketcher Work Bench** and back into the **Part Design Work Bench**.

11.8 After returning to the **Part Design Work Bench** the "**L Shaped Extrusion**" part may appear red for a few seconds. This means that CATIA V5 is in the process of updating the part to match the changes made in the **Sketcher Work Bench**. When CATIA V5 is done updating the part, it will return back to its original color and the base leg will be modified from 1" to 2" as shown in Figure 2.33.

Figure 2.33

11.9 The purpose of the previous steps was to show you how easy it is to modify a part. Now, after all that work, you are going to find out how easy it is to **Undo** all that work; the work completed in Step 11. There are two ways to accomplish this. The first method is to select the **Undo** ↺ button, one step at a time, until your "**L Shaped Extrusion**" base leg is back to 1". If your part remains red after the **Undo** command, you will have to select the **Update** ⊚ tool. Selecting the **Update** tool forces CATIA V5 to update the modification. The part should turn to its normal color and the base leg should go back to 1". The second method is to go back into the **Sketcher Work Bench** and change the constraint back to 1", then **Exit** back to the **Part Design Work Bench**.

NOTE: The **Update** tool is located at the bottom of the screen. If it is not visible, you will have to pull it out on the screen so it is selectible. For future reference, any time the **Update** tool is highlighted, CATIA V5 is signalling that an update is required. All you have to do is select the **Update** tool and CATIA V5 will update the part.

NOTE: The steps for modifying the width of the base leg of the "**L Shaped Extrusion**" can be applied to all of the other geometrical properties of the part such as radii, chamfers and holes (any constraint value). The values can be modified by double clicking on the **Pad.1** branch in the **Specification Tree**. This makes all **Constraints** visible and pickable. You can double click on a constraint which will bring up the **Constraint Definition** window for that particular constraint. It is in the **Constraint Definition** window that you can modify the particular constraint value. Double clicking on the "**L Shaped Extrusion**" part will also make all of the constraints visible for selecting and modifying.

When you get into parts with multiple sketches, you will need to specify the particular plane the sketch was created in. For example, the values specified for the profile sketch of the "**L Shaped Extrusion**" were created in the **Sketcher Work Bench** in the **ZX Plane**. To modify those values, you would need to specify the same plane, the **ZX Plane**. You could not modify the length of the "**L Shaped Extrusion**" in the **Sketcher Work Bench**. The length was created with the **Pad** tool in the **Part Design Work Bench**.

12 Translating The "L Shaped Extrusion"

Translating the part is simply moving the object from one place to another. To demonstrate this command, you will move your "**L Shaped Extrusion**" forward five inches. The following steps describe this process.

12.1 Select the **Translation** tool from the **Transformation Features** tool bar located on the right side of the screen. If this tool is not visible, you may need to drag it up from the bottom right corner and into view. If you are not sure how to drag and drop a hidden tool bar, refer back to Step 10.4 .

Figure 2.34

12.2 The **Translate Definition** window allows you to specify what entity to translate and how far to translate it. Reference Figure 2.34.

Translate Definition	? X
Direction:	Chamfer.1\Edge.4
Distance:	5
OK	Cancel

12.3 If no translation **Direction** has been specified, the defalt value will be "**No Selection**". In order to select a direction for the translation, you must select the the **Direction** box. To do this, select in the middle of the box. It will highlight blue meaning it has been selected.

12.4 Select the bottom edge of the base leg of the "**L Shaped Extrusion**" as shown in Figure 2.35. Notice that the **Direction** box now shows the name of the line selected. The part has also been highlighted meaning that it is the entity that will be translated. Two arrows also appear in the middle of the part pointing in the positive and negative directions of the translation.

Figure 2.35

pos. & neg. direction of translation

Distance = 0in

select this edge for direction

12.5 Now enter **5** in the **Distance** box as shown in Figure 2.34.

12.6 Select the **OK** button. The part will be moved five inches forward. To verify that the part was really translated, double click on the **Translate.1** branch that has just been added to the **Specification Tree**. CATIA V5 will show you where the part was and where it is now, after the translation. The **Translate Definition** window will also appear. This will allow you to modify the selected translation.

12.7 Select the **Cancel** button and the transformation will not be modifed.

Figure 2.36

13 Rotating The "L Shaped Extrusion"

When creating a three-dimensional object, it is very important that you are able to rotate the object to be

able to see the side you want to work on. In CATIA V5 there are several ways to rotate the part which will be be discussed below.

13.1 The first way to rotate a part is using the **Rotate** tool from the **Transformation Features** tool bar. As explained previously, this tool bar may be hidden on the bottom right corner of the screen. You may need to drag it up into view. If the **Rotate** tool is still not visible after pulling up the **Transformation Features** tool bar, select the arrow in the bottom corner of the **Translate** tool. It will be one of the sub-options available (Figure 2.36). To use this command, you will need to select the object to be rotated and specify an axis of rotation and the degree the object is to be rotated. The steps below will demonstrate this.

Figure 2.37

13.1.1 Select the **Rotate** tool from the **Transformation Features** tool bar. The **Rotate Definition** window will appear on the screen as shown in Figure 2.37.

13.1.2 The first option in the window is the **Axis** Specification box. CATIA V5 will only accept a straight line to define the axis of rotation. Select the left edge of the standing leg of the "**L Shaped Extrusion**" as shown in Figure 2.38 . The "**L Shaped Extrusion**" will highlight indcating that it is the entity to be rotated.

Figure 2.38

select this edge for axis of rotation

13.1.3 Now, all that is required is an angle entered in the **Angle** box to tell CATIA V5 how many degrees to rotate the part. Enter in **45** degrees and select the **OK** button.

13.1.4 The part has now been rotated 45 degrees around the line that was selected as the axis.

NOTE: The **Rotate.1** will now appear in the **Specification Tree**. If you need to modify the angle, double click **Rotate.1** in the **Specification Tree**. The pop-up window will appear allowing you to modify the values previously specified.

NOTE: This rotation method changes the orientation of the part in relationship to the 0,0,0 axis. The part moves in relationship to the axis not to you the viewer.

13.2   The next way to rotate a part in CATIA V5 is to use the **Rotate** tool found at the bottom of the screen. This tool does not move the part in relationship to the axis, but moves the viewers perspective of the part. The orientation of the geometry, with reference to the axis or with any other entity, is not effected. Since this does not change the geometry at all, there is no change made to the **Specification Tree**. This same rotation can be accomplished with the mouse only. Push the middle mouse button. Continue to hold the middle mouse button down and push down the left mouse button. This sequence of mouse buttons will bring up the same rotation sphere. For detailed instructions on this process, reference the Introduction and Step 7.1 in this lesson.

13.2.1 To use this command, select the **Rotate** tool. The tool will highlight red meaning it has been selected.

13.2.2 Select any point on the screen and hold down the left mouse button.

13.2.3 The rotation sphere will appear and show the axis of rotation (Figure 2.8).

13.2.4 When you have rotated your point of view to where you want it, release the left mouse button and the rotation will be terminated.

13.3 One other way to rotate a part is using the **Compass** located in the upper right corner of the screen as shown in Figure 2.39. The **Compass** can be used to perform many different tasks besides rotation. Figure 2.39 shows the names of the different parts of the **Compass**.

Figure 2.39

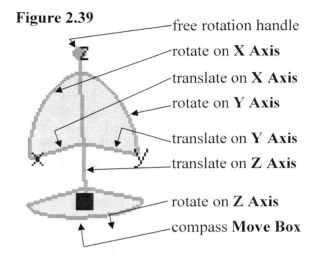

free rotation handle

rotate on **X Axis**

translate on **X Axis**

rotate on **Y Axis**

translate on **Y Axis**

translate on **Z Axis**

rotate on **Z Axis**

compass **Move Box**

13.3.1 One way the **Compass** can be used to rotate a part, is to hold the left mouse botton down on the free rotation handle and move it around. You will notice that as the **Compass** pivots, the part will do the same thing. This type of rotation is much the same as the rotation process explained in Step 13.2.

13.3.2 Figure 2.39 shows the different components of the **Compass.** Each component allows your perspective of the part to be rotated or translated. You might want to play around with these different rotations and translations to see exactly how the movements change your perspecitve of the part.

NOTE: The **Rotate** tool and **Space Ball** method does not change the orientation of the part in relationship to the 0,0,0 axis. The part moves in relationship to the axis not you the viewer. As you rotate and/or translate the part, notice that the planes representing the 0,0,0 locaton change with the part.

13.3.3 Another way of using the **Compass** to rotate a part, is by dragging the compass and placing it on the object you want to rotate. This is done by holding the left mouse button down on the **Move Box** located at the base of the **Compass,** reference Figure 2.39. Drag the **Compass** over the part and release it. The **Compass** will stay grey in color until you highlight the **PartBody** in the **Specification Tree**. Once the **PartBody** is highlighted, the **Compass** will turn green. Once the **Compass** is green, any rotations and/or translations you make will move the part in relationship to the 0,0,0 axis. Use this technique to rotate your "**L Shaped Extrusion**".

13.3.3.1 Drag the the **Compass** over to the "**L Shaped Extrusion**" as explained above and place it on the base leg of the "**L Shaped Extrusion**" as shown in Figure 2.40.

13.3.3.2 Select (highlight) the "**L Shaped Extrusion**" **PartBody** in the **Specification Tree**. The **Compass** will turn green.

Figure 2.40

13.3.3.3 To view the options available to you, click the left mouse button with it on the **Compass**. Select **Edit** at the bottom of the window. This will bring up the **Compass Manipulation** window as shown in Figure 2.41.

Figure 2.41

13.3.3.4 The first option is **Position**. This refers to the position of the compass with reference to the (0,0,0) point. Remember, the (0,0,0) is where the **XY**, **YZ**, and **XZ Planes** intersect in the center of the screen. Enter a zero in the **U**, **V**, and **W** windows and select the **Apply New Position** button. This will change the (0,0,0) location to the point where the **Compass** is located.

NOTE: This rotation method changes the orientation of the part in relationship to the 0,0,0 axis.

NOTE: Step 13.3.3.3 gives you access to many more **Compass Manipulation** tools. Be aware of the options available to you for future reference.

14 Creating A Symetrical "L Shaped Extrusion"

This command is used to transform the part symetrically from one side of a plane or surface to another. The following steps will take you through this process.

14.1 Select the **Symmetry** tool from the tool bars at the right of the screen. It is one of the sub options found when the arrow is selected on the **Transformation Features** tool bar. Reference Figure 2.36 to see where this tool is located in the tool bar.

14.2 The **Symmetry Definition** window will appear on the screen as shown in Figure 2.42.

14.3 The **Reference** box is prompting for a plane or surface to be selected. For this lesson, select the left side surface of the "**L Shaped Extrusion**" as shown in Figure 2.43.

Figure 2.42

Figure 2.43

select this surface

14.4 The outline of the new part will be highlighted in orange to show where the symetrical part will be created. If your screen looks similar to the one in Figure 2.44, select the **OK** button. The "**L Shaped Extrusion**" should now be replaced with a symmetrical part on the other side of the selected surface. Notice that the **Specification Tree** now has a new branch called **Symmetry.1**.

NOTE: **Symmetry** creates a new part that is symmetrical to the original. Once the **Symmetry** is accepted, the orignal part no longer exists. If you want to keep both the original part and the symmetrical part, you need to use the **Mirror** tool, which is covered in the next step.

Figure 2.44

15 Mirroring The "L Shaped Extrusion"

The **Mirror** tool is just like the **Symmetry** tool except when the part is mirrored, the original part will not dissappear. It will be joined to the new mirrored part to make one complete part. The steps below will demonstrate how to mirror the "**L Shaped Extrusion**". The finished product will look more like a "**T Shaped Extrusion**".

15.1 Select the bottom side of the base leg of the "**L Shaped Extrusion**" as shown in Figure 2.45. The entire outline of the surface should highlight in red. If only one line is highlighted, you haven't selected the surface. Reselect the surface until the entire profile is highlighted.

Figure 2.45

select this surface

15.2 Select the **Mirror** tool ![icon] from the right hand side of the screen. The **Mirror Definition** window will appear on the screen. Notice, that in the **Mirror Element** box, it shows that **Face.3** has been selected. This should be the surface you selected in Step 15.1.

15.3 Select the **OK** button and the part will be mirrored around the bottom surface of the base leg of the "**L Shaped Extrusion**" as shown in Figure 2.46. As with the other tools, a **Mirror.1** branch is added to the **Specification Tree**.

15.4 Mirroring the "**L Shaped Extrusion**" changed the part shape from an **L** to a **T**. Save the **CATPart** as "**T Shaped Extrusion.CATPart**" using the **Save As** command. Now you will have two separate **CATParts**, the "**L Shaped Extrusion**" and the "**T Shaped Extrusion**". **The remainder of this lesson, Lesson 3 and Lesson 4 will reference the "T Shaped Extrusion".**

15.5 The current "**T Shaped Extrusion**" is not the standard mill T extrusion. To make the extrusion represent a standard mill T extrusion remove the chamfer created in Step 8. Select **Chamfer.1** from the **Specification Tree** and press the **Delete** key or select the **Cut** ![icon] tool. The orginal part along with mirrored part will update with the chamfer removed as shown in Figure 2.47.

Figure 2.46

Mirror.1 added to the   new **Mirrored** part
Specification Tree

NOTE: The mirrored entity is still part of the same **PartBody**. This means that there is still just one part on the screen (Part1).

NOTE: <u>The remainder of this lesson, Lesson 3 and Lesson 4 will reference the "T Shaped Extrusion", not the "L Shaped Extrusion".</u>

16 Scaling The "T Shaped Extrusion"

The **Scaling** tool in CATIA V5 will make an object larger or smaller by a specified scaling factor. A scaling factor greater than 1 will make the part larger and a scaling factor less than 1 will make the part smaller. CATIA V5 does not recognize a negative number as a scaling factor.

CATIA V5 has two methods for scaling a part. The first method is by selecting a point. The second method is by selecting a face or plane. **Scaling** a part by selecting a point will scale the part equally around that point. **Scaling** a part by selecting a face or plane will only scale the parts of the solid that do not lie on the plane or run parallel to the plane. The following steps will show you how to scale the new "**T Shaped Extrusion**" by selecting a point. **Scaling** a part by selecting a plane will not be demonstrated, but it is recommended that you take some time to try it. To scale the "**T Shaped Extrusion**", complete the following steps.

16.1 Select the point at the top of the standing leg where the radius ends as shown in Figure 2.47. Make sure that only the point is highlighted and not the line.

16.2 Select the **Scaling** tool from the **Transformation Features** tool bar.

16.3 When the **Scaling Definition** window appears on the screen as shown in Figure 2.48, enter **.5** into the **Ratio** box. You will not need to enter anything in the **Reference** box, because the point has already been selected as your reference element.

Figure 2.47   select here

Figure 2.48

Look mom. No more chamfer!

16.4 Select the **OK** button and the part will be scaled to half it previous size. As in the previous processes, a new branch will be added to the **Specification Tree**. The new branch will be labled **Scaling.1** .

17 Applying Constraints In The Part Design Work Bench

In Lesson 1, **Constraints** were added to the two-dimensional sketch to control the profile of the "**L Shaped Extrusion**". The same type of **Constraints** can be used to control three-dimensional parts in the **Part Design Work Bench**. The following steps will show you how to set and modify **Constraints** in the **Part Design Work Bench**.

In Lesson 1, **Constraints** were placed on the sketch of the "**L**" profile. The **Constraints** were green in color. CATIA V5 allows you to modify the colors and appearance of the **Constraints**. The steps below show where to go to access the **Constraints** modification window.

17.1 Select the **Tools** tab from the top of the screen as shown in Figure 2.49.

17.2 In the **Tools** pull down window select **Options** as shown in Figure 2.49.

17.3 When the **Options** window appears , select the **Parameters** branch as shown in Figure 2.50.

Figure 2.49   select here

17.4 From the top right of the window, select the **Symbols** tab.

The **Symbols** window is divided into three boxes. The first box is the **Constraint Style** box, then the **Dimension Style** box, and the last box is the **Display at Creation** box. The following paragraphs will explain the functions of each of these three boxes. This section is intended to be for your information only. There will not be any modifications made to the **Symbols** tab. It will be up to you to experiment with the different settings and decide what works best for you.

Figure 2.50

The **Constraint Style** box controls the colors of the different types of **Constraints**. These colors can be changed by selecting the down arrow to the right of the color box and selecting the color of your choice from the list provided. Selecting the **More Colors** option at the bottom of the list will give you additional color choices.

There is also a **Filter** button in the **Constraint Style** box. Selecting the **Filter** button will bring up the **Constraint Filter** box as shown in Figure 2.51. The **Constraint Filter** allows you to specify which **Constraints** you want to appear on the screen and which **Constraints** you don't want to appear.

The **Dimension Style** box controls the actual geometry of the **Constraint**. The **Scale** option allows you to specify the size of the **Constraint.** The **Gap** option allows you to alter the distance between the part and the extension line of the dimension. The **OverRun** option allows you to specify how much of the extension line of the dimension sticks out past the dimension.

The **Display at Creation** provides a visual picture of how the different **Constraints** will look with the current settings.

Figure 2.51

17.5 Select the **Ok** button to return to the **Part Design Workbench**.

17.6 The first **Constraint** to be placed will be one that defines the height of the standing leg. To place this **Constraint**, select the **Constraint** tool from the right side of the screen. It may be hidden at the bottom of the screen.

17.7 Rotate the part until the bottom surface is visible and select it as shown in Figure 2.52.

Figure 2.52

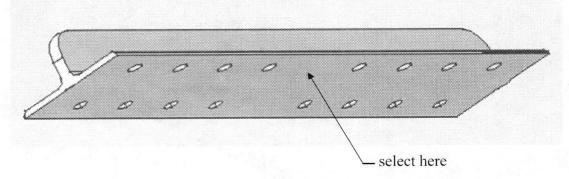

— select here

17.8 Rotate the part back until the top of the standing leg is visible and select it as shown in Figure 2.53.

NOTE: If you are having trouble selecting the entire surface (only one line will select), try zooming in closer and then selecting the surface.

— select here

Figure 2.53

17.9 When the **Constraint** appears on the screen, drag it away from the part and place it as shown in Figure 2.54. The **Constraint** should show **0.5"** in the value box as shown in Figure 2.54.

Figure 2.54

place **Constraint** here

17.10   Now apply what you have learned by creating a constraint that defines the length of the "**T Shaped Extrusion**". When you are done your part should look similar to the one shown in Figure 2.55.

Figure 2.55

18 Applying Material To The "T Shaped Extruison"

A special feature of CATIA V5 is the ability to add a material to the solid entity. CATIA V5 material contains the actual physical properties of the material as well as a specific visual representation. When a material has been added, the solid object takes on all of the characteristics of that material. The following steps will show you how to add material to an existing solid.

18.1   Select **Part1** from the top of the **Specification Tree** as shown in Figure 2.56. Make sure it is highlighted red indicating that it has been selected. Notice that the part will also highlight. **Part1** has to be highlighted so that CATIA V5 knows what to apply the material to.

Figure 2.56

18.2   Select the **Apply Materials** tool from the bottom of the screen.

18.3   The **Library** window will appear as shown in Figure 2.57. The **Library** window contains all of the materials available in CATIA V5. Notice that the materials are divided into categories. Each category has a tab at the top of the window. Each tab can be selected to access all of the materials under that particular category.

18.4   Select the **Metal** tab. This will bring up the metals library.

18.5   Select the **Aluminum** material located in the upper left corner of the window. The **Aluminum** label will highlight indicating it has been selected.

18.6   Select the **OK** button located at the bottom of the window. The **Aluminum** material will be added to the "**T Shaped Extrusion**". An **Aluminum.1** branch will be added to the **Specification Tree**.

Figure 2.57

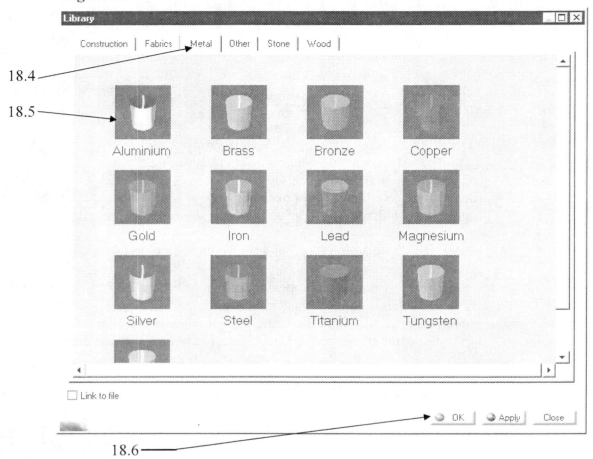

18.4

18.5

18.6

18.7 Right now the material only shows up in the tree. To view the material applied to the part, select the down arrow next to the **Render Style** tool at the bottom of the screen as shown in Figure 2.58.

18.8 When the options appear, select the **Render Style** tool ⌇. This tool is the **Applies Customized Veiw Parameters** tool.

18.9 This will bring up the **Custom View Modes** window. Select the **Materials** box at the bottom of the window as shown in Figure 2.59.

18.10 Select the **OK** button. The **Material** will now be applied to the **Part1** of the "**T Shaped Extrusion**". For all of the other **Reder Style** options, reference the Introduction Lesson.

Figure 2.59

Figure 2.58

Figure 2.60

Custom View Modes ? X

☑ Edges _points

☑ Shading

☐ Outlines

☐ Hidden edges _points

☐ Hidden line removed

☐ Dynamic hidden line removal

☑ Materials

◉ OK   ◉ Cancel

18.8

18.7

19 Managing The Specification Tree

During the creation of complex parts, the **Specification Tree** can become very long and extend below the screen as shown in Figure 2.60. The **Specification Tree** can be expanded or contracted. It can also be zoomed in or out.

Most of the branches in the **Specification Tree** have a sphere with either a plus or minus symbol (**–** **+**). The plus symbol means that a particular branch can be expanded to show more detail branches. The minus symbol means the **Specification Tree** may be compressed to hide the detail branches. The **Specification Tree** can be a very powerful tool if you learn to use it correctly. It is recommend that you spend some time expanding, contracting and manipulating the **Specification Tree**. The following steps explain how to change the size of the **Specification Tree**.

19.1 Select any one of the lines that connects the branches of the **Specification Tree** as shown in Figure 2.60. The part geometry on the screen will be dimmed to show that the **Specification Tree** is the only thing that can be manipulated.

19.2 Select the **+ Magnifying Glass** tool to **Zoom** up (enlarge) the **Specification Tree**. Select the **– Magnifying Glass** tool to zoom out. Use the tool to make the **Specification Tree** smaller. Reference Figure 2.61 for the **Zoom** tools located on the bottom tool bar.

Figure 2.61

19.3 The **Specification Tree** can also be moved to a different location on the screen. Make sure the **Specification Tree** is still selected, the part geometry is dimmed. Select the **Move** tool ✛ located on the tool bar at the bottom of the screen. Select the **Specification Tree**, then drag and drop it where you want it located.

19.4 To unselect the **Specification Tree** so you can go back to working on the part geometry, select anywhere on the line that connects the branches of the **Specification Tree**. When the part is no longer dimmed, all of the tools will be back to normal allowing you to manipulate the part geometry instead of the **Specification Tree**.

19.5 If the **Specification Tree** extends beyond the screen length, you can use the **Move** tool or move your mouse over the tree and select the middle mouse button to activate a scrool bar for the **Specification Tree**. You can move the scroll bar with your mouse. If your middle mouse button has a roller, you can scroll up and down the **Specification Tree** with the scroll button.

20 Customizing The Specification Tree

It is easy to keep track of the **CATPart** entities for simple designs such as **Sketches**, **Pads**, and **Patterns**. But for more complex designs and assemblies, it is critical to keep all of the design information readily available. The "**T Shaped Extrusion**" required only one **Sketch** and CATIA V5 automatically named it **Sketch.1** as shown in the **Specification Tree**. Modifying a parameter and/or **Constraint** in the sketch would be easy, because it would be obvious which sketch the parameters are in. If your design had five sketches, it would be a bit more complicated. If someone else had to modify your design, how would they know what information was in which sketch? Renaming **Sketch.1** to "**L Shaped Sketch**" would help determine the information contained it that sketch. It is suggested that you name the sketch "**L Shaped Sketch**" not **T**, because the sketch profile is still in the shape of an **L**. Remember; it is the **Mirror.1** branch that completes the "**T shaped Extrusion**". CATIA V5 allows you to rename the branches of the **Specification Tree** so it has meaningful information. It is not necessary to rename every branch, use good judgment in what to rename. Renaming particular branches of the **Specification Tree** will be critical in the following lessons. Customize your **Specification Tree** by completing the following steps.

20.1 First you will rename the base of the **Specification Tree**. Select **Part1** so it is highlighted.

20.2 With your mouse over the highlighted **Part1**, push the right mouse button. This will bring up the **Edit** window.

20.3   Select the **Properties** option. Make sure you have the correct entity
       selected. You will change the **Properties** of the selected element only.
       This will bring up the **Properties** window for the **Part1** entity.

20.4   Select the **Product** tab as shown in Figure 2.62. The **Part Number** box
       has **Part1** in it by default. Type in "**T Shaped Extrusion**" in the place of
       Part1.

20.5   Select **OK**. Check that the base of the **Specification Tree** is now named
       "**T Shaped Extrusion**". This step is important, especially when you start
       inserting multiple **Parts** into an assembly.

20.6   The next branch you need to rename is the **PartBody** branch. Use the
       same process as described in the previous steps to rename the **PartBody**
       branch. Rename the **PartBody** branch to "**T Shaped PartBody**". There

Figure 2.62

are some differences in the **Properties** window. The **Name** box is under
the **Feature Properties** tab instead of the **Product** tab. The box you
modify is under **Name** instead of **Part Number**.

20.7   Rename **Sketch.1** to "**L Shaped Sketch**" following the same process as
       described in Step 20.6

If your **Specification Tree** looks similar to what is shown in Figure 2.62 you are ready for the next step. Customizing the **Specification Tree** will become more important as your designs become more complex.

21 Reviewing The Design Process Using The Specification Tree

CATIA V5 supplies you with a tool to review the processes used to create a **CATPart**. This tool automatically takes you through each step of the design process. The following steps will take you through a review of the "**T Shaped Extrusion**" you created.

21.1 From the **Specification Tree** select the **PartBody** branch that you want to review.

21.2 From the top tool bar menu, select the **Edit** option. This will bring up the **Edit** pop-up window.

21.3 Select the **Scan or Define In Work Object** option located near the bottom of the window. This will bring up a **Scan** window as shown in Figure 2.63.

21.4 From the **Scan** window, select the **Forward** button. This will take you to the first step in creating the "**T Shaped Extrusion**", **Pad.1**.

21.5 Select the **Forward** button again. This will take you to the second design step where **EdgeFillet.1** was created.

21.6 Select the **Forward** button again. This will take you to the third design step where **EdgeFillet.2** was created.

21.7 Continue through the design steps by clicking the **Forward** button. This will take you through **Hole.1**, **Hole.2**, **RectPattern.1**, **RectPattern.2**, **Translate.1**, **Symmetry.1**, **Mirror.1** and **Scaling.1**.

21.8 When you get to **Scaling.1,** you will see the finished part which was the last design entity created.

21.9 You have the option of going backwards, by selecting the **Backward** button.

NOTE: If you exit out of the **Scan** window in the middle of the review process CATIA V5 will show the part as it existed at that point in the design process. In other words, it will not show the finished part. Don't panic; you haven't lost the finished part. Bring the **Scan** window back up and select the **Last Feature** button. Then select the **Exit** button.

Figure 2.63

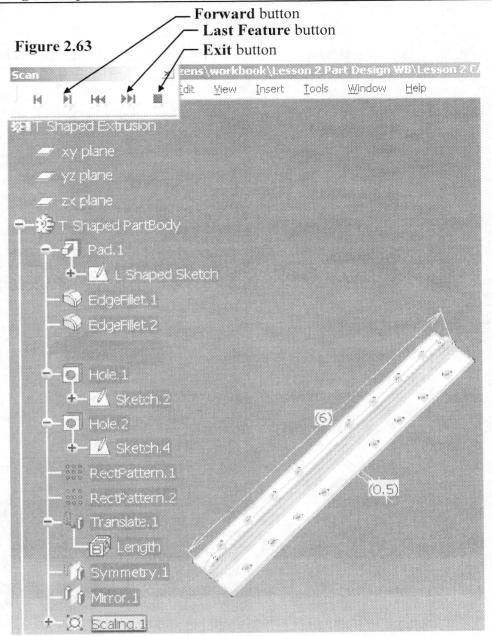

Forward button
Last Feature button
Exit button

22 Save The Completed "T Shaped Extrusion" Before It Gets Away

To save a CATIA V5 work session, complete the following steps.

22.1 Verify that all operations are complete and the "**T Shaped Extrusion**" is the way you want it to be saved. For the following steps reference Figure 1.45 and 1.46 in Lesson 1.

22.2 Select **File** from the top tool bar.

22.3 Select the **Save As** option.

22.4 In the **Save As** window, select the directory you want the part to be saved to.

22.5 In the same window, type in the **File Name**. For this lesson save your part as the "**T Shaped Extrusion**". The extension "**CATPart**" will be added automatically.

22.6 If everything is the way you want it in the **Save As** window, select **Save**.

NOTE: Remember the file name and the directory you saved your file in; you will need to open it back up and use it in Lesson 3 and Lesson 4.

Figure 2.64

23 Exiting CATIA V5

To exit CATIA V5, complete the following steps.

23.1 Make sure you saved the part. If you have made any unsaved changes to the part, CATIA V5 will prompt you to save when exiting.

23.2 Select **File** from the top tool bar as shown in Figure 2.64.

23.3 Select **Exit**.

23.4 Since CATIA V5 is Windows compliant, another way to exit is to select the **Close** tool at the very top right of the screen. Both methods of exiting CATIA V5 will put you back at the **Windows NT Desktop**.

Lesson 2 Summary

The **Part Design Work Bench** gives the designer a variety of powerful, time saving tools to work with. The **Part Design Work Bench** is a natural transition from the **Sketcher Work Bench**. It is important to be able to differentiate between **Sketcher** entities and **Part Design** entities.

Lesson 2 Review

After completing this lesson you should be able to answer the questions and explain the concepts listed below.

1. List two different methods of deleting an entity.
2. What three things must be selected to create a hole that is accurately located in a part?
3. How would you modify the diameter of a hole that is already created?
4. How would you modify the location of a hole that is already created?
5. CATIA V5 gives you a choice of five different types of holes. List all five.
6. CATIA V5 gives you several methods to rotate a part (changing the parts relationship to the 0,0,0 point). List two of them.
7. **T** or **F** Applying **Material** to your part automatically updates the visual representation of the part.
8. How can the **Specification Tree** be expanded to show additional branches?
9. What key on the keyboard do you hold down to multi-select two lines at the same time?
10. The **Rectangular Pattern** tool is found in which tool bar?
11. What color (by default) does CATIA V5 shade the part when it is in the process of updating?
12. What two things must be selected in order to use the **Rotate** command from the **Transformation Features** tool bar?
13. Name the five tool bars discussed in this lesson.
14. When creating a chamfer, what are the two different mode options available in the **Chamfer Definition** box?
15. How do you make the part dim so you can manipulate the **Specification Tree**?
16. What lets you know there are hidden tool bars at the bottom right side of the screen?
17. What tool would you use to move an object from one location to another?
18. **T** or **F** **Constraints** can be used in the **Sketcher Work Bench** only.
19. Why is it important to rename the specific branches in the **Specification Tree**?
20. Explain what the **Compass** can be used for.

Lesson 2 Practice Exercises:

Now that your CATIA V5 toolbox has more tools in it, put them to use on the following **Practice Exercises**. The shapes are simple and can be completed in one sketch. The dimensions represent the constraints you are to use in the **Sketcher Work Bench** prior to extruding them in the **Part Design Work Bench**. This lesson does not have any suggested steps, but there are helpful hints for each of the **Practice Exercises**.

Each **Practice Exercises** has a suggested name to use when saving the exercise; this is critical, because some of these exercises are used later on in this workbook. Good Luck!

1. This first exercise will get you more familiar with the **Chamfer** and **Hole** commands. Save this part as "**Lesson 2 Exercise 1.CATPart**".

HINT: Sketch the part with square edges. Add the two big chamfers to the part after it has been extruded into a part using the **Chamfer** tool ⬦ . Use the **Hole** tool ⬛ to add the hole in the part.

2. This part is pretty simple. Save this part as "**Lesson 2 Exercise 2.CATPart**".

HINT: The two holes can be put in at the same time. Use the **Up To Next** option in the **Extension** tab as shown in Figure 2.19.

3   This part provides good practice with the **Fillet** 🔲 and **Hole** 🔲 tools. Save this part as "**Lesson 2 Exercise 3.CATPart**".

HINT: Use the **Sketcher Work Bench** to create the part using three rectangles. Add the radii in the **Part Design Work Bench** using the **Fillet** tool 🔲 . Don't forget, you need to use the **Pad** 🔲 tool in the **Part Design Work Bench** prior to using the **Fillet** tool. The 1.55 radius can be created using two fillets of the same radius.

4 This part will give you more practice with the **Fillet** 🗆 and **Hole** 🗆 tools. Save this part as "**Lesson 2 Exercise 4.CATPart**".

HINT: For some practice using the **Mirror** tool 🗆 , create one half of the I-beam in the **Sketcher Work Bench**. Extrude it using the **Pad** tool 🗆 in the **Part Design Work Bench**. Use the **Mirror** tool to create the other half. Also, create the first hole in the channel and use the **Rectangular Pattern** tool 🗆 to create the rest of the holes.

NOTES:

Introduction To The Drafting Work Bench

In this lesson you will create a production drawing of the "**T Shaped Extrusion**" created in Lesson 1 and Lesson 2. The Lesson 3 format is the same as Lesson 1 and Lesson 2 in that it is not a comprehensive lesson on the **Drafting Work Bench**. It is not the intent of this lesson to be a comprehensive reference, but a basic step-by-step for the most common tools and functions in the CATIA V5 **Drafting Work Bench**.

Lesson 3 Objectives

This lesson will introduce you to the basics of creating sheets and views using the **Drafting Work Bench**. Lesson 4 covers the text and dimensioning found in the **Drafting Work Bench**.

This lesson covers the following areas:

- How to select the **Drafting Work Bench**
- The **Drafting Work Bench** layout
- How to customize the **Drafting Work Bench**
- How to create **Sheets**
- How to create **Views**
- How to modify an existing view
- How to move a view from on sheet to another
- How to create a **Detail**, **Section** and **Auxiliary Views**
- How to **Save** the newly created sheets (drawings) "***.CATDrawing**"
- How to **Print** the newly created sheets (drawings)

Drafting Work Bench Tool Bars

There are thirteen standard tool bars found in the **Drafting Work Bench**. Six of the thirteen tool bars are shown below. The other seven will be covered in Lesson 4. The individual tools found in each of the six tool bars are labeled to the right of the tool icon. This chapter will not cover every tool found in the **Drafting Work Bench**.

The **Select** Tool Bar

Tool Bar	Tool Name (default)	Tool Type Options
	Select	Selection Trap, Intersecting Trap, Polygon Trap, Paint Stroke Selection
	Free Rotation	

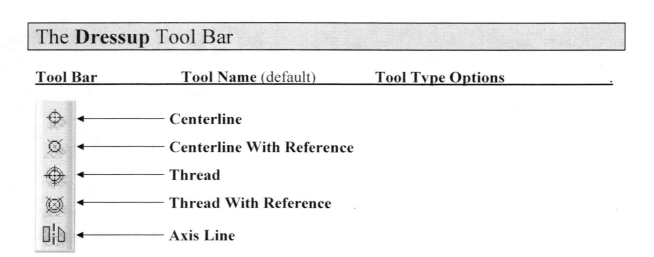

The **Dressup** Tool Bar

Tool Bar	Tool Name (default)	Tool Type Options
	Centerline	
	Centerline With Reference	
	Thread	
	Thread With Reference	
	Axis Line	

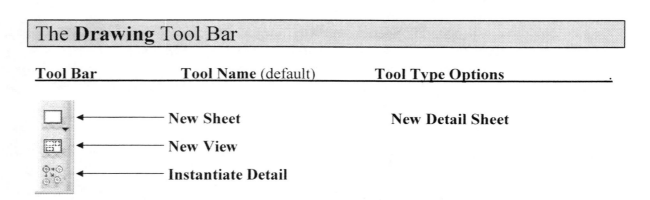

The **Drawing** Tool Bar

Tool Bar	Tool Name (default)	Tool Type Options
	New Sheet	New Detail Sheet
	New View	
	Instantiate Detail	

The **Views** Tool Bar

Tool Bar	Tool Name (default)	Tool Type Options
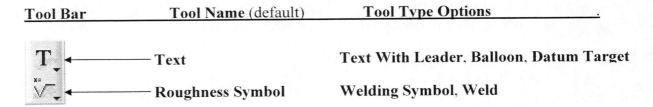	Front View	Unfolded, Projection, Auxiliary, Isometric
	Offset Section	Aligned, Offset Cut, Aligned Cut
	Detail View	Detail Profile, Quick Detail, Quick Profile
	Clipping View	Clipping View Profile
	View Creation Wizard	"Front, Top & Left", "Front, Bottom & Right", All Views

The **Annotations** Tool Bar

Tool Bar	Tool Name (default)	Tool Type Options
	Text	Text With Leader, Balloon, Datum Target
	Roughness Symbol	Welding Symbol, Weld

The Graphic Properties Tool Bar

Pattern

Copy Object Format

Line Type

Thickness

Color

Steps To Creating Sheets And Views Using The Drafting Work Bench

CATIA V5 uses the files created in the **Part Design Work Bench** to create drawings. As previously stated, the files created in the **Part Design Work Bench** are saved with the "**CATPart**" extension. The **Drafting Work Bench** uses the file created in the **Part Design Work Bench,** but is saved as a separate file. The **Drafting Work Bench** files have a "**CATDrawing**" extension. Both the "**CATPart**" and "**CATDrawing**" files are linked together. To pull up the "**CATDrawing**" file, CATIA V5 must be able to locate the related "**CATPart**" file. If CATIA V5 cannot find the linked file, you will get an error. If you move a "**CATPart**" file to a different directory, the "**CATDrawing**" file linked to it will not be able to locate the "**CATPart**" file. You will have to update the directory where the "**CATPart**" exists.

This lesson takes you through one of the more common methods of accessing, creating and manipulating a part ("**CATPart**" file) into a drafting or drawing format ("**CATDrawing**" file). There are multiple methods of creating a drawing. This lesson will introduce you to one method and several of the tools. You are encouraged to explore other methods to find out what works best for your requirements.

1   Start CATIA V5

If you need to review this step refer to Lesson 1 Step 1.

2   Select The Part Design Work Bench

Yes, this lesson covers the **Drafting Work Bench,** but it is easier to specify what "**CATPart**" you are bringing into the **Drafting Work Bench** by making it active in the **Part Design Work Bench**.

3   Open The "T Shaped Extrusion.CATPart" File

Open the "**T Shaped Extrusion**". The "**T Shaped Extrusion**" started in Lesson 1 as the "**L Shaped Extrusion**". In Lesson 2 the "**L Shaped Extrusion**" was mirrored into a T shaped extrusion; thus, at the completion of Lesson 2 the part was saved as the "**T Shaped Extrusion.CATPart**". Once your "**T Shaped Extrusion**" part is on the screen, select the very top branch labeled "**T Shaped Extrusion**" in the **Specification Tree** as shown in Figure 3.1. The default **Part1** label was revised in Lesson 2 to "**T Shaped Extrusion**". Make sure "**T Shaped Extrusion**" is highlighted.

Figure 3.1

T Shaped Extrusion ← select here
— xy plane
— yz plane
— zx plane

4   Select The Drafting Work Bench

This step uses the "**T Shaped Extrusion.CATPart**" to create a production drawing using the **Drafting Work Bench**. With a few simple menu selections, CATIA V5 will automatically produce an orthographic layout of your part. The steps are defined below.

Figure 3.2

4.1   Using one of the methods described in Lesson 1 select the **Drafting Work Bench**.

4.2   Selecting the **Drafting Work Bench** will bring up the **New Drawing Creation** pop-up window shown in Figure 3.3. The **Drafting Work Bench** has many options. This step will show you how to create a drawing relatively quick.

Drafting work Bench

Figure 3.3

4.3   Select the **Modify** button in the **New Drawing Creation** window as shown in Figure 3.3.

4.4   This selection will bring up an additional pop-up window, the **New Drawing** window as shown in Figure 3.4.

Figure 3.4

4.5 Select the arrow under the **Standard** option. This will give you several options for the standard you want to use for your drawing.

    4.5.1 For this lesson select "**ANSI**", as shown in Figure 3.4.

    4.5.2 For the **Format** box, select "**B ANSI**". The size of "**B ANSI**" will show up in the **Width** and **Height** boxes.

    4.5.3 Set the **Orientation** to "**Landscape**" and the **Scale Of Sheets** to "**1**".

    4.5.4 When all of the options are defined, select the **OK** button.

4.6 At this point, the **New Drawing** window will disappear leaving the **New Drawing Creation** window as shown in Figure 3.5. The information displayed in the window should be updated to show the options you just defined, such as the **Standard**, **Format**, and **Orientation**. This window gives you four drawing layout options. For this lesson, select the third option: **Front**, **Bottom** and **Right**.

Figure 3.5   select here

4.7   Select **OK**. The pop-up window will disappear and the CATIA V5 drafting screen will appear. The "**T Shaped Extrusion**" part will appear in the three views you just defined: **Front**, **Bottom** and **Right**. Reference Figure 3.6 for the CATIA V5 drafting screen.

Figure 3.6

5   The Drafting Work Bench Layout

One of the first things you should notice is that the screen looks significantly different than the **Sketcher** and **Part Design Work Benches**. The **Drafting Work Bench** is truly limited to two dimensions. All of the rotation and other 3D capabilities are gone. Your 3D part is now being represented in orthographic projection, the foundation on which drafting is based.

5.1   **Tool Bars**: By default there are thirteen tool bars in the CATIA V5 **Drafting Work Bench**. Thirteen tool bars is too many to possibly show on one side bar. By default, CATIA V5 adds a tool bar across the top of the screen. This is still not enough room to represent all of the tool bars. Notice, both the side tool bar and top tool bar have the double arrow symbol signifying that there are additional tool bars avalaible, but not visible. To help you get familar with all of the tool bars, pull all thirteen tool bars out on the screen so they are visible and available for selection.

5.2   **Sheet.1**: CATIA V5 automatically created **Sheet.1** for you. The size was specified by you in the **New Drawing Creation** window. You selected "**B ANSI**" which is 17" X 11". The sheet is represented by the shadowed box in Figure 3.6.

5.3   **View Layout**: You determined the view layout in the **New Drawing Creation** window. You selected the third choice, which included the **Front**, **Bottom** and **Right** views. By default, the views include the **View Name** and **View Scale**. You will be shown how to modify this later in this lesson.

5.4   **Drafting Work Bench Specification Tree**: CATIA V5 creates a **Specification Tree** for the **Drafting Work Bench**. The **Specification Tree** is separate from the **Part Design Specification Tree,** but has similar qualities and can be manipulated (modified) in the same manner.

5.5   Modifiying the **Drafting Work Bench Standards**: As in the **Sketcher** and **Part Design Work Benches**, the standards are quick and easy to change.

The only action required by you in this step is to pull all thirteen tool bars out on the screen so they are visible and can be easily selected. If you have completed this task you can continue on to Step 6.

Figure 3.7

6   Customizing The Default Values

If you are going to change anything about the **Drafting Work Bench** defaults, now would be the best time. Customizing the **Drafting Work Bench** is similar to the customizations made in Lesson 1 and Lesson 2. The steps are detailed below.

6.1   Go to the top tool bar (pull down menus) and click on **Tools**, **Options** as shown in Figure 3.7. This brings up **File Tab** options on the right side of the screen and **File Type** options on the left. From the options on the left, select **Drafting**. The tabbed options on the right change accordingly.

6.2   Under **Drafting,** there are six tabs. They are **General**, **Layout,**

Figure 3.8

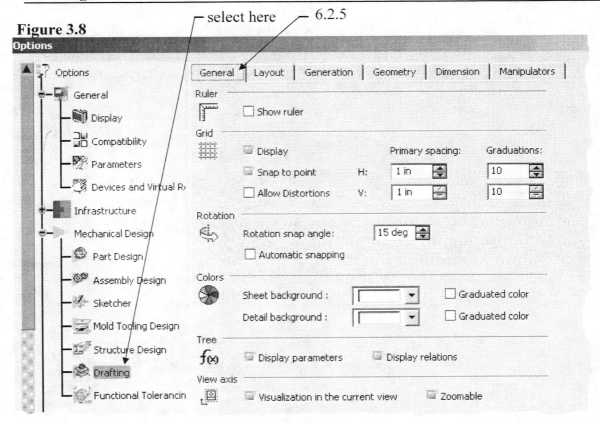

Generation, Geometry, Dimension and **Manipulators**. The following is a breif explanation of the different tabs.

6.2.1   **General**: Figure 3.8 shows the different sections of the **General** tab and the variables they control. The controls are similar to the **Sketcher** and **Part Design** controls. For this step set the **Grid primary Spacing** value to **1"** and the **Graduations** to **10**. Turn the **Grid Display** and **Snap To Point** on.

6.2.2   **Layout**: Figure 3.9 displays the togle controls in the **Layout** tab. This tab controls the default setup of the drawing views. For this step set up your **Layout** the same as shown in Figure 3.9.

Figure 3.9

| General | Layout | Generation | Geometry | Dimension |

View creation
- View name
- Scaling factor
- View frame
- Propagation of broken and breakout specfications

New Sheet
- Copy background view

Source sheet: ● First sheet
                      ○ Other drawing

6.2.3   **Generation**: The toggle control for the **Generation** tab is displayed in Figure 3.10. Set up your **Generation** tab the same as shown in Figure 3.10.

Figure 3.10

6.2.4   **Geometry**: This tab controls how the geomentry created in the **Drafting Work Bench** will be displayed. Some of the togle controls also appear in the bottom tool bar such as **Constraint Visualization**, reference Figure 3.11 and Figure 3.6. Set up your **Geomtry** tab the same as is shown in Figure 3.11.

6.2.5   **Dimension**: This tab controls how the dimensions are created and visualized. There are additional windows with more controls. This tab is not covered in detail but you now know where the controls are. As you create dimensions you are encouraged to test the different controls. For this step set up the tab as shown in Figure 3.12.

6.2.6   **Manipulators**: This tab controls the tools that allow you to modify the dimensions. For this step set up the tab as shown in Figure 3.13.

Figure 3.11

Figure 3.12

Figure 3.13

| Layout | Generation | Geometry | Dimension | Manipulators |

Manipulators

Reference size: .118 in

☐ Zoomable

Dimension Manipulators

		Creation	Modification
☐	Modify overrun:	☐	☐
☐	Modify blanking:	☐	☐
▼	Insert text before:	☐	☐
▼	Insert text after:	☐	☐
⟨⟹	Move value:	☐	☐
	Move dimension line:	☐	☐
	Move dimension line secondary part:	☐	☐

6.3   You are encouraged to try some of the other modifications. When the changes have been made, select the **OK** button at the bottom of the **Options** windows. The changes you specified will be displayed, such as the **Grid** and **Graduations**.

7   Creating A New Sheet

The orthographic layout of the "**T Shaped Extrusion**" on **Sheet.1** does not leave much room for any additional views. To add an additional view, you will need to create a new sheet. To do this, complete the following steps.

7.1   Creating new and/or additional sheets for your drawing is very simple. First you have to be in the **Drafting Work Bench**.

7.2   In the **Drafting Work Bench,** select the **New Sheet** tool ☐. This will create a new sheet every time you click on the tool. For this lesson create **Sheet.2**.

7.3   There are two ways you can verify that a new sheet has been created. One way is, at the top left of the **Drafting Work Bench** screen there are **Sheet** tabs representing each existing sheet as shown in Figure 3.14. The tabs will be labeled **Sheet.1** and **Sheet.2** in successive order. The second method of

new sheet

Figure 3.14

verifying a new sheet was created, is by checking the **Drafting Specification Tree**. The **Sheets** will also show up as branches as shown in Figure 3.15. The branches will be labeled the same as the tabs. The newly created sheet will become the active sheet. If you want to go back to the previous sheet, click on the file tab representing the desired sheet number. The sheet can also be selected from the **Drafting Specification Tree**.

7.4   Each newly created sheet will, by default, have the sheet size and drafting standard defined when you first enter the **Drafting Work Bench**.

Figure 3.15

7.5   No new views have been defined for the newly created **Sheet.2**. As the views are defined, the **Drafting Specification Tree** will also include the defined views.

The sheets are as easy to delete as they are to create. You can select the sheet from the **Specification Tree**, then select the **Cut** tool ✂ at the bottom of the screen. Be careful, you can delete a sheet even if it has existing views defined.

8   Creating A New View

Now that you have created a new sheet, you can create additioinal views as required and/or desired. There are several different ways to add new views to the newly created sheet; two of the most common methods are listed below.

NOTE: It is important that you know what view and orientation of the part is best for what you want to accomplish. To fully visualize what you are creating in the **Drafting Work Bench** and selecting from the **Part Design Work Bench**, split the screen horizontally so that half of the screen shows the **Drafting Work Bench** and the other half displays the **Part Design Work Bench**. To split the screen horizontally, select the pull down window labled **Window** at the top center of the screen. Select **Tile Horizontally**

Figure 3.16

as shown in Figure 3.16. This selection will split all of the active windows horizontally on the screen. You will be required to select a plane or surface from the **Part Design Work Bench**. The plane or surface you select will be applied to the **Drafting Work Bench**. So, before proceeding, be sure you have the **Part Design Work Bench** and the **Drafting Work Bench** windows split on the screen as shown in Figure 3.17. This is a common window function.

Figure 3.17 (Windows tiled horizontally)

8.1   Select the **View Creation Wizard** 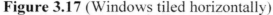 tool from the **Views** tool bar.

8.2   This will bring up a pop-up window labeled "**View Wizard (Step ½): Predefined Configurations**". The window allows you, the user, to define the specific orthographic projections and/or isometric views. Select the first choice (top left) "**Configuration 1 using the 3rd angle projection method**". This option will place three orthographic views on the pop-up window. At this point, you can modify the placement of the views by selecting the individual views and dragging them to the new location. Once you have the placement of the three views similar to Figure 3.18, select the **Next** button at the bottom of the pop-up window.

Figure 3.18

select here first

select here second

8.3   The next window allows you to select additional views (Figure 3.19). In this step you will want to add an isometric view (bottom left choice). Select the **Isometric** button and then select the location you want the isometric view to be presented. For this lesson, place the isometric view at the top right of the existing views.

Figure 3.19

isometric view

place view here

when done select here (8.4)

8.4   When you have the view layout as you desire, or similar to Figure 3.19, select the **Finish** button at the bottom middle of the pop-up window.

8.5   CATIA V5 will then prompt you to "**Select a reference plane on a 3D geometry**". The plane or surface you are being prompted for is refering to the part in the **Part Design Work Bench**. For this lesson, select the surface shown in Figure 3.20.

Figure 3.20

Blue Compass

select this surface

8.6   After you select the surface, four green rectanglar frames will appear in the **Drafting Work Bench** screen. The rectanglar frames will be labeled with the views you defined in the Steps 8.2 and 8.3. The part will be displayed in the **Front View**, with the surface you selected in Step 8.5 as the front view, normal to the viewer as shown in Figure 3.20. If you drag your mouse over the other views, you will notice that the part appears in the view the mouse is over. If you move the mouse over the **Top View,** the part will appear in that view, oriented as the **Top View**.

8.7   You should also notice a **Blue Compass** in the upper right hand corner of the **Drafting Work Bench** shown in Figure 3.20. The **Blue Compass** allows you to modify the views prior to completing the view orientation. The four arrows pointing 90 degrees apart will rotate the part 90 degrees in the rotational direction you select. In other words, currently the length of the "**T Shaped Extrusion**" is shown in the **Front View**, if you selected the arrow pointing to the right on the **Blue Compass,** the part would rotate 90 degrees. The orientation would change and the length of the part would be shown in the **Right View**. The half circled arrows will not change the part orientation/view relationship, but will rotate the part in the view every 15 degrees. Notice the green ball on the outside of the **Blue Compass** rotates around indicating the degree of rotation. The 15 degree rotation is the standard default. This should be enough to get you started in creating the views you need. The best way to find out what these tools are really capable of is to test and try them, don't be afraid of making a mistake.

Figure 3.21

Angle of rotation

8.8   Once you have the views oriented the way they are shown in Figure 3.22, select anywhere on the sheet to lock and complete the view orientation. Notice that the **Blue Compass** disappears and the part shows up on all of the views in their correct orientation.

Figure 3.22

8.9   If you were testing the **Blue Compass** capabilities and oriented your part
         in such a way that you could not get back to where you started, delete
         what you have and start at Step 8.1 again. Starting at Step 8.1 may sound
         like a lot of work, but the steps are quick and easy. You should be able to
         recreate the views again in a matter of a few seconds. For this lesson
         make sure your view and part orientation look similar to the ones shown in
         Figure 3.22.

NOTE: The default incremental angle of rotation on the **Blue Compass** can be
                modified by holding the mouse over the green ball and pressing the right
                mouse button. This brings up a window that allows you select **Free
                Hand Rotation, Incremental Hand Rotation** and **Set Increment**.

9   Modifying An Existing View

Now that you have been briefly introduced to the process of creating a view, you will
need to know how to modify a view. This step will cover modification of a view,
meaning changing the view properties, appearance, location, scale, moving to a
different sheet, copying, pasting and deleting. Being able to modify an existing view
is a powerful and important aspect of creating a drawing using the **Drafting Work
Bench**. These steps show you how to modify a view.

9.1   **Modifing View Properties**.

9.1.1   Select the view to be modified. The view has to be the active view. The active view will be underlined in the **Drafting Specification Tree** as shown in Figure 3.23.

Select view border or select view in **Drafting Specification Tree**

Figure 3.23

9.1.2   With the mouse over the selected view border push the right mouse button. This will bring up the **Properties** pop-up window. Reference Figure 3.24 for all of the properties options. No changes are necessary at this time.

9.2   **Deleting a view from a sheet**.

9.2.1   Select the view so it is highlighted. This is done by moving the mouse over the view border and selecting it.

9.2.2   With the view highlighted, select the **Scissors** tool in the bottom left corner of the screen. You can also use the **Edit, Cut** or **Delete** options (**Windows** functions).

9.2.3   The view you selected will be deleted, as well as every entity attached to it such as text, 2D geometry and dimensions.

9.3   **Moving a view around on a sheet**.

9.3.1   Select the view so its border is highlighted.

9.3.2   Select the view border with the left mouse button and hold the mouse button down. This will hold the view. Drag the mouse to the location you want the view. When you get the view where you want it, release the mouse button and the view will stay in that location.

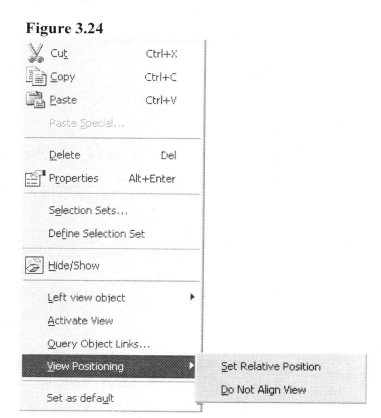

Figure 3.24

9.3.3   If the view was created as an **Auxiliary View** , the view will be locked at the angle the view was projected from. **Alignment** to a view means you can move the view closer or farther away, but you can not move the view to either side; it will stay in the same direction it was projected from. You can override the orthographic projected alignment by selecting **View Positioning** found in the **Properties** window. Then select the **Do Not Align View** option. This will allow you to move the view anywhere you want. If you want to re-align the view complete the same steps, except select **Align View**.

9.4   **Moving a view from one sheet to another sheet**. This process is the same for moving a view and/or copying a view.

9.4.1 Go to the sheet with the view to be moved.

9.4.2 Select the view to be moved.

9.4.3 Use one of the multiple window functions to copy the view to the **Windows** clip board: $\boxed{\text{Ctrl}}$ $\boxed{\text{C}}$, **Edit/Copy** or the **Copy** command in the **Properties** pop-up window reference Figure 3.24 and 3.25 .

9.4.4 Go to the sheet where the view is being moved to.

Figure 3.25

9.4.5 Use one of the multiple **Window** functions to paste from the windows clip board: $\boxed{\text{Ctrl}}$ $\boxed{\text{V}}$, **Edit/Paste** or the **Paste** command in the **Properties** pop-up window reference Figure 3.24 and 3.25 .

✂ Cut	Ctrl+X	
📋 Copy	Ctrl+C	9.4.3
📋 Paste	Ctrl+V	9.4.5
Paste Special...		

9.4.6 The view will appear on the new sheet. You may have to relocate the view within the new sheet (Step 9.3).

9.4.7 The **Drafting Specification Tree** gives you one other method of moving a view from one sheet to another. In the **Drafting Specification Tree,** select the view you want to move and drag and drop it onto the sheet you want to move it to.

9.5 **Scaling a view**. To modify the scale of a view you need to go to Step 10.6.

9.6 **Changing the size of the view window**. As you create dimensions and/or drafting geometry, the view window will expand to encompass the new geometry. CATIA V5 adjusts the view frame automatically. The frame can be larger than the sheet as long as the geometry is contained with in the sheet boundary. The views and geometry do not have to be inside the sheet boundary other than for printing purposes.

10 Creating A Detail View

Detail Views are used to show detailed areas of a part that are too small to see and/or dimension in a standard orthographic view. Detail views are usually scaled up several times to show the needed detail.

CATIA V5 makes creating **Detail Views** quick and easy. The steps below show you how to create a **Detail View** from an existing view. In this exercise you will create a **Detail View** of the "**T Shaped Extrusion**". The current standard orthographic views do not allow enough room for all of the dimensions required to fully define the "**T Shaped Extrusion**". To create a **Detail View** complete the following steps.

10.1 In this step you will be using the **Right View** on **Sheet.2**. Go to **Sheet.2** and activate the **Right View**. This is done by double clicking on the border of the view or by double clicking on the **Right View** in the **Drafting Specification Tree**. You can tell which view is the active view, because the border will be highlighted. Make sure the **Right View** is highlighted.

10.2 Select the **Detail View** tool .

10.3 The prompt zone will read "**NullState**". Determine and then select the center point of the **Detail View**. When selecting the center point, you may want to turn off the "**Snap To Grid**". The "**Snap To Grid**" may make it difficult to select the exact center of the **Detail View.**

For this lesson, make the center of your **Detail View,** the end of the left base leg of the "**T Shaped Extrusion**". This will allow you to dimension the chamfer on that base leg as shown in Figure 3.26. Dimensioning will be covered in the next lesson. You will need to **Zoom** in on the **Right View** to select the left side accurately.

Figure 3.26

select here for center
of **Detail View**

10.4 With the center of the **Detail View** selected, move the mouse away from the selected center. The distance you move away from the center determines the size of, and scope covered by, the **Detail View** . Notice the view grows as you move the mouse away from the selected center. CATIA V5 will prompt you to "**Select a point or click to define the circle radius**". When you move the mouse out, sufficient enough to show the chamfer as shown in Figure 3.27. Confirm the view size by selecting the location with the mouse.

Figure 3.27

drag circle approximately
to this location

10.5 Once you have determined the size of the view by selecting the circle, CATIA V5 automatically creates the **Detail View**. Now all you have to do is determine the location of the view. You determine the location by dragging the mouse around to where you want the view located. When you get the view where you want it, select the location and the view will freeze in that location. The view will by default be created at a scale of 2 to 1. Notice CATIA V5 automatically creates a link from the standard orthographic view to the **Detail View**. By default the view is labled **View A**. Reference Figure 3.28 for the link between the **Right View** and **Detail View A**. This default labeling may be revised.

Figure 3.28

10.6 **Detail View A** will have to be scaled from the default of 2:1 to 7:1. To modify the **View Scale,** complete the following steps.

10.6.1 Make sure the **Detail View** is active, then double click on it so it is highlighted. Remember you can also select the **Detail View** from the **Drafting Specification Tree**.

10.6.2 Move the mouse so it is on top of the view border as shown in Figure 3.29. Push the right mouse button. If the mouse is on any other enity, the **Properties** window will be for that entity, not the view properties.

Figure 3.29   place mouse here

Figure 3.30

10.6.3 A pop-up window will appear. Select the **Properties** option as shown in Figure 3.30.

10.6.4 This will bring up all of the properties that define the **Detail View** you just created.

10.6.5 Select the **View** tab at the top left of the window. One of the variables under the **View** tab is **Parameters,** which includes the **Scale.** Type in **7** to **1** in the place of **2** to **1** as shown in Figure 3.31. Select **Apply** at the bottom right of the screen. **Apply** will allow you to preview the change before commiting to it. Notice the other view variables that can modified.

Figure 3.31
Change the 2 to a 7

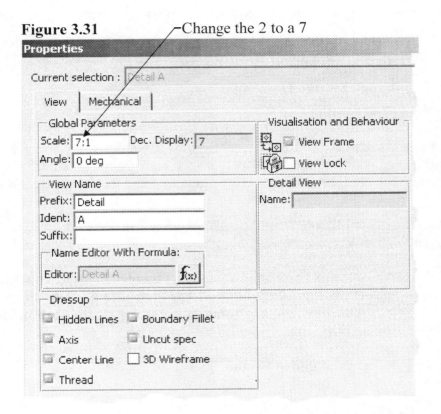

10.6.6 Select **OK**, and the modification will be completed. CATIA V5 automatically updated the scale value for you.

10.6.7 Notice, under **Sheet.2** in the **Drafting Specification Tree** that view **Detail A** has been added, reference Figure 3.32 .

Figure 3.32

Detail View A can now be dimensioned and modified just like any other view. Congratulations! You have just created your first detail view!

11 Creating A Section View

Creation of **Section Views** has never been easier. To get the full picture of what you are creating, it is suggested that you have the screen split between the **Drafting Work Bench** and the **Part Design Work Bench**. Refer to Step 8 on splitting the screen between the two work benches.

There are four options under the **Section View** tool, they are;

    1   **Aligned Section View** .

    2   **Offset Section View** .

    3   **Aligned Section Cut** .

    4   **Offset Section Cut** .

The **View** and **Cut** are similar, except for the **Cut** options show only what is on the cutting plane; whereas, the **View** includes the background geometry. Study the difference between the **Offset Section View** tool and the **Offset Section Cut** tool.

For this lesson you will be using the **Aligned Section View** . To create an **Aligned Section View,** complete the following steps.

    11.1 Activate the **Top View** , reference Figure 3.33. The **Top View** is the view that shows the holes true size. The view is looking down on the standing leg. **The view you are going to use to create the section view must be the active view.**

    11.2 Select the **Aligned Section View** tool.

Figure 3.33 Top View

                         Top view
                         Scale: 1:1

    NOTE: Using the **Drafting Work Bench,** you are going to create a line that cuts across the part. This line will be represented in the **Part Design Work Bench** as a plane that cuts perpendicular through the part. As you create the line in the **Drafting Work Bench,** you can simultaniously see the cutting plane in the **Part Design Work Bench**.

After you select the **Aligned Section View** tool, CATIA V5 will prompt you with "**FirstState**". This prompt is asking you to select the starting point for your line. Your mouse will now be accompanied by the **Autodetector** ⊕.

11.3 Move the **Autodetector** to the **Top View,** directly over the center of the hole farthest to the left of the **Top View**. Notice, as the **Autodetector** passes over the hole location, CATIA V5 creates a connecting line from the center of the hole to the **Autodetector**. This connecting line is telling you when the cutting line passes through the center of a hole. For this step you want the cutting line to pass through the center of this hole. Move the **Autodetector** about one **Primary Spacing** above the part. Reference Figure 3.34 for approximate target location. Once you have the **Autodetector** located as described, click the left mouse button once. This selection defines the starting location for the cutting plane.

Figure 3.34 ——Place **Autodetector** here

Top view
Scale: 1:1

11.4 CATIA V5 will now prompt you to "**Select an object or a command**". This prompt is asking you to select the second point of the cutting line. Move the mouse directly down through the part, the **Autodetector** will soon follow. Notice as you move the **Autodetector** through the part, you are creating a cutting line through the part in the **Drafting Work Bench,** as shown in Figure 3.35. This cutting line is visible in the **Part Design Work Bench** as a cutting plane as shown in Figure 3.36. As you move the mouse around, a visible representation is created in both the **Drafting Work Bench** (represented as a line) and the **Part Design Work Bench** (represented as a plane). The cutting line in the **Drafting Work Bench** also shows the angle of the cutting plane. For this lesson, pull the line down through the entire part and one additional **Primary Spacing** below the part. Keep the angle at 90 degrees as shown in Figure 3.35.

11.5 CATIA V5 allows you to create additional cutting planes by continuing the process of clicking and moving. For this lesson, only one cutting plane is required. Move the **Autodetector** to the location described in

Step 11.4 as shown in Figure 3.35 and double click the mouse. Double clicking the mouse will end the process of creating the **Section View**.

Figure 3.35

Top view
Scale: 1:1

Figure 3.36

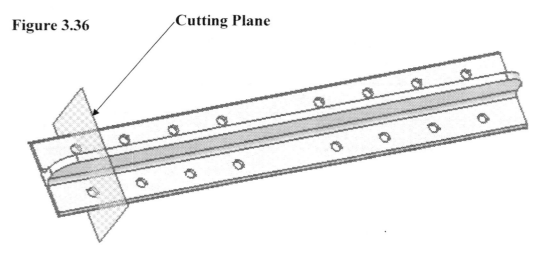

11.6 The **Aligned Section View** is created but not yet located. The **Aligned Section View** will be framed in a green border and will follow your mouse movement.

11.7 Drag the mouse to where you want the **Aligned Section View** and select that location. The **Aligned Section View** will now be frozen in the selected location. When you select the location, the part goes away and the **Section View** remains similar to what is shown in Figure 3.37. CATIA V5 will automatically call the view **Section View B-B**. You might have to go back to a full screen view and/or **Zoom Up** on the view to

Figure 3.37

B-B

Section view
Scale: 1:1

see all the detail clearly. If you selected the center of the hole location, you will be able to see that the **Section View** shows the holes and their centerlines.

11.8   You can modify the location, title and scale of **Section View B-B**. You can also use the **Show/No Show** tools to modify the appearance of **Section View B-B**. To change the **Properties** of the **Section View B-B,** refer to Step 9. For this step, no properties need to be modified.

NOTE: CATIA V5 has saved you a lot of work. It has automatically created and labled the Section view and linked it Top View. The **Drafting Specification Tree** added the the new **Section View B-B** to the current sheet as shown in Figure 3.38. CATIA V5 has taken the responsibility of naming the views, but allows you the flexibility to modify them if so desired.

Figure 3.38

This is a very powerful drafting tool. Although this lesson does not go into any more detail on this tool, you now have an introductory knowledge of how to apply it to your drawings. You can now expand that basic knowledge by applying it to different parts. The **Practice Exercises** at the end of this lesson will give you that opportunity.

12 Creating An Auxiliary View

Orthographic projection can usually show enough part detail to show all dimensions and surfaces "**True Size**". When standard orthographic views can not show all of the required detail, auxiliary views are used to show the required detail. CATIA V5 has made the creation of **Auxiliary Views** quick and easy. This step will take you through creating an **Auxiliary View** of the "**T Shaped Extrusion**". The standard orthographic views show all of the dimensions required on this part, except for the chamfer on the base leg. To show the chamfer surface "**True Size**", an **Auxiliary View** is required. Complete the following steps to create an **Auxiliary View**.

12.1   Activate the **Right View**, the view shown in Figure 3.22. The **Right View** shows the edge of the chamfer the best. It is the edge of the chamfer that you will use to project the **Auxiliary View** from.

12.2 Select the **Auxiliary View** tool . This tool is found in the **Views** tool
bar. It is not the default tool, so you may have to select the little arrow at
the bottom to access the **Auxiliary View** tool.

12.3 CATIA V5 will prompt you to "**Sketch a projection plane**". This prompt
is asking you to draw a line in the active view. The line will be used to
project the new view 90 degrees from the line. What you need to
accomplish in this step is to show the chamfered surface "**True Size**" in
your **Auxiliary View**. To do this, you must create a line that is parallel to
the chamfered edge in the **Right View**.

12.4 Move your mouse to the **Right View**, the **Autodetector** will follow.
Notice, as you move your mouse past the chamfered edge, the edge
highlights. This signifies that you are parallel with that line. When the
chamfer edge is highlighted, select the point as shown in Figure 3.39.
This will be the starting point for your projection line.

Figure 3.39   select here

12.5 CATIA V5 will prompt you for a "**Second_State**". This means, select the
second or ending point for your projection line. If you drag the mouse
along (parallel to) the chamfered edge, the chamfered edge will remain
highlighted. This signifies that you are still parallel to the chamfered edge
line. Drag it parallel and past the part as shown in Figure 3.40, then select
the point.

Figure 3.40

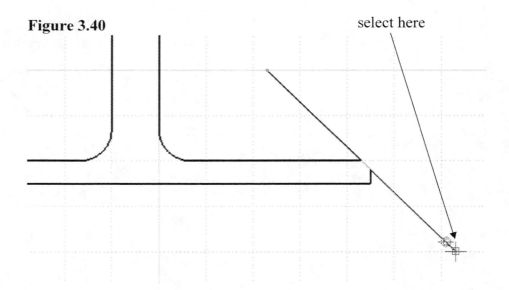

select here

12.6 CATIA V5 will prompt you to "**Click the view position**". CATIA V5 has created the **Auxiliary View,** but is asking you where to place it. Drag the mouse 90 degrees away from the projection line you created in Steps 12.3 thru 12.5. As you drag the mouse away, you will notice the new **Auxiliary View** trailing the mouse movement. Move the mouse to an open spot on your sheet and select that location as shown in Figure 3.41. The new **Auxiliary View** will be locked in that location. The view location can be modified, but location is limited. Since the view was created 90 degrees from the projection line, the view is locked into the line of projection. You can move the view away from the projection line, but not from side to side.

Figure 3.41   **Auxiliary View**

Auxiliary view C
Scale: 1:1

Right view
Scale:1

12.7 Once you lock in the view location, the view name and scale appear as shown in Figure 3.41. An automatic link is made to the **Auxiliary View** and the view it was projected from. CATIA V5 creates the projection lines and reference to the **Auxiliary View**.

12.8 The newly created **Auxiliary View** is very long and takes up a lot of room on the sheet. If a small portion of the view will show all the information needed, you can clip the view. The **Clipping** tool allows you to show only the portion of the view you select. Select the **Clipping View Profile** tool located in the **View** tool bar. All you need to do is draw a frame around the part of the view you want to be visible. The portion of the view outside of the frame will not be visible. The frame is created using successive lines, then double clicking to end. For this lesson, use the **Clipping View Profile** tool to hide the overall length of the "**T Shaped Extrusion**", reference Figure 3.42 and 3.43.

Figure 3.42

make this box

A   C

C

Right view
Scale:1

```
Auxiliary view C
Scale:  1:1
```

Figure 3.43 (after **Clipping** has been performed)

A
C
C

```
Auxiliary view C
Scale: 1:1
```

Right view
Scale: 1:1

The combination of the tools available give you a limitless possiblity of view creation and manipulation. This lesson was a brief introduction to the possiblities. This lesson did not cover all of the tools available. The other tools are similar, so if you get the idea of what you need to do, you can easily and quickly learn the other tools.

13 Saving Your Newly Created Drawing

This process is basically identical to saving a file covered in Lesson 1. The only difference is that it will be saved with the name you give it followed by the extension of "**CATDrawing**". This "**CATDrawing**" file will be linked to the "**CATPart**" file it used to create the views. Next time you bring up this "**CATDrawing**" file, it will go to the same directory looking for the "**CATPart**" file. If the "**CATPart**" file has been deleted or moved to another directory, you will get a warning that it can not find the "**CATPart**" file required to complete the CATIA Session. You will have the option to bring up just the "**CATDrawing**" file, but the part will not be loaded. If the file was moved to another directory, you will have the opportunity to type in the new directory so the file can be linked.

For this lesson, save your newly created drawing as "**T Shaped Extrusion.CATDrawing**".

14 Printing The Newly Created Sheets

Printing the final product is very similar to almost any other **Windows** printing process. To print **Sheet.1** and/or print **Sheet.2**, complete the following steps.

Figure 3.44

    14.1 Before you print, go to the the **Page Setup** window found in the **File** pull down menu. The **Page Setup** window shown in Figure 3.44, allows you to change the **Format** of your sheet, including the standard size (**Width & Height**). It allows you change the **Orientation** to **Landscape** or **Protrait**. If you have not changed your units to inches in the **Tools**, **Options**, **General** menu, the **Width** and **Height** will be in mm. The last option is to modify the **Background**. If you have made the appropriate changes along the way, this should be just a verification process. Reference Figure 3.44 for the layout of the **Page Setup** window.

    14.2 Select the **File**, **Print Preview** option. The **Print Preview** window will pop up. The window will give you a good idea of what your print will look like before you commit it to paper. If you are satisfied with the what is shown on the **Print Preview** window, select the **Print** tool to print.

    14.3 If you already know that your sheet is set up the way you want it, you can skip Step 2 and select the **Print** option. This will bring up the **Print** pop-up window. The **Print** window offers all the print options any **Windows** application does; **Printer**, **Print Range**, **Copies**, **Print Preview** and **Options** buttons. For the **Print** window layout and options, reference Figure 3.45. You were instructed to selected the "**B ANSI**" sheet size which is 11" X 17". If you have a printer/plotter, that will plot that size, you are good to continue. If you have a standard 8.5" X 11" printer, you will have to select the "**Fit to printer format**" option. This will print the 11" X 17" on 8.5" X 11"; hence, the print will not be to scale.

Figure 3.45

14.4 If everything is set up the way you want it, select the **OK** button at the bottom of the **Print** window. A click of the **OK** button and your masterpiece should be on its way!

This lesson does not require you to print any of the sheets you created. However, it would be a good idea to try printing now. Future lessons will refer back to this step when printing is required.

Lesson 3 Summary

Creating a drawing is no small task. CATIA V5 has gone a long way in simplifying and automating the process, where possible. The best thing CATIA V5 has done is to make the process easier to learn. This lesson supplies the introductory tools required to start producing drawings immediately. You now have enough knowledge to explore and learn the more advanced options.

Lesson 3 Review

After completing this lesson you should be able to answer the questions and explain the concepts listed below.

1. A file created in the **Drafting Work Bench** has what type of file extension?
2. What are the similarities between the **Drafting Work Bench** and the **Sketcher Work Bench**?
3. **T or F** A line created in the **Drafting Work Bench** is a three-dimensional entity.
4. List at least three types of **Views** CATIA V5 creates automatically for you.
5. **T or F** The **Drafting Work Bench** has a **Specification Tree**.
6. **T or F** CATIA V5 allows a maximum of 5 views per sheet.
7. **T or F** CATIA V5 allows you to transfer a view from one sheet to another.
8. **T or F** By default, all of the tool bars are visible when entering into the **Drafting Work Bench**.
9. How do you toggle the **Snap to Grid** on and off?
10. How do you modify the **Primary Spacing** of the grid?
11. **T or F** You have to use the **View Creation Wizard** to create a sheet.
12. What tool bar contains the following tools: **Centerline, Centerline With Reference, Thread, Thread With Reference** and **Axis Line**?
13. **T or F** CATIA V5 allows you to create an unlimited amount of projected views.
14. What is the function of the **View Creation Wizard**?
15. **T or F** When creating a **Section View**, CATIA V5 helps you visualize it by creating a cutting plane through the part in both the **Drafting Work Bench** and the **Part Design Work Bench**.
16. How do you activate the **Properties** window for a view?
17. **T or F** CATIA V5 saves the drafting sheets created in the **Drafting Work Bench** and parts created in the **Part Design Work Bench** in the same file with the same extension.
18. Does the **Drafting Work Bench** have tools to create drafting geometry, such as 2-D lines, arc, circles etc.?
19. Explain how you can modify an **Auxiliary View** so you can move it anywhere on the sheet and not just in the direction of the created projection (hint: **Alignment**).
20. How do you split the screen so you can see the **CATDrawing** screen and the **Part Design** screen at the same time?

Lesson 3 Practice Exercises

The practice exercises for this lesson require you to use the "**CATPart**" files you created back in Lesson 1 and extruded in Lesson 2. Each practice part has its own list of special requirements. The requirements are a minimum, so you have to use the tools learned in this lesson. This workbook is not meant to teach any drafting standards; although, good practices are strongly encouraged. It is up to you to layout the drawings as to the best of your experience and/or education will allow. Remember text and dimensions will be covered in Lesson 4. The file extension used in the **Drafting Work Bench** is "**CATDrawing**". Good Luck!

1   Use the "**Lesson 2 Exercise 1.CATPart**" to create a drawing with the following sheet and view requirements.

    1.1   Create a drawing with three standard orthographic views of this part.

    1.2   Put the drawing on **ANSI B** sheet.

    1.3   Create a second sheet.

    1.4   Create an **Aligned Section View**. Run the section view vertically through the center of the hole.

    1.5   Create an **Auxiliary View** off of the angled surface noted in the drawing below.

    1.6   Create a **Detail View** of the chamfer shown on the drawing below. Scale the detail view 4:1.

    1.7   Save the drawing as "**Lesson 3 Exercise 1. CATDrawing**".

create an **Auxiliary View** from this surface

Create a **Detail View** from this surface

Create an **Aligned Section View** from this cutting plane

2   Use the "**Lesson 2 Exercise 2.CATPart**" to create a drawing with the following
      sheet and view requirements.

   2.1   Create a drawing with three standard orthographic views of this part.

   2.2   Put the drawing on **ANSI B** sheet.

   2.3   Create a second sheet.

   2.4   Create an **Aligned Section View**. Run the section view vertically through
          the center of the holes.

   2.5   Create an **Aligned Section Cut**. Run the section cut vertically through the
          center of the holes.

   2.6   Create an **Auxiliary View** off of the angled surface noted in the drawing
          below.

   2.7   Save the drawing as "**Lesson 3 Exercise 2.CATDrawing**".

use this plane to
create an **Aligned
Section View** and
**Aligned Section
Cut**

create an
Auxiliary view
from this surface

3 Use the "**Lesson 2 Exercise 3.CATPart**" to create a drawing with the following sheet and view requirements.

    3.1 Create a drawing with three standard orthographic views of this part.

    3.2 Put the drawing on **ANSI C** sheet.

    3.3 Create a second sheet.

    3.4 Create an **Aligned Section View**. Run the section view vertically through the center of the hole.

    3.5 Save this part as "**Lesson 3 Exercise 3. CATDrawing**".

use this plane for **Aligned Section View**

4   Use the "**Lesson 2 Exercise 4.CATPart**" to create a drawing with the following sheet and view requirements.

     4.1   Create a drawing with three standard orthographic views of this part.

     4.2   Put the drawing on **ANSI A** sheet.

     4.3   Create a second sheet.

     4.4   Create an **Aligned Section View**. Run the section view vertically through the center of the holes.

     4.5   Create an **Aligned Section Cut**. Run the section cut vertically through the center of the holes.

     4.6   Save this part as "**Lesson 3 Exercise 4. CATDrawing**".

use this plane to create an **Aligned Section View** and **Aligned Section Cut**

Lesson 4

Introduction To Creating Text And Dimensions Using The Drafting Work Bench

This lesson continues from Lesson 3 with the **Drafting Work Bench**. You will use the **Sheets** and **Views** of the "**T Shaped Extrusion.CATDrawing**", created in Lesson 3. This lesson will instruct you on how to add the text and dimensions to the views created in Lesson 3. Like Lesson 3, this is not a comprehensive lesson on the **Drafting Work Bench**.

Figure 4.1

Lesson 4 Objectives

The objective of this lesson is to supply you with enough instruction that you can complete a production drawing of the "**T Shaped Extrusion**" as shown in Figure 4.1. You should be able to apply this newfound knowledge to the exercise parts and any other part that requires a production drawing. This chapter will not cover every tool found in the **Drafting Work Bench**. It is not the intent of this lesson to be a comprehensive reference, but a basic step-by-step for the most common tools and functions in the CATIA V5 **Drafting Work Bench**.

The tools and processes covered in this lesson are listed below.

- Additional **Drafting Work Bench** tools
- Review of lesson 3
- How to create and modify **Text**
- How to create and modify **Leaders**
- How to create and modify **Dimensions**
- How to create a **Border** and **Title Block**
- How to insert the **Bill Of Materials**
- How to insert **Picture Files**
- Review how to **Save** and **Print** the completed drawing sheets (**CATDrawing**)

Drafting Work Bench Tool Bars

There are thirteen standard tool bars found in the **Drafting Work Bench**. Six of the thirteen tool bars were covered in Lesson 3. The remaining tool bars are covered in this lesson. The individual tools found in each of the thirteen tool bars are labeled to the right or beneath the tool icon.

The **Text Properties** Tool Bar

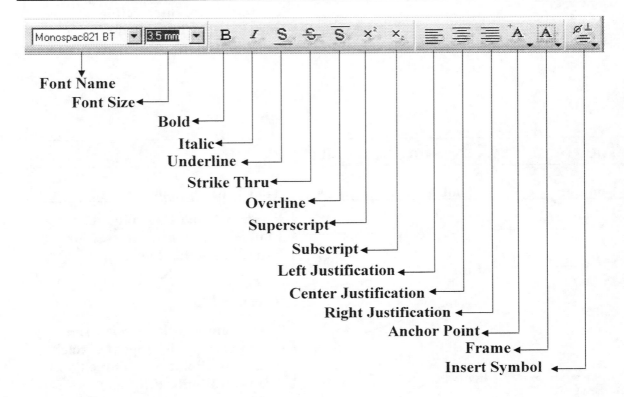

Font Name

Font Size

Bold

Italic

Underline

Strike Thru

Overline

Superscript

Subscript

Left Justification

Center Justification

Right Justification

Anchor Point

Frame

Insert Symbol

The **Dimension Properties** Tool Bar

Precision

Unit

Tolerance

Tolerance Type

Dimension Line

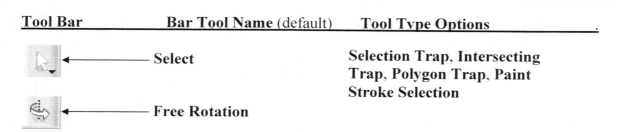

The **Select** Tool Bar

Tool Bar	Bar Tool Name (default)	Tool Type Options
	Select	Selection Trap, Intersecting Trap, Polygon Trap, Paint Stroke Selection
	Free Rotation	

The **Geometry Creation** Tool Bar

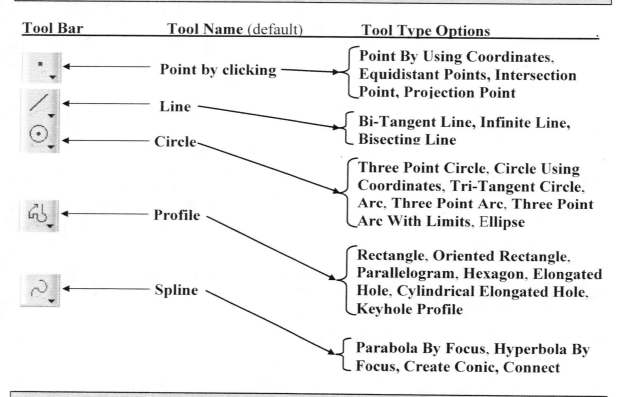

Tool Bar	Tool Name (default)	Tool Type Options
	Point by clicking	Point By Using Coordinates, Equidistant Points, Intersection Point, Projection Point
	Line	Bi-Tangent Line, Infinite Line, Bisecting Line
	Circle	Three Point Circle, Circle Using Coordinates, Tri-Tangent Circle, Arc, Three Point Arc, Three Point Arc With Limits, Ellipse
	Profile	Rectangle, Oriented Rectangle, Parallelogram, Hexagon, Elongated Hole, Cylindrical Elongated Hole, Keyhole Profile
	Spline	Parabola By Focus, Hyperbola By Focus, Create Conic, Connect

The **Generation** Tool Bar

Tool Bar	Tool Name (default)	Tool Type Options
	Generating Dimensions	Generating Dimensions Step By Step, Generated Balloons

The **Dimensioning** Tool Bar

__Tool Bar__	__Tool Name__ (default)	__Tool Type Options__

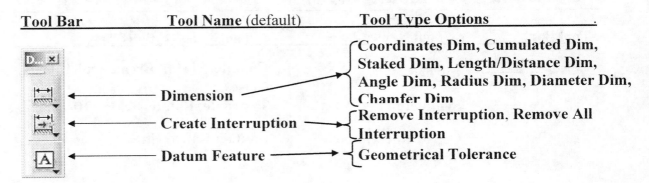

__Dimension__ → Coordinates Dim, Cumulated Dim, Staked Dim, Length/Distance Dim, Angle Dim, Radius Dim, Diameter Dim, Chamfer Dim

__Create Interruption__ → Remove Interruption, Remove All Interruption

__Datum Feature__ → Geometrical Tolerance

The **Dressup** Tool Bar

__Tool Bar__	__Tool Name__ (default)	__Tool Type Options__

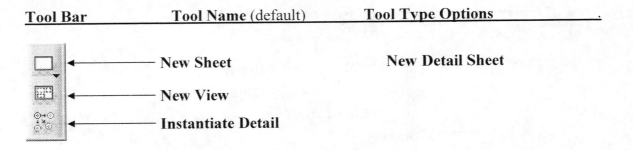

__Center Line__   __Center Line With Reference, Thread, Thread With Reference, Axis__

__Fill Area__

The **Drawing** Tool Bar

__Tool Bar__	__Tool Name__ (default)	__Tool Type Options__

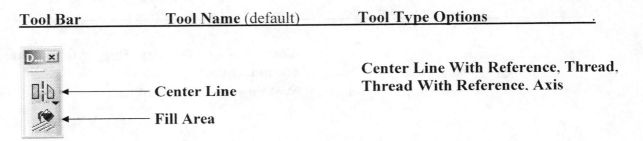

__New Sheet__   __New Detail Sheet__

__New View__

__Instantiate Detail__

The **Geometry Edition** Tool Bar

Tool Bar	Tool Name (default)	Tool Type Options
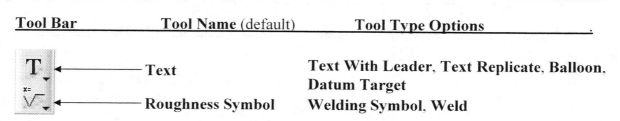	Corner	Chamfer, Trim, Break, Quick Trim, Close
	Symmetry	Translate, Rotate, Scale, Offset
	Constraints Defined In Dialog	Contact Constraint

The **Annotations** Tool Bar

Tool Bar	Tool Name (default)	Tool Type Options
	Text	Text With Leader, Text Replicate, Balloon, Datum Target
	Roughness Symbol	Welding Symbol, Weld

The **Graphic Properties** Tool Bar

- Pattern
- Copy Object Format
- Line Type
- Thickness
- Color

The **Style** Tool Bar

 Use Default

Adding Text And Dimensions To Drawings Using The Drafting Work Bench

CATIA V5 uses the files created in the **Part Design Work Bench** to create drawings. As previously stated, the files created in the **Part Design Work Bench** are saved with the "CATPart" extension. The **Drafting Work Bench** uses the file created in the **Part Design Work Bench**, but is saved as a separate file. The **Drafting Work Bench** files have a "CATDrawing" extension. Both the "CATPart" and "CATDrawing" files are linked together. To pull up the "CATDrawing" file, CATIA V5 must be able to locate the related "CATPart" file. If CATIA V5 cannot find the linked file, you will get an error. If you move a "CATPart" file to a different directory, the "CATDrawing" file linked to it will not be able to locate the "CATPart" file. You will have to update the directory where the "CATPart" exists. This can be done using the **Edit**, **Links** tools. This lesson takes you through the steps of accessing and adding text and dimensions to your existing "**T Shaped Extrusion.CATDrawing**" file. There are many different methods and standards to dimension a drawing. This lesson concentrates on how to create, place and modify text and dimensions. This lesson does not attempt to teach any one dimensioning standard or style. You are encouraged to explore other methods; find out what works best for your requirements.

1   Start CATIA V5

If you need to review this step, refer to Lesson 1.

2   Select The Drafting Work Bench

In this lesson you do not need to open the **Part Design Work Bench** because you already made the "**CATPart**" to "**CATDrawing**" link in Lesson 3. Select the **Drafting Work Bench**. The **New Drawing** pop-up window will appear. Select the **Cancel** button since you will be working on an existing drawing.

3   Open The "T Shaped Extrusion. CATDrawing" File

This lesson uses the "**T Shaped Extrusion.CATDrawing**" you created in Lesson 3. Open the "**T Shaped Extrusion.CATDrawing**".

4   The Drafting Work Bench Layout

The **Drafting Work Bench** layout was covered in Lesson 3. It is mentioned in this lesson, because it would be a good idea to review the layout, where everything is and how to access all of the tool bars. You are encouraged to go back to Lesson 3 and review the **Drafting Work Bench** layout.

Since you have opened an existing "**CATDrawing**" file, your layout will be a bit different than the **Drafting Work Bench** without any sheets or views created. The following steps cover the same items as Step 5 in Lesson 3, except the information is specific to the opened "**T Shaped Extrusion.CATDrawing**".

4.1   **Tool Bars**: Lesson 3 covered six of the thirteen **Drafting Work Bench** tool bars. This lesson will cover the remaining tool bars. Pull all of the tool bars up on the screen so they are visible and pickable. It would be beneficial to preview all the tools you will be using in this lesson. If you have any detailed questions on the tool bars, refer back to Lesson 3.

4.2   **Sheets**: When you opened the "**T Shaped Extrusion.CATDrawing**", a minimum of two sheets should appear on the sheet tab at the top left of the screen. If you created any additional sheets in Lesson 3, they should also be represented on a tab.

4.3   **View Layout**: You determined the view layouts in Lesson 3 when you created the drawing and added the additional views.

4.4   **Drafting Work Bench Specification Tree**: All of the sheets and views you created in Lesson 3 will be represented in the **Drafting Specification Tree**.

4.5   **Modifiying the Drafting Work Bench Standards**: As in the **Sketcher** and **Part Design Work Benches** the standards are quick and easy to change.

The only action required by you in this step, was to review the tool bars from Lesson 3 and preview the tool bars for this lesson. If you have completed this task, you can continue on to Step 5.

5 Customizing The Default Values

Customizing the default values was covered in detail in Lesson 3. This is a critical step, so it was left in this lesson as a reminder. You need to think about them before you get started. If you have any questions on how to modify any of the default values, refer back to Lesson 3 Step 6. If you do not have any questions on this subject, continue on to the next step.

6 Creating And Modifying Text

CATIA V5 does not have all of the functions of a true word processor, but it is a vast improvement from past CAD system attempts to incorperate text functionality. True **Windows NT** functionality gives CATIA V5 several ways to create and modify text. If you are familiar with **Windows** functions, the **Text** tool bar is almost idenitical. If you look at the top tool bar, you should be able to recognize many similar tools such as **Font Style, Font Size, Bold, Italics, Under Line, Align Right, Align Center, Align Left** and so on.

The **Annotation** tool bar has two options. The first one is the **Text** tool $\mathbb{T}$ which has four options, they are:

1 The **Text** tool $\mathbb{T}$. This is the tool used to create text.

2 The **Text With Leader** .

3 The third option is **Balloon** ⑥. **Balloon** places a balloon around a drawing annotation such as a part number.

4 The last option is **Datum Target** .

The other option on the **Annotation** tool bar is the **Bold Symbol** tool. The **Bold Symbol** tool has three options, they are:

1 The **Roughness Symbol** .

2 The **Welding Symbol** .

3 The **Weld Symbol** .

This lesson will not be using any of the last three options, but you might want to know them for furture projects.

To add text to your "**T Shaped Extrusion.CATDrawing**", complete the following steps.

6.1   Text will be attached (linked) to the view that is active at the time the text is created. You must activate the view you want the text to be attached to. If the view is deleted, the attached text will be deleted with it. For this step you will be required to put text in the **Top View**, so activate that view. Select the **Top View** by selecting the border of the **Top View** or by selecting the **Top View** in the **Drafting Specification Tree**.

     6.1.1   Select the **Text** tool **T** in the **Annotation** tool bar.

     6.1.2   CATIA V5 will prompt you to **"Indicate The Text Anchor Point"**. Move the mouse to the location in the active view where you want the text created and select that location. This is where the text will be anchored (located). For this step, select a location just under and to the left of the "**View Title**" and "**Scale Value**" as shown in Figure 4.2. The text can be easily relocated later if you change your mind.

Figure 4.2

select somewhere in this area

Top view
Scale:1

     6.1.3   A **Text Editor** pop-up window will appear as shown in Figure 4.3. As the name indicates, this is the text editor. For this step, you will be adding a note specifying the material type. In the **Text Editor** window,

Figure 4.3

Text Editor

Material type is 6064 Aluminum in the T6 Conditio

OK   Cancel

type in the following: "**Material Type is 6064 Aluminum in the T6 Condition**".

6.1.4 When you've entered the text as shown in Figure 4.3, select the **OK** button. The **Text Editor** window will disappear and the text will show up where you indicated in Step 6.1.2. Your **Top View** should now look similar to the view shown in Figure 4.4.

6.1.5 You may need to move the text around a little if it isn't similarly located as shown in Figure 4.4. The newly created text is created within a text window. The text window can be moved by selecting it and dragging it around to where you want it. This is a **Windows** drag and drop operation.

6.1.6 You can change the size of the text window by selecting one of the window handles (box) and moving the mouse accordingly, reference Figure 4.5 .

Figure 4.4

Figure 4.5

6.1.7   The text can be edited by double clicking on the text. Double clicking on the text brings up the **Text Editor** pop-up window with the text you just selected in the window. You can delete, add and/or modify the text as you would in any other **Windows** text editor. When you have completed all of the text modifications, select the **OK** button to apply the modifications.

6.1.8   To change the properties of the text, move the mouse over the text window as shown in Figure 4.6. The text window will highlight. While the mouse is over the text window, right click the mouse. From the pop-up window that appears, select the **Properties** option. This will bring up the **Properties** pop-up window as shown in Figure 4.7.

Figure 4.6   place the mouse here

Material type is 6064 Aluminum in the T6 Condition

The **Properties** window has three main tabs, they are:

1   **Font**, reference Figure 4.7 .

2   **Text**, reference Figure 4.8 .

3   **Graphic**, reference Figure 4.9 .

Figure 4.7

Figure 4.8

Figure 4.9

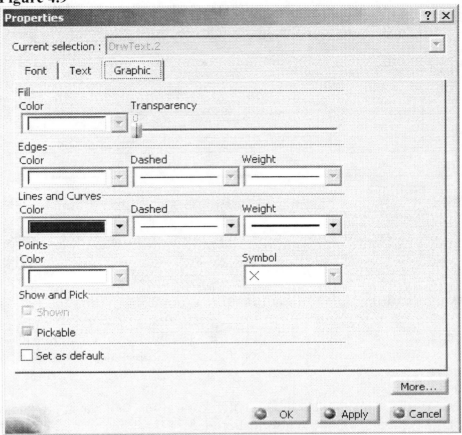

Once all the changes have been made, select **Apply** to verify that the changes are indeed what you expected. If the applied changes are as you expected, select **OK** and the changes will become permanent.

Make the following modifications to the text you created in Step 6.1.3.

1 **Edit** the text so the material type is in the "**T4**" condition instead of "**T6**". Reference Step 6.1.7.

2 Change the **Font** to **ROM3**. Reference Step 6.1.8 under the **Font** tab.

3 Change the **Style** to **Bold**. Reference Step 6.1.8 under the **Font** tab.

4 Change the **Size** to **.15**. Reference Step 6.1.8 under the **Font** tab.

5 Change the the **Color** to **Green**. Reference Step 6.1.8 under the **Font** tab.

6 Change the **Justification** to **Center**. Reference Step 6.1.8 under the **Text** tab.

After completing the changes listed above, the **Top View** should look
similar to the one in Figure 4.10.

Figure 4.10

Top view
Scale:1

Material type is 6064 Aluminum in the T4 Condition

7   Creating And Modifying Leaders

This step is actually a continuation of Step 6. The process of creating a leader is the
same as creating text, with one additional step. The following explain the process of
creating **Leaders**.

The **Text With Leader** tool is found in the **Annotation** tool bar, it is a sub option
under the **Text** tool. All of the information in Step 6 applies to the **Text With
Leader** tool, except that the first point selected is the starting point of the leader.
CATIA V5 will prompt you to "**Select Element Or Indicate The Leader Anchor
Point**". The second point is actually the "**Text Anchor Point**". Once you have
selected the leader anchor point and text anchor point, the process is identical to the
Text tool. The text created with the **Text With Leader** tool can be modified the
same as the text created with the **Text** tool, covered in Step 6. The leader anchor
point and text anchor point can also be modified. Select the text and leader so they
are highlighed. Once the leader text is highlighted, handles on the leader and text box
show up. You can select and drag each handle to the location you want.

For this step create a leader anchored to the top right hole in the **Top View**. Anchor
the text a little above and to the right of the part. In the **Text Editor** window, type
"**#30 Pilot Holes Typical**". The **Top View** should look similar to Figure 4.11.

Figure 4.11

Top view
Scale: 1:1

Material type is 6064 Aluminum in the T4 Condition

8   Creating And Modifying Dimensions ⬌

CATIA V5 has simplified the dimensioning process and at the same time added some powerful tools. CATIA V5 knows what kind of dimensions to create by the different entities you select. There are several different ways of creating dimensions.

This step concentrates on the **Dimensioning** tool bar. The tools in the **Dimensioning** tool bar are listed below.

> 1   The **Dimension** tool ⬌ .
>
> 2   The **Datum Feature** tool 🅰 .
>
> 3   The **Coordinate Dimension** tool 📧 .
>
> 4   The **Geometric Tolerance** tool 🎛 .

This step will show you how to create several of the basic types of dimensions using the **Dimensioning** tool. This step also will show you how to modify the dimensions created.

Another more advanced method of creating dimensions is using constraints created in the **Sketcher** and **Part Design Work Benches**. The **Constraint** method is a powerful concept, but also one that takes some up front planning and time to get a handle on. Even though this book does not cover the process, for your reference, the tools are **Generating Dimensions** and **Generating Dimensions Step By Step,** both found in the **Generation** tool bar.

Figure 4.12

There are two main things that affect how your dimensions look and are created. The first thing is your dimension standards. Select the **Tools**, **Options** as shown in Figure 4.12. This will bring up the **Options** window.   Select the **Drafting** branch, you may have to expand the **Mechanical Design** branch to access the

Tools

f(x) Formula...

Image   ▶

Macro   ▶

Customize...

Options...

Drafting branch. Select the **Dimension** tab. This will bring up the dimension options, your window should look similar to the one shown in Figure 4.13. This step does not require you to change any of the standards, just be aware what options are available.

Figure 4.13

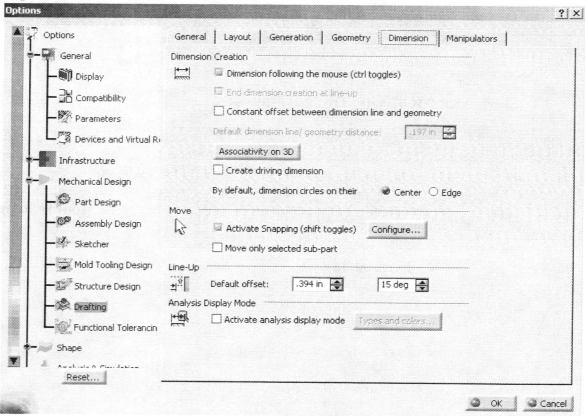

The second critical thing in creating dimensions is located in the top right tool bar, the **Dimension Properties** tool bar. This is where you control the **Dimension Line**, **Tolerance Type**, **Tolerance**, **Unit** and **Percision**, reference Figure 4.14. There is one more thing that should be considered when creating dimensions, the units the "CATPart" file was created in. CATIA V5 will allow you to create the "CATPart" in one unit and dimension it in another. Be sure you have the units set the way you want. For this step and lesson, everything is in inches.

Figure 4.14

The following step will show you how to create and modify several of the basic dimension types.

8.1   Before you actually create a dimension, set the **Dimension Properties** to the following specifications.

8.1.1   Set the **Dimension Line** to where the value is between the dimension lines (reference Figure 4.15).

8.1.2   Set the **Tolerance Description** to **DIN_NUM2** (reference Figure 4.15).

8.1.3   Set the **Tolerance** to **+-.030** (reference Figure 4.15).

8.1.4   Set the **Numeric Display Description** to **NUM.DIMM** (reference figure 4.15).

8.1.5   Set the **Precision** to three places to the right of the decimal (.001) (reference Figure 4.15).

Figure 4.15

Now you are ready to create some dimensions. Follow the steps listed below.

8.2   Select the **Dimension** tool in the **Dimensioning** tool bar. CATIA V5 will prompt you to "**Select The First Element For Dimension Creation**". If you select only one element, it will create a **Dimension** for the one element. For example, if you select one edge of the part, you will get the length of that one edge. If you select a circle you will get a diameter **Dimension**. In this step you are going to create the overall length of the extrusion in the **Top View**.

8.3   Select the left most edge of the "**T Shaped Extrusion**" in the **Top View**. A dimension length of the edge selected will be created, ignore it! Reference Figure 4.16.

Figure 4.16

select this edge

.357 ± .030

#30 Pilot Holes Typical

Top view
Scale: 1

ignore this **Dimension**

8.4   Select the right most edge of the "**T Shaped Extrusion**" in the **Top View**. The length **Dimension** created in Step 8.3 will be replaced with a distance **Dimension** between the two ends of the part. Your newly created **Dimension** should look similar to the one shown in Figure 4.17.

distance **Dimension**   select this edge

Figure 4.17

B

6.000 ± .030

#30 Pilot Holes Typical

Top view
Scale:1

8.5   The newly created **Dimension** can be modified by completing the following steps.

8.5.1   Select the **Dimension** so it is highlighted.

8.5.2   Selecting the part of the **Dimension** that you want to change and drag it to the new location. For example, the dimension created in Figure 4.17 is too close to the part, select the dimension line to modify it's location.

8.5.3   Drag the **Dimension** line to a position similar to the one shown in Figure 4.19.

Figure 4.18

Figure 4.19

8.6   In this step you will create a radius dimension using the **Front View**.
       There are several different ways you can accomplish this. The most
       common method would be to use the **Dimension** tool bar. An alternative
       method is shown in Figure 4.20. Select **Insert** from the top pull-down
       menu. Select **Dimensioning, Dimensions** and **Radius Dimensions.** Then
       select the radius on the right side of the standing leg of the "**T Shaped
       Extrusion**" in the **Front View** as shown in Figure 4.21. Indicate the
       location of the radius dimensions. You can right click on the radius
       dimension to change the **Properties**. The **Properties** window allows you
       to modify the **Dimension Text, Font, Text** and **Graphic**.

Figure 4.20

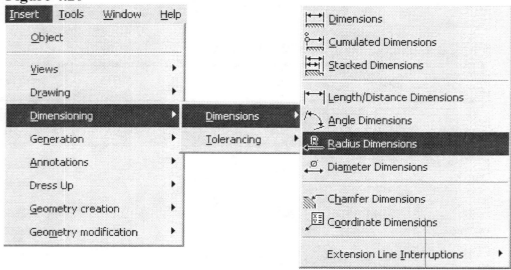

8.7   This time select the **Diameter Dimension** tool located in the **Dimension** tool bar. Select the top left hole in the **Top View**. A diameter **Dimension** will be created. The arrows will be pointing in toward the center of the circle. Selecting one of the arrows will reverse the direction of the arrows to where they point out away from the center of the circle.

Figure 4.21

select this radius ⟶

The hole is too small to clearly show the arrows this way, so switch them back by selecting the arrows again, reference Figure 4.22.

Figure 4.22

8.8   CATIA V5 knows to put the degree symbol in a **Angled Dimension**, reference the **Dimension Properties** tool bar at the top right of the screen; the **Unit** defaults to degrees. The one catch to this, is that CATIA V5 does not change the **Tolerance** or the **Precision**. In most cases, the **Tolerance** and **Precision** are different than the length and/or distance **Dimension**. The **Tolerance** and **Precision** can be modified after creation. In this step you will create an **Angle Dimension** using the **Right View**.

       8.8.1   Change the **Dimension** defaults prior to creating a **Dimension**. In the **Dimension Properties** tool bar, select the **Tolerance** arrow so all of the sub options show up. Select the **+-0.030** , reference Figure 4.23.

Figure 4.23

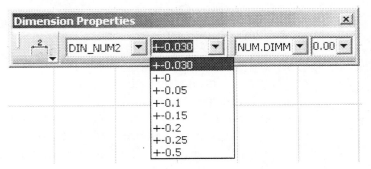

       8.8.2   **Zoom Up** on the **Section View B-B** so the chamfer can be clearly identified and pickable, similar to what is shown in Figure 4.24.

       8.8.3   From the **Dimension** tool bar select the **Angle** tool.

       8.8.4   Select the right side of the standing leg of the **"T Shaped Extrusion"** in the **Section View B-B**. Figure 4.24 points out the location of selection 1.

8.8.5

Figure 4.24

8.8.6   Select the top right side of the horizontal leg of the "**T Shaped Extrusion**" in the **Section View B-B**. Figure 4.24 points out the location of selection 2. This will create the **Angled Dimension**. If the **Dimensions** bunch too close together don't worry, a few quick mouse clicks and the **Dimension** can be modified just the way you want it. The **Dimension** created should read 90 degrees with no tolerance as shown in Figure 4.25.

Figure 4.25 (**Angled Dimension** as created by default)

8.8.7   To move the **Dimension,** select the **Dimension** arrow (arc) and drag it to the upper right quadrant of the view.

Figure 4.26

8.8.8   To move the text, select the text and drag it in either direction along the dimension arrow (arc). Notice the **Dimension** value is tied to the arc. If the **Dimension** value is too close to the part, you will have to reselect the arrow **Dimension** (arc) and drag it farther away from the part, similar to what is shown in Figure 4.26.

As with the other **Dimensions**, you can add prefix/suffix text to the dimensions. This is done by selecting the text and then bringing up the **Properties** window. The **Dimension Test** tab has a text box for prefix and suffix text. For this step, add the suffix text that reads "**Typical**" as shown in Figures 4.27.

Figure 4.27

Suffix text added

8.9   The preceeding steps introduced you to creating the basic types of **Dimensions**. Your assignment now is to complete the **Dimensions** required to complete the drawing of the "**T Shaped Extrusion**". You now have the basic tools to **Dimension** the drawing. Good luck! Don't worry, you're not totally abandoned. Figure 4.31 is meant to be a guide and/or a suggestion as to what your completed dimensioned drawing should look like.

9   Creating A Border/Title Block Using The Geometery Creation Tool Bar

One of the main components of a production drawing is the title block. Title blocks can vary from simplistic to complex depending on how much information you are required to present. This lesson will give you the basic tools to create a title block.

How complex the title block is, is up to you. The tools and processes used to create the title block are almost identical to the tools in the **Sketcher Work Bench**. If you have any detail questions on how to use the **Profile, Line, Trim, Corner** and even the **Constraints** tools, refer back to Lesson 1 on the **Sketcher Work Bench**. Figure 4.31 is an example of an average title block.

The title block can be saved and imported to any other drawings, so you won't have to recreate a title block for every drawing. CATIA V5 allows you to import graphic files into your title block, so you can import your school and/or company logo as a graphics file. The **SUU** (Southern Utah University) and **MTI** (Metalcraft Technologies, Inc.) logo on the title block in Figure 4.31 are .tif files imported into the title block. To create a title block, complete the following steps.

9.1 Make sure all of your views fit on the sheet. This may require you to move a few of the views around (Lesson 3 Step 9). You may also discover that you do not have enough room on the current sheet, so you may have to create a new sheet (covered in Lesson 3 Step 7).

9.2 Turn on the **Grid Lines**, if not already on. It is the tool at the bottom right of the screen. The tool toggles the grid lines **On** and **Off**. If the **Primary Spacings** on the grid lines do not balance with sheet outlines, modify the grid spacing (Lesson 3 Step 6.2.1).

Figure 4.28

9.3 Turn on the **Snap To Grid** if not already on. It is the ▦ tool at the bottom right of the screen. The tool toggles the **Snap To Grid On** and **Off**.

9.4 Select the **Edit, Background** option located at the bottom of the pull down window as shown in Figure 4.28. This will turn off all of the current views making it so that they can not be modified. The title block option in CATIA V5 can only be used in the **Background** mode.

9.5 Select the **Insert** pull down window from the top of the screen as shown in Figure 4.29.

9.6 From the **Insert** pull down window, select the **Drawing** option and then the **Frame And Title Block** option. This will bring up the **Insert Frame and Title Block** window, shown in Figure 4.30. From inside this window the title block can be set to specific dimensions. Since you are going to make the title block fit your style, select the **OK** button and you will be able to drag and stretch the title block to the size you need.

Figure 4.29

Figure 4.30

9.7   Move the lines of the title block around until they are in the locations you want. To move them, select the line and drag it to the location you want. Figure 4.31 gives you an example of what the title block could look like. Your title block doesn't have to look exactly like the one shown in Figure 4.31.

9.8   The default line weight for the title block is too thin. To make the border line thicker, complete the following.

      9.8.1   Bring the **Properties** window up for one of the lines in the title block you just created, reference Figure 4.32

      9.8.2   Select the **Graphic** tab.

      9.8.3   Go down to the **Lines And Curves** section.

      9.8.4   Select the arrow to the right of the **Thickness** option. Selecting the arrow will show you the different line weight options available to you.

      9.8.5   Select the line that is one weight thicker than the default line.

      9.8.6   Select **Apply** to preview the change.

      9.8.7   Select **OK** to accept the change.

Figure 4.31

9.8.8   Repeat Steps 9.8.1 thru 9.8.7 to change the line thickness of the remaining lines of the title block.

9.8.9   Now, verify that the border line is thicker.

9.9   Add the **Text** to the title block where appropriate. Remember, Figure 4.31 is for your reference. Reference Step 6 of this lesson on how to use the **Text** tool. This is a good opportunity to use your creative side. This step does not have any exact requirement, other than to complete the title block.

NOTE: The **Geometry** tool bar can be used to create additonal lines and other draw entities that your generic title block does not have. These commands work similar to the **Sketcher Work Bench** explained in Lesson 1.

Figure 4.32

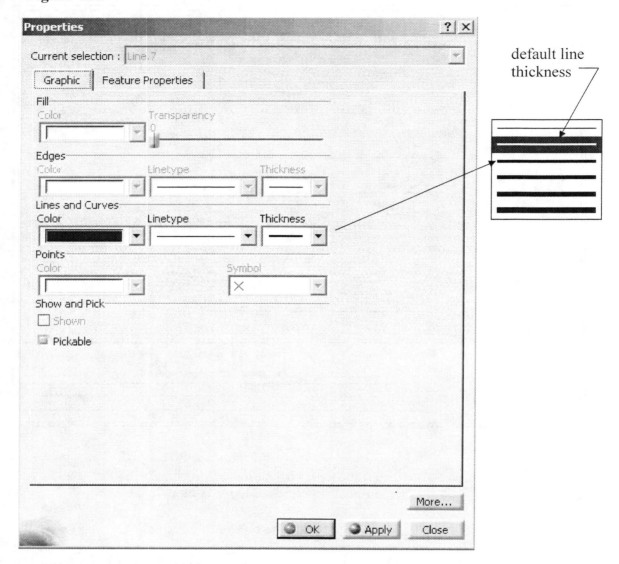

10 Inserting Bill Of Materials To the Title Block

CATIA V5 allows you to automatically add the **Bill of Materials** to the title block as Figure 4.29 shows. The only catch is, it requires a "***.CATProduct**" file. So far you have created "***.CATPart**" and **.CATDrawing**" files. Lesson 5 and 6 cover "***.CATProducts**", the lessons also explain how to add the **Bill of Materials** to your drawings. This is a powerfull and time saveing tool and is worth mentioning, but for detailed instructions, reference Lessons 5 and 6.

11 Inserting Picture Files Into The Title Block

CATIA V5 allows you to customize your **Title Blocks** by inserting your choice of picture files. Figure 4.34 gives you a sample of all the options you have for importing into the **Title Block**. The following steps detail the process of adding a picture file to your title block. This can be any picture file you want, but you need to supply it. This step uses a sample file for demonstation purposes only.

Figure 4.33

    11.1 Things you need to know before you start.

        11.1.1 Make sure you know what kind of graphics file you are going to import.

        11.1.2 Make sure the size and quality is what you expect.

        11.1.3 Make sure you know where the file is located and what the name of the file is.

    11.2 Select the **Insert** tool from the top pull down menu as shown in Figure 4.33.

    11.3 Select the **Object** option. This will bring up an **Insert Object** window as shown in Figure 4.34.

Figure 4.34

select

11.4   From the **Insert Object** window select the **Create From File** option as shown in Figure 4.34.

11.5   From the same window, select the **Browse** option. This will bring up the **Standard Windows Browse** window which allows you to search through the directories for the specific picture file.

Figure 4.35

select

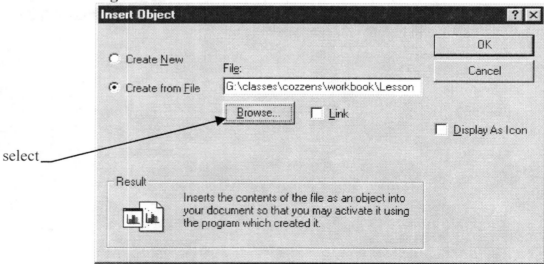

11.6   Find the graphics file you want to insert and select it.

NOTE: If you want the picture to be displayed make sure the "**Display As Icon**" is not selected, reference Figure 4.35.

11.7   Select **Ok**.

11.8   The graphic will be placed on the (0,0) point on the active sheet.

11.9   To move the graphic to the proper location, use the drag and drop process.

11.10 If your School/Business icon is placed on your title block similar to what is shown in Figure 4.31 you are ready to move on.

12 Saving Your Updated Drawing

This process is basically identical to saving a file covered in Lesson 1. The only difference is that it will be saved with the name you give it followed by the extension of "**CATDrawing**" as explained in Lesson 3.

13 Printing The Finished Drawings

This process is covered in detail in Lesson 3 Step 14. Remember to make sure all of the veiws fit on the sheets. You can use the **Print Preview** window to preview the print and make the necassary adjustments. Figure 4.36 shows the "**T Shaped Extrusion**" in the **Print Preview** window. If the views do not fit within the sheet boundaries, review Lesson 3 Step 9 for detailed information on how to move views around. For this lesson print out all of the drafting sheets you created.

Figure 4.36

Lesson 4 Summary

Creating a complete drawing is no small task. CATIA V5 has come a long way in simplifying and automating the process where possible. One of the best things CATIA V5 does is to make the process of learning quicker and easier. This lesson supplies the introductory tools required to start producing drawings almost immediately. You now have enough knowledge to explore and learn the more advanced options on your own.

Lesson 4 Review

After completing this lesson, you should be able to answer the questions and explain the concepts listed below.

1. A file created in the **Drafting Work Bench** has what type of file extension?
2. **T** or **F** When you create a **CATDrawing** from a **CATPart**, CATIA V5 makes a link between the two different files.
3. **T** or **F** The **Drafting Work Bench** has some similarities to the **Sketcher Work Bench**.
4. Justify your answer to question 3.
5. List at least three types of views that CATIA V5 automatically creates for you.
6. **T** or **F** CATIA V5 does not allow dimensions to be modified. You must delete the dimension and start over.
7. **T** or **F** It is possible to generate dimensions from **Constraints** created in the **Sketcher Work Bench**.
8. **T** or **F** To create a radius dimension, you use the same **Dimension** tool you would use to create an angled dimension.
9. Does the **Drafting Work Bench** have a **Specification Tree**?
10. **T** or **F** By default, all of the tool bars are visible when entering the **Drafting Work Bench**.
11. How do you toggle the **Snap To Grid**, **On** and **Off**?
12. How do you modify the **Primary Spacing** and **Graduations** of the drafting grid?
13. What tool bar contains the following tools: **Centerline**, **Centerline With Reference**, **Thread**, **Thread With Reference** and **Axis Line**?
14. **T** or **F** Modifying CATIA V5 text is as simple as double clicking on the text to be modified to bring up the **Text Editor** window, making the changes to the text and then selecting **OK** to apply the changes.
15. **T** or **F** Dimensions created in a view will show up on the **Drafting Specification Tree**.
16. What tool bar controls the dimension tolerance?
    a. **Dimensioning**
    b. **Graphic properties**
    c. **Dimension Properties**
    d. **Generation**
    e. None of the above
17. What must be done to a sheet prior to inserting a CATIA V5 title block?
18. **T** or **F** Once the title block is inserted you can go back and modify the views.
19. What tools are required to insert a picture file into your title block?
    a. **Insert**
    b. **Object**
    c. **Import Picture**
    d. Both b and c
    e. Both a and b

20. **T** or **F** CATIA V5 allows two-dimensional entities to be created in the **Drafting Work Bench** to help supplement the three-dimensional views.

Lesson 4 Practice Exercises

The practice exercises for this lesson require you to use the "**CATDrawing**" files you created Lesson 3. Complete the drawings started in Lesson 3 using the **Text** and **Dimensioning** tools. Create a border/title block for each of drawings. It is not the intent of this book to teach any drawing and/or drafting standard; therefore, the standard and style is up to you.

Remember the file extension used in the **Drafting Work Bench** is **CATDrawing**. Good Luck!

1   Open "**Lesson 3 Exercise 1.CATDrawing**". Add the required text, dimensioning and border/title block information to make the sheets a completed production drawing. Insert a picture file of your school and/or company logo. Save the drawing as "**Lesson 4 Exercise 1. CATDrawing**".

2   Open "**Lesson 3 Exercise 2.CATDrawing** ". Add the required text, dimensioning and border/title block information to make the sheets a completed production drawing. Save the drawing as "**Lesson 4 Exercise 2. CATDrawing**".

3   Open "**Lesson 3 Exercise 3.CATDrawing** ". Add the required text, dimensioning and border/title block information to make the sheets a completed production drawing. Save the drawing as "**Lesson 4 Exercise 3. CATDrawing**".

4   Open "**Lesson 3 Exercise 4.CATDrawing** ". Add the required text, dimensioning and border/title block information to make the sheets a completed production drawing. Save the drawing as "**Lesson 4 Exercise 4. CATDrawing**".

NOTES:

Lesson 5   Cᴏᴍᴘʟᴇx & Mᴜʟᴛɪᴘʟᴇ Sᴋᴇᴛᴄʜ Pᴀʀᴛs

Introduction To Creating Complex And Multiple Sketch Parts

In Lesson 1 you created a sketch and in Lesson 2 you extruded the sketch into a three-dimensional part. Lesson 1 taught you that an unclosed sketch could not be extruded. This statement is still true. In this lesson you will learn how to create multiple sketches that make one part. This means that you will go into the **Sketcher Work Bench** several times to create separate sketches. The separate sketches will be extruded in the **Part Design Work Bench** to form one part. The **Specification Tree** will show only one part (**Part.1**). The difference is, **Part.1** will be made up of several sketch branches. Figure 5.1 shows you the first multiple sketch part you will create in this lesson. Figure 5.2 shows the **Specification Tree** for **Part.1**. Notice the multiple sketches are all under the **PartBody** branch, which make up the **Part.1 Specification Tree**.

Figure 5.1

Figure 5.2

The first part of this lesson will teach you the tools needed to create the complex and multiple sketch parts. The second part of this lesson gives step-by-step instructions on creating three different parts. The first part will be the **Swivel**. The **Swivel** will be created using multiple sketches. The second part is the **Top U-Joint**. It will also be created using multiple sketches. The third part is the **Bottom U-Joint**. You will use **Boolean Geometry** to create this part.

The three parts created in this lesson will be used in Lesson 6, "**Introduction To The Assembly Design Work Bench**".

Lesson 5 Objectives

The objective of this lesson is to:

1   Re-enforce what was learned in Lessons 1 and 2.

2   Show different approaches to creating parts using the **Sketcher** and **Part Design Work Benches**. This will be accomplished by creating a part that requires multiple sketches.

3   Create the detail parts for Lesson 6, "**Introduction To Creating An Assembly Using The Assembly Design Work Bench**".

4   Introduce you to some of the tools found in the **Product Structure Work Bench**.

5   Use **Boolean Geometry** to create parts (yes **Boolean Geometry** still exists).

The step-by-step instruction will not be as detailed as in Lesson 1 and 2. It will be assumed the tools used in the first two lessons are now common knowledge. If they are not, you are encouraged to go back and review the subjects you have questions on.

Tools Used For Complex & Multiple Sketch Parts

For the most part the tools used in this lesson are the same tools used in Lesson 1 and Lesson 2. If you have questions on any of the **Part Design Work Bench** and/or the **Sketcher Work Bench**, review Lesson 1 and Lesson 2.

This lesson does use a new work bench, the **Product Structure Work Bench**. The **Product Structure Work Bench** and the associated tools are shown next with a brief explanation. The **Product Structure Work Bench** is very helpful when you start to deal with multiple **CATPart**s, as you will in this lesson.

The **Body** and **Boolean Geometry** tools are also shown, as you will be using them later in this lesson.

The **Product Structure Work Bench** has several tool bars. This lesson uses only one of the tool bars. The tool bar is labeled "**Product Structure**" tool bar. Only four of the tools are used or discussed in this lesson, they are the tools with the * beside them. The same tools can be accessed from the <u>I</u>nsert pull down window when the **Product Structure Work Bench** is active. Note that the **Insert** pull down window will be different depending on what work bench is active (in use). Additional **Product Structure Work Bench** tools will be discussed in Lesson 6.

The **Product Structure** Tool Bar

Tool Bar	Tool Name (default)	Tool Type Options

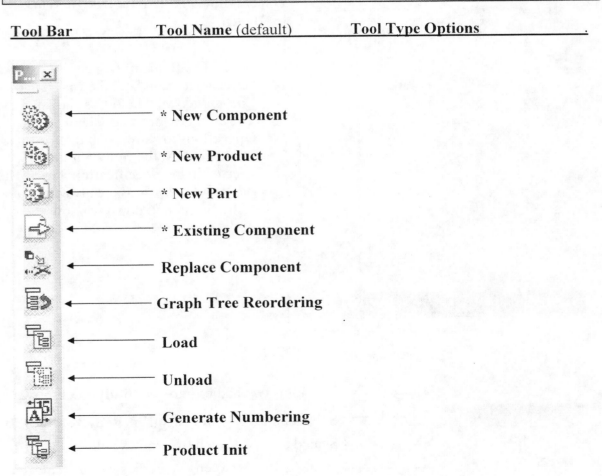

* New Component

* New Product

* New Part

* Existing Component

Replace Component

Graph Tree Reordering

Load

Unload

Generate Numbering

Product Init

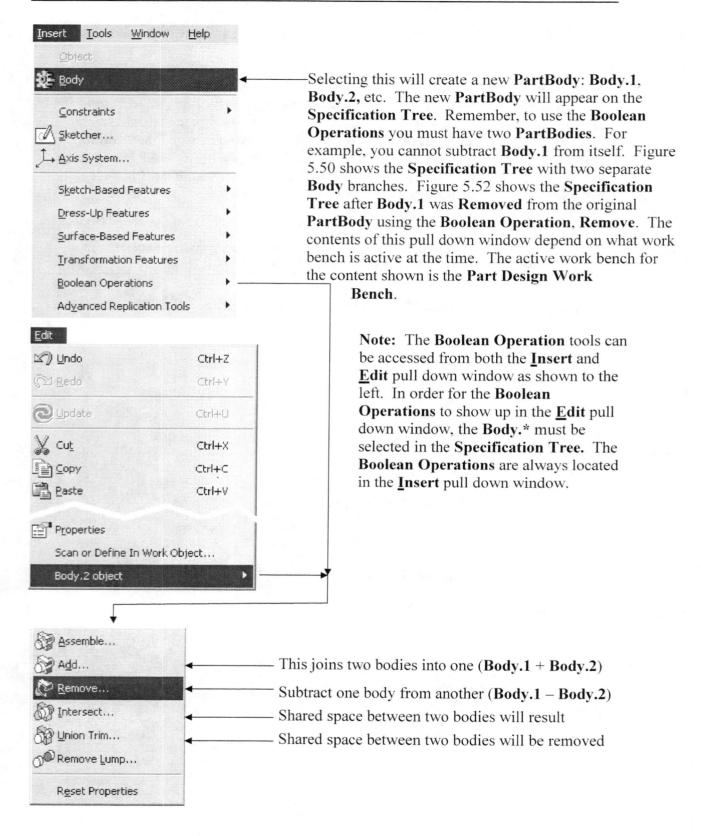

Selecting this will create a new **PartBody**: **Body.1**, **Body.2**, etc. The new **PartBody** will appear on the **Specification Tree**. Remember, to use the **Boolean Operations** you must have two **PartBodies**. For example, you cannot subtract **Body.1** from itself. Figure 5.50 shows the **Specification Tree** with two separate **Body** branches. Figure 5.52 shows the **Specification Tree** after **Body.1** was **Removed** from the original **PartBody** using the **Boolean Operation**, **Remove**. The contents of this pull down window depend on what work bench is active at the time. The active work bench for the content shown is the **Part Design Work Bench**.

Note: The **Boolean Operation** tools can be accessed from both the **Insert** and **Edit** pull down window as shown to the left. In order for the **Boolean Operations** to show up in the **Edit** pull down window, the **Body.*** must be selected in the **Specification Tree**. The **Boolean Operations** are always located in the **Insert** pull down window.

This joins two bodies into one (**Body.1** + **Body.2**)

Subtract one body from another (**Body.1** – **Body.2**)

Shared space between two bodies will result

Shared space between two bodies will be removed

Steps To Creating Complex & Multiple Sketch Parts

Figure 5.3

1 Creating The "Swivel" Using Multiple Sketches

There are multiple methods to start creating a **CATPart**. A few of them have been used and/or explained in the earlier lessons. This lesson will show you a few more ways of accomplishing the same thing. Figure 5.3 shows the dimensions that will be used to create the "**Swivel**". Complete the following steps to create the "**Swivel**" as shown in Figure 5.3.

    1.1   Start CATIA V5. (the obvious!).

    1.2   Verify that the default **Properties** are set the way you want them such as **Units, Primary Spacing** and **Graduations**. For this step, set the **Units** to inches, the **Primary Spacing** to 1 inch and the **Graduations** to **10**.

    1.3   By default CATIA V5 will bring up the **Product Structure Work Bench**. If your CATIA V5 default has been changed select the **Product Structure Work Bench**. Select **Product1** from the **Specification Tree**. With the **Product1** branch highlighted select the **New Part** tool from the **Product Structure Work Bench** as shown in Figure 5.4. This will bring up the **New Part** window as shown in Figure 5.5. It is important that the **Product1** branch is selected otherwise the **Part Number** window will not pop up.

Figure 5.4

New Part

Figure 5.5

Figure 5.6

1.4   For the **New Part Number** box type in "**Swivel**". This method allows you to name the part as you create it rather than modifying the name after the part is created as you did in Lesson 1 and Lesson 2.

1.5   Select **OK** to create the **Swivel.CATPart**. Notice that a **Swivel (Swivel.1)** branch was just created in the **Specification Tree**. If you expand the **Swivel (Swivel.1)** branch you will have a **Specification Tree** similar to what is shown in Figure 5.6.

1.6   Now you need to enter the **Part Design Work Bench**. There are several different methods you can use to accomplish this. One method is to expand the **Swivel (Swivel.1)** branch as shown in Figure 5.6 and then double click on the next branch labeled "**Swivel**". This will bring up the **Part Design Work Bench**. The second method is to expand the **Swivel (Swivel.1)** branch and select (highlight) the next branch, **Swivel** then select the **Part Design Work Bench** from either the **Start** pull down menu or the **Welcome To CATIA V5** window. Reference Lesson 1 about the **Welcome To CATIA V5** window.

1.7   Enter the **Sketcher Work Bench** using the **ZX Plane** as shown in Figure 5.7.

1.8   Create a **Circle** at the coordinates (0,0) with a radius of **.5** inches as shown in Figure 5.8.

Figure 5.7

ZX plane

Figure 5.8

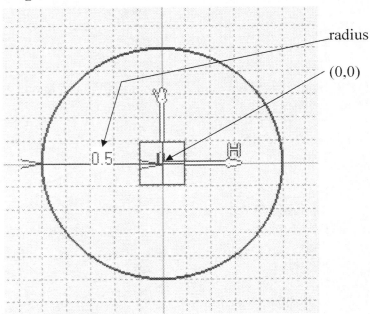

radius

(0,0)

0.5

1.9   Exit the **Sketcher Work Bench**. Remember, this will put you back into the **Part Design Work Bench**.

1.10 Select the **Pad** tool.

1.11 When the **Pad Definition** window appears, as in Figure 5.9, select the **More** button. This will expand the **Pad Definition** window to show the **Second Limit** box. Figure 5.10 shows the **Pad Definition** window expanded to include the **Second Limit**.

Figure 5.9   **Figure 5.10 (Pad Definition** window extended)

— **More** button

— **Mirrored Extent** button

1.12 In the **First Limit** area, enter "**1in**" for the **Length** box. Leave the **Type** box set at "**Dimension**", as shown in Figure 5.10.

1.13 In the **Second Limit** area, enter "**1in**" for the **Length** box, as shown in Figure 5.10.

1.14 Select the **OK** button. Notice that the circle has been extruded 1 inch in both directions, reference Figure 5.11.

1.15 Select the **ZX Plane,** reference Figure 5.7. Enter the **Sketcher Work Bench**. Notice Step 1.7 created **Sketch.1**. This step creates an additional sketch, **Sketch.2**.

Figure 5.11

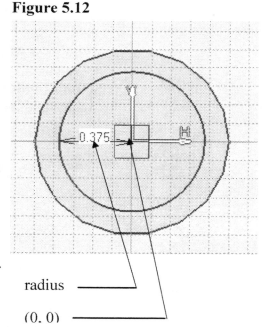

1.16 Create another **Circle** at the coordinates (0,0) with a radius of **.375** as shown in Figure 5.12.

Figure 5.12

1.17 Exit the **Sketcher Work Bench.** Select the **Pad** tool.

1.18 Enter "**1.6**" as the **First Limit Length**. Instead of selecting the **More** button and entering a length for the **Second Limit Length**, select the **Mirrored Extent** button, reference Figure 5.10. As long as the extrusion length is symmetrical you can use this button.

1.19 Select the **OK** button. The part should look similar the part shown in Figure 5.13.

0.375

radius ———

(0. 0) ———

Figure 5.13

1.20 You now need to create or duplicate **Pad.1** and **Pad.2** in the **YZ Plane.** You could create two new sketches and extrude them using the **Pad** tool, but that would be more work and time consuming than necessary. The **Circular Pattern** tool will allow you to use the geometry you already created. You will want to apply the **Circular Pattern** to both **Pad.1** and **Pad.2** in the same operation. For this step hold the ☐**Ctrl** button down as you select **Pad.1** and **Pad.2** from the **Specification Tree**, this is the Windows multi-select process. Reference Figure 5.14.

Figure 5.14

1.21 With **Pad.1** and **Pad.2** highlighted select the **Circular Pattern** tool ⬡. It is found in the **Transformation** tool bar. You may have to expand the **Rectangular Pattern** tool to locate it, as shown in Figure 5.14.

1.22 This will bring up the **Circular Pattern Definition** window as shown in Figure 5.15. Fill in the boxes as shown in Figure 5.15. Make sure the **Angular Spacing** is **90deg** and **Pad.1** and **Pad.2** show up in the **Object To Pattern** box.

1.23 Select the **Reference Element** box, and then select the **XY Plane** from the **Specification Tree**. This will bring up a **Feature Definition Error** window.

Figure 5.15

1.24 In the **Feature Definition Error** window, select **OK**. Your screen should look similar to what is shown in Figure 5.15. CATIA V5 is looking for some entity to rotate the pattern around. You could have created a line and/or used other existing entities to define the rotation, but no other elements exist at this point. You get a warning when using the **XY Plane** but it still lets you use it, notice it shows up in the **Reference Element** box.

Figure 5.16

1.25 In the **Circular Pattern Definition** window select the **OK** button. At this point your part should look similar to the one shown in Figure 5.16.

1.26 Create a .04 radius fillet on the outer edges of **Pad.1** (the large cylinder), reference Figure 5.16. You can create the fillet on all four edges and add only one **Fillet** branch to the

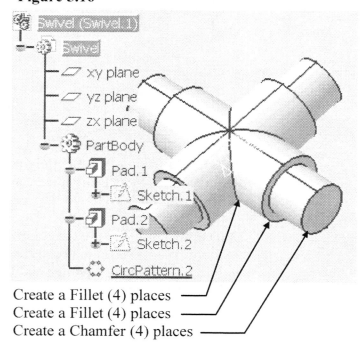

Create a Fillet (4) places ———
Create a Fillet (4) places ———
Create a Chamfer (4) places ———

Specification Tree by using the Windows multi-select method (Select the edges while you hold down the [Ctrl] key).

1.27 Create a .06 radius fillet at the intersection of the **Pad.1** (large cylinder), reference Figure 5.16. Use the Windows multi-select method so you only create one **Fillet** branch to the **Specification Tree**.

1.28 Create (.060 X 45 deg.) **Chamfer**s on the ends of all four smaller pins as shown in Figure 5.16. Again, use the Windows multi-select method.

Figure 5.17

1.29 Select **Product1** from the base of the **Specification Tree**. Rename **Product1** to **U-Joint Assembly**. Reference Lesson 2 Step 20 on how to rename **Specification Tree** branches the process is the same for **Product**s, **Parts**, **PartBodys** and all other **Specification Tree** branches.

1.30 Apply **Iron** material to the "**Swivel**" part. Remember you must select (highlight) the **Part** you are applying the material to. You must also apply the **Material Visualization**. Reference Lesson 2 Step 18 for detailed instructions.

1.31 If your '**Swivel**' looks similar to what is shown in Figure 5.17, you are ready to continue to the next step.

1.32 To add a new part to the "**U-Joint Assembly.CATProduct**" double click
      on the "**U-Joint Assembly.CATProduct**". This will take you out of the
      Part Design Work Bench and bring up the **Product Structure Work
      Bench**.

1.33 With the "**U-Joint Assembly.CATProduct**" selected (highlighted), select
      the **New Part** tool 🔲 This will bring up the **New Part Number**
      window, the same as in Step 1.3 and Figure 5.5.

1.34 Name the new part "**Top U-Joint**". Notice the new part "**Top U-Joint**"
      part will show up on the **Specification Tree**.

1.35 A **New Part Origin** window will come up. Select to keep the same **Part
      Origin**.

1.36 Save the "**U-Joint Assembly**". The file will be saved as a **CATProduct**,
      not a **CATPart**. If you saved the file prior to adding the new part the file
      would have been saved as a **CATPart**. A **CATProduct** is two or more
      CATParts.   Lesson 6 will go into detail on how existing **CATPart**s are
      brought into a **CATProduct**.

2   Creating The "Top U-Joint" Using Multiple Sketches

The "**Top U-Joint**" is the second of three parts you will create in this lesson,
reference Figure 5.18. You will create the "**Top U-Joint**" using the same method you
did in Step 1, using multiple sketches. There are many possible methods of creating
this part. Step 1 is a suggested
method. At this point, you should   **Figure 5.18**
be capable of creating this part on
your own. You are encouraged to
try your own method, maybe even
use the following steps as helpful
hints. General steps to create this
part are provided below if you are
not ready to attempt this on your
own. Since this part will be used in
Lesson 6, **Assembly Design Work
Bench**, it is critical that the
dimensions shown in Figure 5.18
are used.

2.1   The "**Top U-Joint**" part
      is a new part and
      completely separate from

the "**Swivel**" part you just created. Since the "**Top U-Joint**" part is a new part, you will need double click on the "**Top U-Joint**" branch of the **Specification Tree**. This will bring up the **Part Design Work Bench** for the selected part, the "**Top U-Joint**".

2.2   Select the **YZ Plane**, shown in Figure 5.19.

Figure 5.19

YZ Plane

2.3   Enter the **Sketcher Work Bench**.

2.4   Sketch the profile shown in Figure 5.20. There are many different ways this sketch could be created and most of them would be correct. This step is not limiting you to one particular method as long as you get the desired result. The method used in Figure 5.20 is a sample or suggested method. Since the part is symmetrical only half of the sketch was created. Complete the following steps to create the sketch as shown in Figure 5.20. Reference Figure 5.20 for the remaining steps.

2.4.1   Create the first half of the sketch as shown in Figure 5.20. The first half of the sketch is on the left hand side in the dark lines.

2.4.2   Create a vertical axis on the horizontal **0** point, using the **Axis** tool. An **Axis** is created the same as a line, it has a start point and end point, but it is represented as dashed lines. The **Axis** is needed to define the point of symmetry.

2.4.3   Use Ctrl select (Windows multi-select) to select all of the sketch entities (all of the entities to symmetry about the axis).

2.4.4   With sketched entities highlighted, select the **Symmetry** tool. The prompt zone will prompt you to select the line or axis that the entities will symmetry around.

2.4.5   Select the **Axis** you created in step 2.4.2. The second half of the sketch will appear completing the sketch.

2.4.6   If the second half of the sketch is not constrained anchor the **Axis**. The **Anchor** tool is found in the **Constraints Defined In A Dialog Box** tool. Anchoring the axis constrains the second half of the part without over constraining it.

2.4.7   If your sketch looks similar to the one shown in Figure 5.20 you are ready to move on the next step.

2.5   Exit the **Sketcher Work Bench**.

Figure 5.20

first half of sketch

Axis line used for **Symmetry** tool

second half of sketch created using the **Symmetry** tool.

Anchor on the **Axis** to lock down the second half of the sketch

the "**Swivel.CATPart**" is a reference part since you are working in the **CATProduct** mode.

2.6   Select the **Swivel (Swivel.1)** branch of the **Specification Tree**.

2.7   With the **Swivel (Swivel.1)** branch highlighted select the **Hide/Show**
       tool at the bottom of the screen. This will place the **Swivel** in **Hide** mode.
       It will still be there it is just moved from view. Notice the **Swivel**

(Swivel.1) branch is dimmed, this signifies that the branch is in **Hide** mode.

Figure 5.21

Swivel.CATPart is in **Hide** mode

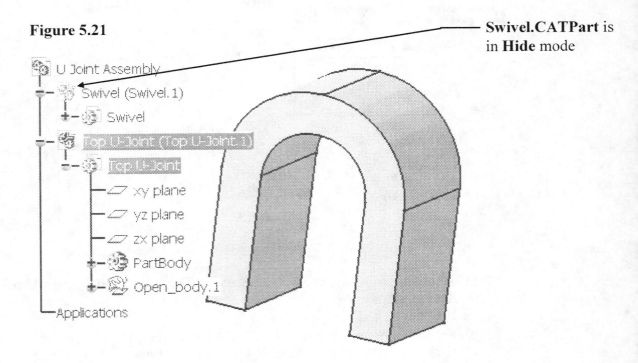

2.8   Use the **Pad** tool to extrude the profile 1 inch, then select the **Mirrored Extent** option so the extrusion will be a total of 2 inches thick but centered on the **YZ Plane**. Your newly created pad should look similar to what is shown in Figure 5.21.

2.9   The next step is to create a **2."** diameter rounded edge on the bottom of both legs. This process can be simplified by using the **Tritangent Fillet** tool. By default, the **Tritangent Fillet** tool will be a sub option under the **Edge Fillet** tool. To select the **Tritangent Fillet** tool, select the arrow next to the **Edge Fillet** tool. This will display the sub options available, reference Figure 5.22.

Figure 5.22

2.9.1

2.9.2

2.10   Select the **Tritangent Fillet** tool. This will bring up the **Tritangent Fillet Definition** window as shown in Figure 5.23. The first box is the **Faces To Fillet** box. This box allows you to select two faces to be joined with a fillet. The second box is **Face To Remove** box. This box allows you to select the face that will be removed and replaced with the fillet.

Figure 5.23   **Figure 5.24**

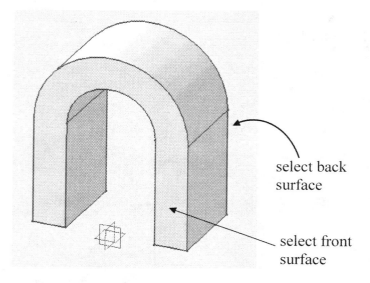

select back surface

select front surface

2.11 Select the front and back surfaces as the **Faces to Fillet** on the "**Top U-Joint**", as shown in Figure 5.24.

2.12 Select the bottom surface of the right leg. This surface joins the front and back surfaces. It is the **Face to Remove**, as shown in Figure 5.25.

Figure 5.25

Figure 5.26

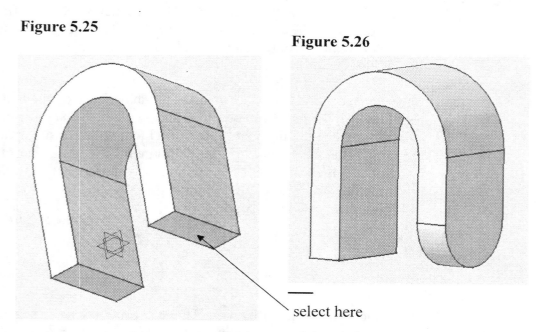

select here

2.13 Select the **OK** button. The bottom

surface selected will be removed and replaced with a radius. The radius will be the same size as the length of the surface it replaced, reference Figure 5.26.

2.14 Repeat Steps 2.9 thru 2.13 to create the radius on the other leg. With the radii created on both legs, the part should look similar to the one shown in Figure 5.27.

Figure 5.27

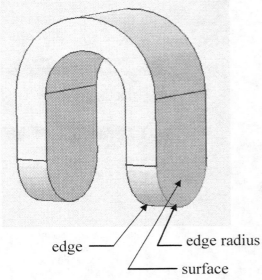

edge ——— ——— edge radius

——— surface

2.15 To put the **.75** inch diameter hole in the two legs of the part, multi select the edge and surface shown in Figure 5.27. If you have questions on this process, reference Lesson 2.

2.16 Select the **Hole** tool ⬛. In the **Hole Definition** window, enter ".75" inches for the **Diameter** box and select "**Up To Last**" as the **Hole Type**. This will create the hole in both legs at the same time.

Figure 5.28

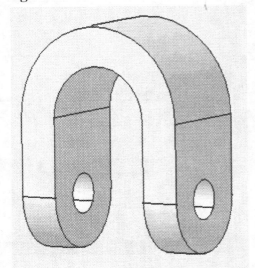

2.17 Select **OK** to create the hole. Your part should look similar to the one in Figure 5.28.

NOTE: Selecting the edge of the radius before selecting the **Hole** tool will create the hole at the center of that radius as shown in Figure 5.27. Selecting an arc is the same as multi selecting two edges to locate the hole.

2.18 The next step is to create the shaft on the top of the "**Top U-Joint**". To accomplish this you will need to create a **Plane** that will represent the top of the shaft. This **Plane** is where you will create the sketch for the shaft. Since the **Plane** tool is not a default tool in the **Part Design Work Bench**, you will have to add it to the tool bar or

Figure 5.29 ——— select

Tools Window Help

ƒ(x) Formula...

Image ▶

Macro ▶ ——— select

Parent/Children...

Customize...

enter the **Generative Shape Design Work Bench**. Since the **Generative Shape Design Work Bench** has not been covered, complete the following steps to add the **Plane** tool to the **Part Design Work Bench**.

2.18.1 Select the **Tools, Customize** options from the top pull down menu as shown in Figure 5.29.

Figure 5.30   — select here first, then here —

Figure 5.31

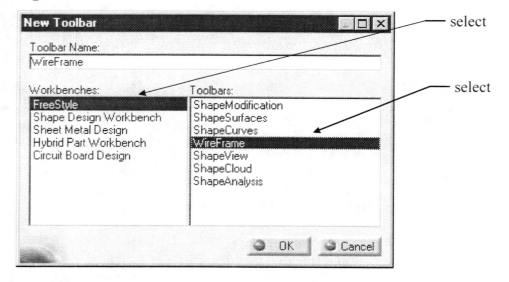

2.18.2 When the **Customize** window appears on the screen, select the **Toolbars** tab and then select the **New** button located on the right side of the window as shown in Figure 5.30.

2.18.3 When the **New Toolbar** window appears, select **FreeStyle** as the **Work Bench** and **WireFrame** as the **Toolbar** as shown in Figure 5.31.

2.18.4 The **WireFrame** tool bar that contains the **Plane** tool will appear on the screen as shown in Figure 5.32. If a different tool bar appeared, select the "**X**" in the top right corner of the incorrect tool bar to remove it and repeat Steps 2.18.1 thru 2.18.4.

Figure 5.32

Plane tool

2.18.5 Select the **OK** button in the **New Toolbar** window to accept the new tool bar. Select the **Close** button in the **Customize** window to remove it from the screen. You can now move the **WireFrame** tool bar to a convenient location on the screen. This was the long method of accessing the **Plane** tool, but it also taught you how to customize your tool bars. Just because you are in the **Part Design Work Bench** does not mean you cannot have access to tools from other work benches.

2.18.6 You can access the **Plane** tool quickly by selecting the **View** pull down menu on the top of the screen. Select **Toolbars** (the first option). This will bring up a long list of tool bars. The ones that are checked are the tool bars you currently have access to on the right side of your screen. Check the tool bar labeled **Reference Elements (Extended)**. This will add the **Reference Element** tool bar to the right side of your screen. This tool bar contains the **Plane**, **Point** and **Line** tools.

2.19 Select the **Plane** tool from the **Reference Elements** tool bar just added. This will bring up the **Plane Definition** window. Set the **Plane Type** to **Offset From Plane**. Select the **XY Plane** as the **Reference**. Enter **6.05** inches as the **Offset**. Reference Figure 5.33.

2.20 Select the new **Plane**. With the new **Plane** highlighted select the **Sketcher** tool to enter the **Sketcher Work Bench**. If the part goes off the screen use the "**Fit All In**" tool to bring it back. Make sure the **PartBody** is highlighted so the sketch will be created in the **PartBody** branch and not the **Open Body.1** branch. If the sketch is created in the **Open Body.1** branch of the **Specification Tree** you will not be able to use the **Pad** tool to create the solid part.

Figure 5.33

new **Plane**

2.21 Create a **Circle** with a radius of **.6** inches, and **Constrain** it as shown in Figure 5.34.

Figure 5.34

2.22 Exit the **Sketcher Work Bench** and extrude the circle down to the top surface of the "**Top U-Joint**" as shown in Figure 5.35.

HINT: To extrude the circle down to the top of the "**Top U-Joint**" without having to enter in the exact distance, set the **Type** box to "**Up To Next**". This will extrude the circle down until it hits the top surface of the "**Top U-Joint**". If the extrusion arrow is pointing away from the "**Top U-Joint**" surface, select the "**Reverse Direction**" button in the **Plane Definition** window. This will invert the arrow.

2.23 Add a **.15** inch **Chamfer** to the top edge of the shaft as shown in Figure 5.36.

Figure 5.35   **Figure 5.36**

2.24 Add a **.2** inch radius **Fillet** to all of the exterior edges of the solid as shown in Figure 5.36.

2.25 Add a **.2** inch radius **Fillet** where the **Pad.1** (U- shaped sketch) intersects with **Pad.2** (shaft). Reference Figure 5.36.

2.26 The next few steps will take you through the process of creating the gears on the shaft. Complete the following steps to create the gears.

    2.26.1 Create the sketch shown in Figure 5.37 on the **ZX Plane**. The sketch consists of one straight line.

Figure 5.37

sketch consisting of one straight line

2.26.2 **Constrain** the sketch as shown in Figure 5.37. Notice the sketch is not a closed sketch. The **Slot** tool does not require a closed sketch, but it is important that you **Constrain** the sketch as shown. Future modifications will not work if the sketch is not constrained as shown in Figure 5.37.

2.26.3 Exit the **Sketcher Work Bench**.

Figure 5.38

— Profile Sketch

2.26.4 Create another sketch; select the same **Plane** that was used to create the shaft sketch. Create the sketch that is shown in Figure 5.38.

2.26.5 **Constrain** the sketch as shown in Figure 5.38.

2.26.6 Exit the **Sketcher Work Bench**.

2.26.7 Select the **Slot** tool . This will bring up the **Slot Definition** window as shown in Figure 5.39.

2.26.8 For the **Profile** box select the sketch you created in Figure 5.38, in this case it is **Sketch.10**.

2.26.9 For the **Center Curve** box, select the sketch you created in Figure 5.37, in this case it is **Sketch.9**.

2.26.10 Select the **OK** button to create the **Slot**. Figure 5.40 represents what the completed slot should look like.

Figure 5.39

Sketch.9 (Center Curve)

Sketch.10 (the Profile)

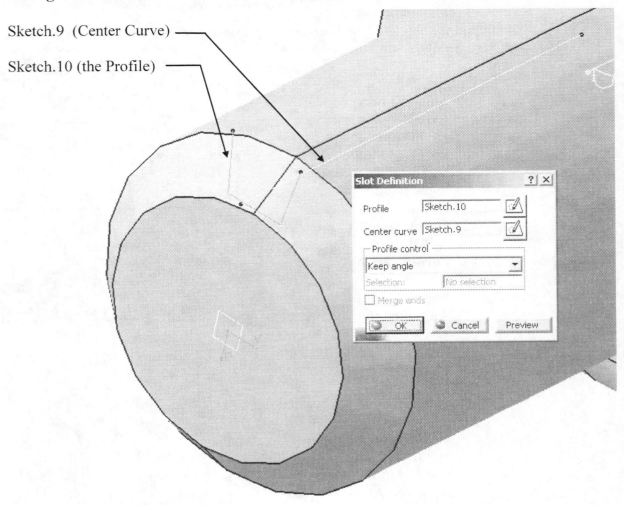

Figure 5.40   (completed slot)

Reference Element for
Circular Pattern

2.27 The original slot is complete. Now you can use the original slot to create a circular pattern around the shaft. The following steps detail this process.

Figure 5.41

2.27.1 Select the **Slot** tool. This will bring up the **Circular Pattern Definition** window as shown in Figure 5.41. Make sure that **Slot.1** is highlighted.

2.27.2 Select **Angular Spacing & Total Angle** for the **Parameters** box.

2.27.3 Enter **45 deg** for the **Angular Spacing** box.

2.27.4 Enter **360 deg** for the **Total Angle** box.

Figure 5.42

2.27.5 Select the rounded surface on the end of the shaft for the **Reference Element**. Figure 5.40 shows that it was **Fac.4**. For this particular selection (**Angular Spacing & Total Angle**) you can select a circular edge to define the circular pattern. Other selections require a line or axis.

2.27.6 For the **Object To Pattern** box, select the slot you created in the previous steps, in this case it was **Slot.1**.

2.27.7 Select the **Preview** button. If the preview shows the slot being rotated and duplicated around the rounded edges as shown in Figure 5.42, select the **OK** button to create the **Circular Pattern**.

2.27.8   If your "**Top U-Joint**" looks similar to the one shown in Figure 5.42 you are ready to move on.

2.28   You are done adding features to the "**Top U-Joint**" but not quite finished with the part. Add "**Brass**" material to the "**Top U-Joint**". The only reason for applying brass as the material is so the part can easily be differentiated from the other parts (the "**Swivel**" and "**Bottom U-Joint**"). Remember that you must change the **Visualization** mode before the material will be applied to the part, reference Lesson 2 on **Applying Material**.

2.29   Earlier in this lesson you were instructed to put the "**Swivel**" part in **Hide** mode so it would not get in the way while you constructed the "**Top U-Joint**". Now is a good time to bring it back so you can see both parts (the "**Top U-Joint**" and "**Swivel**"). To do this, select the "**Swivel**" branch of the **Specification Tree**. Then select the **Hide/Show** tool at the bottom of the screen. This will bring the "**Swivel**" back into view

2.30   Double click on the "**U Joint Assembly**", the base of the **Specification Tree**. Remember this will take you to the **Product Structure Work Bench**. Save the "**U-Joint Assembly**". Remember, you must be in the **Product Structure Work Bench** to save as a "**U-Joint Assembly.CATProduct**". If the "**Swivel**" part is active in the **Part Design Work Bench**, only the "**Swivel.CATPart**" will be saved.

2.31   Step 3 will take you through the process of creating the "**Bottom U-Joint**" using a different approach.

3   Creating The "Bottom U-Joint" Using Boolean Geometry

The third and last part you will create in this lesson is the "Bottom U-Joint", shown in Figure 5.64. The "**Bottom U-Joint**" is identical to the "**Top U-Joint**". In Industry, you would create the "**Bottom U-Joint**" as efficiently as possible, which would be by duplicating the "**Top U-Joint**". Since it is this books objective to show you how to use as many tools as possible, this step will use a different method in creating the "**Bottom U-Joint**". At the moment, this may not be the most efficient method, but it will help you be a more efficient and knowledgeable CATIA V5 user. This additional method will be recognized by anyone who has experience on the older legacy solid modeling programs. The method still has applications in the solid modeling world. The method is, creating and manipulating solids using **Boolean Geometry**. The following instructions step you through the process of creating the "**Bottom U-Joint**" using **Boolean Operations**.

Figure 5.43

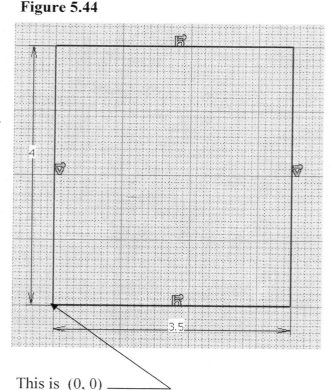

3.1   Start a new part by selecting **File**, **New** from the Windows tool bar. This will bring up the **New** window as shown in Figure 5.43.

Figure 5.44

3.2   From the **New** window, select **Part**. This will create a new part with a new **Specification Tree**. The part number will depend on how many parts you have started/created since you stated the session. Rename the part to "**Bottom U-Joint**". Remember, you can rename by selecting the part branch and right clicking on **Properties**, reference Lesson 2. It will bring up the **Part Design Work Bench**.

This is (0, 0)

NOTE: Yes, it would have been more efficient to select **New Product** in the **Product Structure Work Bench** as you did when creating the "Swivel" and "Top U-Joint". There is a method to this madness (additional work). This process will allow you use additional tools and processes that you otherwise would not have the opportunity to experience. So, please continue as instructed.

3.3   In the **Part Design Work Bench** and the **Part Specification** branch renamed to "**Bottom U-Joint**", create a sketch in the **ZX Plane**.

3.4   Create a rectangle in the **Sketcher Work Bench** as shown in Figure 5.44.

3.5   Exit the **Sketcher Work Bench**, extrude the sketch 1 inch and mirror the extent so the total thickness is 2 inches. Reference Figure 5.45.

3.6   Select the **Insert** tab from the top pull down menu as shown in Figure 5.46.

3.7   From the **Insert** window, select the **Body** option. This will insert a **New Body** into the **Specification Tree** as shown in Figure 5.45.

3.8   Select the **New Body**, **Body.2** in the **Specification Tree**. This will make **Body.2** the active branch.

3.9   Select the front surface of the box as shown in Figure 5.45 and enter the **Sketcher Work Bench**. The selected surface defines the sketcher plane, the same as the plane in previous lessons. The new sketch will show up on the **Specification Tree** under the **Body.2** branch.

Figure 5.45

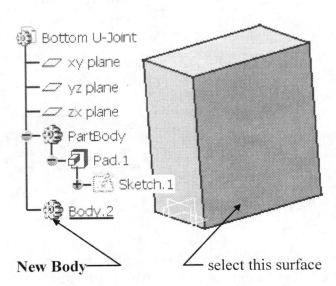

New Body — select this surface

Figure 5.46

3.10 Sketch the profile shown in Figure 5.47. CATIA V5 will allow you to **Constrain** the new sketch to the edges of the existing box (**Sketch.1**) as shown in Figure 5.47.

Figure 5.47

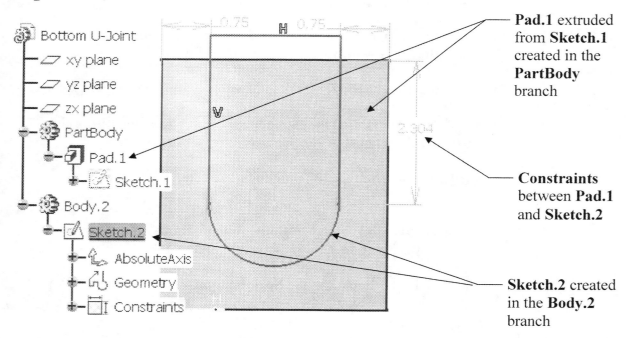

Pad.1 extruded from **Sketch.1** created in the **PartBody** branch

Constraints between **Pad.1** and **Sketch.2**

Sketch.2 created in the **Body.2** branch

3.11 Exit the **Sketcher Work Bench** and select the **Pad** tool.

3.12 In the **Pad Definition** window, select the **More** button. Figure 5.48 shows the **Pad Definition** window already expanded.

3.13 In the **First Limit** box for the **Length**, enter "**2.5in**" as shown in Figure 5.48.

Figure 5.48

3.14 In the **Second Limit** box for the **Length**, enter "**.5in**" as shown in Figure 5.48.

3.15 Select the **OK** button. The extruded solid should look similar to the one shown in Figure 5.49. If the solid was extruded in the wrong direction you may need to hit the **Reverse Direction** button to reverse the direction of the extrusion.

NOTE: As **Sketch.2** was being created, it was being recorded in the **Specification Tree** under the **Body.2** branch. The new **Body** was inserted in the **Specification Tree** in Step 3.6. Figure 5.50 shows what the **Specification Tree** should look like with the **Body.2** branch inserted.

Figure 5.49

Figure 5.50

Pad.1

Pad.2

3.16 Select the branch, **Body.2**, from the **Specification Tree**. This should highlight indicating it has been selected. The corresponding solid on the screen, **Body.2**, will also highlight. If **Body.2** is not selected, the following steps will not work!

Figure 5.51

3.17 Select the **Insert** tab from the top pull down menu as shown in Figure 5.51.

3.18 Select **Boolean Operations** from the bottom of the **Insert** window as shown in Figure 5.51.

3.19 Select **Remove** from the list of **Boolean Operations** as shown in Figure 5.51. This will remove (subtract) the second pad from the first pad. Reference Figure 5.52. Selecting the **Edit**, **Body.2 Object**, **Remove** options will give you the same result. A **Remove.1** branch was added to the **Specification Tree**.

Figure 5.52

Figure 5.53

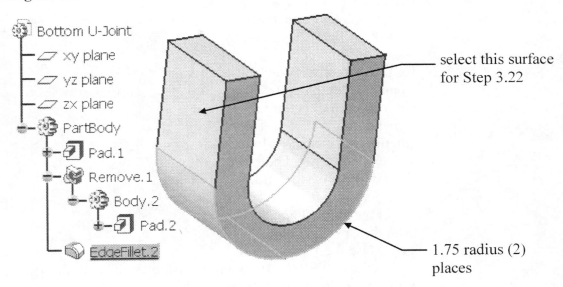

select this surface for Step 3.22

1.75 radius (2) places

3.20 Create a **1.75** radius **Fillet** on the bottom two edges of the part. This can be accomplished with one fillet if you multi-select the two edges to be filleted, otherwise you will have to do it in two separate fillet operations. Figure 5.53 was completed in one fillet operation.

3.21 Add a **New Body** to the **Specification Tree**. Review Steps 3.5 thru 3.7 on how to add a **New Body**.

3.22 Select the left side surface of the part as shown in Figure 5.53 and enter the **Sketcher Work Bench**.

Figure 5.54

3.23 Create a **Circle** with a **.375** inch radius and **Constrain** it as shown in Figure 5.54.

Figure 5.55

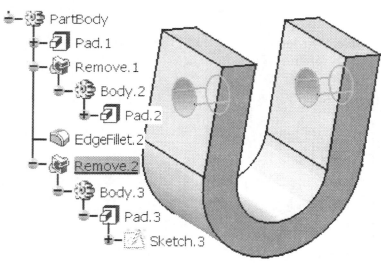

3.24 Exit the **Sketcher Work Bench** and extrude the circle in both directions as shown in Figure 5.55. The length is not critical as long as it extends beyond both sides of the U-shaped **Body**.

3.25 Select the **Body.3** branch from the **Specification Tree**. Use the **Remove** tool as described in Step 3.19 to remove **Body.3** (the cylinder you just created). You can use the **Edit** or **Insert** method.

3.26 If your "**Bottom U-Joint**" looks similar to the one shown in Figure 5.56 you are ready to continue on to the next step.

Figure 5.56

3.27 The next step in creating the "**Bottom U-Joint**" is creating the shaft. It would be simpler to create the shaft using the same method you used for the "**Top U-Joint**". This step will have you create another **Body** so you can experience the **Add** operation in the **Boolean Geometry** tool bar. This will also allow you to see the difference in how it affects the **Specification Tree.** So, for this step, create another **New Body**. The **New Body** should be **Body.4**.

Figure 5.57

Figure 5.58

select this surface

3.28 Select the **Plane** tool. When the **Plane Definition** window appears, set the **Plane Type** box to "**Offset From Plane**" as shown in Figure 5.57. If the **Plane** tool is not available, refer back to Step 2.18 to add the tool to the **Part Design Work Bench.**

3.29 Figure 5.58 shows the surface to select as the reference **Plane**.

3.30 Enter "**6.05**" in the **Offset** box as shown in Figure 5.57.

3.31 Select the **OK** button to create the **Plane**.

3.32 Select the new **Plane** and enter the **Sketcher Work Bench.** Create a **Circle** with a **.6in** radius and **Constrain** it as shown in Figure 5.59.

Figure 5.59

3.33 Exit the **Sketcher Work Bench** and extrude the sketch up to the bottom surface of the part. Your "**Bottom U-Joint**" should look similar to the one shown in Figure 5.60.

Figure 5.60

3.34 If you select the shaft, you will notice that only the shaft will highlight (**Body.4** in the **Specification Tree**), reference Figure 5.61. The shaft is separate from the U-shaped solid. In Step 2 you created the shaft using the same method, but as the same body. To make the "**Bottom U-Joint**" as one complete part, you must add the two solid parts (**Bodies**) together. This is done in the same menu window as Step 3.19. The only difference is you select the **Add** tool instead of the **Remove** tool. Add the two **Bodies** (**Body.1** and **Body.4**) together.

3.35 After completing the **Add** operation, your **Specification Tree** should look similar the one shown in Figure 5.62. Compare the difference between the **Specification Tree** in Figure 5.61 and Figure 5.62. Notice where the **Body.4** is located, it was added to the **PartBody** branch.

3.36 The next step is to create a **2.00"** diameter rounded edge on both legs. For this step, you will use the same tool used in Step 2, the **Tritangent Fillet** tool. Create the **Tritangent Fillet** exactly as you did in Step 2.9. For detailed instruction, refer back to Step 2.9 through 2.14.

Figure 5.61 (**Bodies** not joined)

only **Body.4** is highlighted

Figure 5.62

separate body, **Body.1**

3.37 Add a **.15in Chamfer** to the top edge of the shaft as shown in Figure 5.63.

3.38 Add a **.2in** radius **Fillet** to all of the exterior edges of the solid as shown in Figure 5.63. Notice you can do this in one **Fillet** operation using the Windows multi-select, but you must be sure to select only the edges that require the fillet. Any line that is highlighted will receive a fillet. If you have trouble completing the fillet in one operation, you can use as many as you need (one edge at a time). For this step the **Specification Tree** shows that all of the fillets were created in one operation (**EdgeFillet.3**).

Figure 5.63

Figure 5.64

3.39 Create the gears for the shaft the same as you did for the "**Top U-Joint**", using the **Slot** tool. Refer to Steps 2.26 & 2.27 and the related figures on how to use the **Slot** tool and **Circular Pattern** tool.

3.40 In the design process you realize that the shaft is 2 inches too short. CATIA V5 gives you the tools to modify the design without requiring you to re-create any entities. CATIA V5 offers these powerful (time saving) tools, but you the user must have the knowledge and fore thought in the design process to take advantages of these tools. In this case you were instructed to constrain the **Center Curve Sketch** of the **Slot** in such a way that you can modify the **Reference Plane** the **Shaft** sketch was created on, and everything else would automatically be updated. Try it by completing the following steps.

3.40.1 Go to the **Open Body** branch of the **Specification Tree**.

3.40.2 Expand the **Specification Tree** so the **Offset** branch is showing.

3.40.3 Double click on the **Offset** branch. This will bring up the **Edit Parameters** window.

3.40.4 The offset distance in the **Edit Parameters** window will be **6.05**. This is the value that was assigned when creating the **Plane** using the **Offset** option. Now, modify the **6.05** inches value to **8.05** inches.

3.40.5 Select the **OK** button. The length of the shaft will go from **6.05** to **8.05** inches along with the **Slot** and **Circular Pattern** that make up the gear.

3.41 One of the last requirements for "**Bottom U-Joint**" is to apply the **Titanium** material and update the **Render Style** so the material is displayed.

3.42 If your "**Bottom U-Joint**" looks similar to the one shown in Figure 5.64, save the file. Make sure you save the file as "**Bottom U-Joint.CATPart**". The file will be required in the subsequent lesson.

Lesson 5 Summary

The tools and principals covered in Lesson 1 and Lesson 2 still apply, but with the ability to create multiple (limitless) sketches, the **Part Design Work Bench** becomes even more powerful. The **Product Structure Work Bench** helps you to keep things organized as you create multiple parts. If you like to create parts using the **Boolean Geometry**, CATIA V5 allows that option. CATIA V5 allows for many ways to create and design.

Lesson 5 Review

After completing this lesson you should be able to answer the questions and explain the concepts listed below.

1. Name the two types of **Fillets** used in this lesson.
2. Explain the differences between the two types of **Fillets**.
3. What is one of the two methods used to reverse the direction of a profile being extruded (using the **Pad** tool)?
4. What button is used to expand the options in the **Pad Definition** window?
5. What are the steps required to create a **New Body**?
6. What determines the size of the **Fillet** when the **Tritangent Fillet** tool is used?
7. When you were creating the hole in the legs of the "**Top U-Joint**", why was the edge of the radius selected instead of the straight edge of the part?
8. The **Part Design Work Bench**, by default, does not contain the **Plane** tool. How can you make the **Plane** tool available for entities in the **Part Design Work Bench**?
9. **T** or **F** In the **Specification Tree**, a **Plane** falls under the **Open_Body** branch.
10. What "**Type**" option in the **Pad Definition** window is used to extrude a cylinder up to the surface without having to specify the exact distance?
11. The "**Top U-Joint**" and the "**Bottom U-Joint**" parts are identical, but were created using different methods. Which method was the quickest and easiest?
12. What two pull down menus allow you access to the **Boolean Operations**?
13. How could you tell what method was used to create the "**Top U-Joint**" part?
14. **T** or **F** To complete a **Boolean Operation**, you must have two separate **Bodies**; for example, **Body.1** and **Body.2**.
15. What two **Boolean Operations** were used in this lesson?
16. List the other **Boolean Operations**.
17. Describe the process required to subtract one body from another.
18. What method did you use to create the holes in the "**Top U-Joint.CATPart**"?
19. What method did you use to create the holes in the "**Bottom U-Joint.CATPart**"?
20. **T** or **F** The **Specification Tree** will have two separate **Body** branches after completing an **Add** operation (adding two different **Bodies** together).

Lesson 5 Practice Exercises

You now have some knowledge, and a little bit of experience, in creating complex parts that require multiple sketches. The following parts will help you improve and further develop your skill and knowledge.

1   This part is a good starter part. It requires multiple sketches, but is quite simple. If you apply what you have learned in this lesson, you should not have any problems. Save the part as "**Lesson 5 Exercise 1.CATPart**".

Suggested steps:

1.1   Create the box first. Create the sketch on the base plane. Extrude the box 1.50 inches.

1.2   Create the 2.25 inch diameter cylinder. You can use the base plane or the top of the new box as the sketch plane for the cylinder. The only difference it will make is how far you extrude it.

1.3   Use the **Hole** tool to hollow out the cylinder. Remember, you can select the outside radius of the cylinder to locate the hole in the center of the cylinder.

1.4   Use the **Hole** tool again to create the first of four .50 thru holes. Use two of the edges of the box to properly locate the hole. Use the first hole to create the **Pattern** of holes.

2   This part is an excellent opportunity to use both the multiple sketch and **Boolean Geometry** methods of creating a part. There are many possible methods of creating this part. Use your brief experience and your ingenuity to create this part. Remember, at this point there is no right or wrong method. Save your completed part as "**Lesson 5 Exercise 2.CATPart**".

HINT: Create a base solid to begin with and then begin subtracting the different slots and channels. The only feature that requires **Boolean Geometry** subtracted out is the 1 inch square slot. Remember you need to create a **New Body** in the **Specification Tree** before you create the solid.

3   This part will give you more practice with joining and subtracting different bodies. Save the part as "**Lesson 5 Exercise 4.CATPart**".

4   This part involves the same operations as the previous parts. When you are done, save the part as "**Lesson 5 Exercise 5.CATPart**".

5   This part gives more practice with parts that contain multiple bodies. When you are done, save this part as "**Lesson 5 Exercise 6.CATPart**".

Extra Credit: If you like a challenge, this one is for you. When you are done, save the part as "**Lesson 5 Exercise 3.CATPart**".

Suggested steps:

EC.1   The individual features of this part are not that difficult. What makes this part difficult is how the different features are oriented to the other features. Most of the parts used thus far have had parallel and perpendicular sketch planes. When deciding which plane to use in sketcher, select the profile that shows the most detail. In this case it would be the plane labeled **Sketch Plane 1**.

EC.2   Create the standing box profile **Sketch Plane 2** using the bottom of the base plane. Create it parallel to the base and then rotate it the 30 degrees by using the **Rotation** tool found in the **Transformation Features** tool bar.

EC.3   Create a **New Body** on the sketch plane labeled **Sketch Plane 3** and subtract it from the body created in Step EC.1.

EC.4   Create the holes using the **Hole** tool.

NOTES:

Introduction To Creating An Assembly Using The Assembly Design Work Bench

This lesson uses the three detail parts created in Lesson 5. The three parts are the "**Swivel**", the "**Top U-Joint**" and the "**Bottom U-Joint**". This lesson will take you through a step-by-step process of assembling the three detailed parts using the **Assembly Design Work Bench**.

Assembly Design

The first part of this lesson will introduce you to all of the default tool bars found in the **Assembly Design Work Bench**. The second part of this lesson gives step-by-step instructions for entering the **Assembly Design Work Bench**, inserting detail parts into the **Assembly Design Work Bench**, moving detail parts around in the **Assembly Design Work Bench** and assembling the detail parts. Upon completion of this lesson, your assembly should look similar to the one shown in Figure 6.1. As in the previous lessons, not all of the **Assembly Design Work Bench** tools will be used and/or explained in this lesson.

Following the step-by-step instructions, there are 20 **Review Questions** to help you solidify your assembly knowledge.

The last section of this lesson has some **Practice Exercises**.

Figure 6.1

"**Top U-Joint.CATPart**"

U Joint Assembly
- Swivel
- Top U-Joint
- Bottom U-Joint
- Annotations Set.1
- Constraints
  - Fix.1
  - Surface contact.2
  - Coincidence.3
  - Coincidence.4
  - Surface contact.5
- Applications
- Camera

"**Swivel.CATPart**"

"**Bottom U-Joint.CATPart**"

Lesson 6 Objectives

The objective of this lesson is to:

1   Learn how to use some of the basic tools in the **Assembly Design Work Bench**.

2   Learn how to insert existing components into an assembly.

3   Learn how to move individual components around in an assembly.

4   Learn how to constrain individual components in an assembly.

5   Learn how to create additional components in the **Assembly Design Work Bench**.

This lesson teaches these concepts first by giving step-by-step instruction followed by sample problems. Concepts covered in the previous lessons will not be covered in detail, you will be expected to know it.

Assembly Design Work Bench Tool Bars

There are seven default tool bars in the **Assembly Design Work Bench.** The individual tools found in each of the seven tool bars are labeled to the right of the tool icon.

As explained in the previous chapters, the arrow located at the bottom right of the tool icon indicates more than one variation of that tool is available. For a review and/or more information on how to select another variation refer back to Lesson 1.

The **Move** Tool Bar

Tool Bar	Tool Name (default)	Tool Type Options

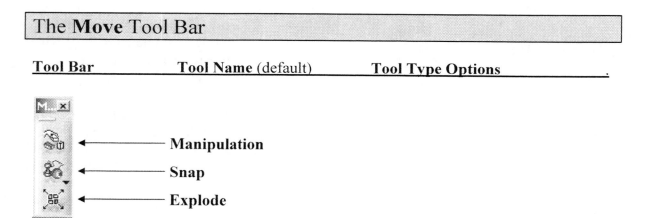

Manipulation

Snap

Explode

The **Product Structure** Tool Bar

Tool Bar	Tool Name (default)	Tool Type Options	.

New Component

New Product

New Part

Existing Component

Replace Component

Graph Tree Reordering

Generate Numbering

ProductInit

Manage Representations

Fast Multi Installation   **Define Multi Installation**

The **Measure** Tool Bar

Tool Bar	Tool Name (default)	Tool Type Options	.

Measure Between

Measure Item

The **Annotation** Tool Bar

Tool Bar	Tool Name (default)	Tool Type Options	.

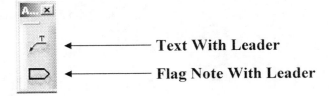

Text With Leader

Flag Note With Leader

The **Constraints** Tool Bar

Tool Bar	Tool Name (default)	Tool Type Options

Coincidence Constraint

Contact Constraint

Offset Constraint

Angle Constraint

Fix Component

Fix Together

Quick Constraint

Flexible/Rigid Sub-Assembly

Change Constraint

Reuse Pattern

The **Assembly Features** Tool Bar

Tool Bar	Tool Name (default)	Tool Type Options

Split Hole

Hole

Pocket

Add

Remove

The **Weld Planner** Tool Bar

Tool Bar	Tool Name (default)	Tool Type Options

← Weld Planner

Steps To Creating An Assembly Using the Assembly Design Work Bench

In Lesson 5 you created the detail parts, the "**Top U-Joint**", "**Bottom U-Joint**" and "**Swivel**". Now you get the opportunity to assemble them together. This is a simple assembly, but it will show you the basic process of bringing together parts and constraining them. Not all of the assembly tools will be used in this lesson. After completing the instructions in this lesson, you are encouraged to try some of the other tools. The instructions in this lesson will give you a good foundation to build on; it's up to you to expand on your basic understanding.

1 Entering the Assembly Design Work Bench

In Lesson 1, you were taught two different methods of selecting a particular work bench. The second method depends on the default settings. You can only select the work benches that show up on the "**Welcome To CATIA V5**" window. Lesson one did not have you add the **Assembly Design Work Bench** to the "**Welcome To CATIA V5**" window. Lesson 1 gives step-by-step instructions on how you can add a work bench the "**Welcome To CATIA V5**" window. You can also select the **Assembly Design Work Bench** by selecting the **Start**, **Mechanical Design**, **Assembly Design Work Bench**.

Figure 6.2

You may have already realized it but you have already started your assembly. In Lesson 5 you created both the "**Top U-Joint**" and the "**Swivel**" in the same file. The file was saved as "**U-Joint Assembly.CATProduct**". For this step **Open** the "**U-Joint Assembly.CATProduct**" created in Lesson 5, reference Figure 6.2. The default work bench will be the **Product Structure Work Bench**. You can select the base of the **Specification Tree** "**U-Joint Assembly**" and then select the **Assembly Design Work Bench**. This will make the **Assembly Design Work Bench** the current work bench.

> **NOTE:** The **Product Structure Work Bench** comes up by default with **Product.1** as the base of the **Specification Tree**. The **Product.1** will not change as you select and enter into the **Assembly Design work Bench**.

2   Inserting Components Into The Assembly Design Work Bench

The detail parts that make up the assembly were created in Lesson 5. Before the detail parts can be assembled, you will need to insert them into the **Assembly Work Bench**. The follow steps explain how this is done.

2.1   Verify that you are in the **Assembly Design Work Bench**. If you are not in the **Assembly Design Work Bench** select it.

2.2   The top of the **Specification Tree** must be selected before components can be inserted into the **Assembly Design Work Bench**. In this case, the top of the **Specification Tree** is labeled "**U-Joint Assembly**" as shown in Figure 6.2.

2.3   With "**U-Joint Assembly**" highlighted, select the **Existing Component** tool. The **Insert an Existing Component** window will appear on the screen as shown in Figure 6.3.

> **NOTE:** If you select the **Existing Component** tool and the **Insert An Existing Component** window does not appear on the screen, it may mean that the base of the **Specification Tree**, the "**U-Joint Assembly**" is not highlighted.

Figure 6.3

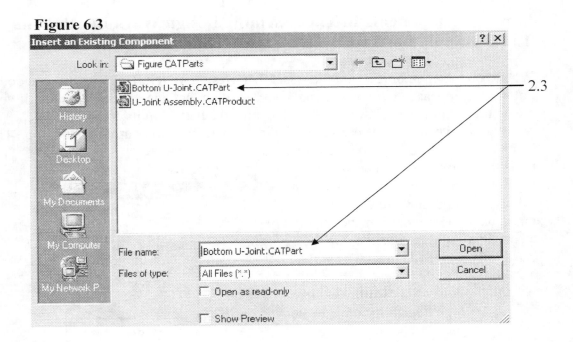

2.3

2.4   In the **Insert An Existing Component** window, find the file that was
saved earlier in Lesson 5 named "**Bottom U-Joint.CATPart**". Select the
Open button. The part should appear on the screen. If it does not, verify
you selected the correct file and then repeat Steps 2.1 thru 2.3. Your
screen should show the "**Bottom U-Joint**" part similar to what is shown in
Figure 6.4.

Figure 6.4

"**Top U-Joint**"

"**Bottom U-Joint**"

"**Swivel**"

3   Moving Components In The Assembly Design Work Bench Using The Manipulation Tool.

When you insert an object into the **Assembly Design Work Bench**, the object does not always appear in the position and/or orientation that you expect. Usually, if you create the detail parts relative to the same axis, the parts will insert in the same orientation. There will be parts that you insert that have no relative orientation. This is not a problem. CATIA V5 has supplied tools that allow easy and accurate manipulation of part orientation. The following steps show you how to manipulate the orientation and location of a part that has been inserted into the **Assembly Design Work Bench**.

Figure 6.5

3.1   Select the **Manipulation** tool from the right side of the screen.

3.2   The **Manipulation Parameters** window will appear on the screen as shown in Figure 6.5. This window allows you to move or rotate the components along any of the three axes.

3.3   Select the "**Y**" direction box.

3.4   Move the pointer with the mouse onto the "**Top U-Joint**" part. The entire part should highlight. Drag it to the approximate location shown in Figure 6.6. Compare the location of the "**Top U-Joint**" to Figure 6.4.

Figure 6.6

Figure 6.7

3.5   Select the "**X**" direction box from the **Manipulation Parameters** window as shown in Figure 6.6.

3.6   Move the pointer onto the "**Swivel**" part. Drag it to the approximate location shown in Figure 6.7.

3.7   Select the **OK** button in the **Manipulation Parameters** window to exit the **Manipulation** command. The three parts that were inserted are now separated so that each can clearly be seen.

4   Moving Components In The Assembly Design Work Bench Using The Compass

The location and orientation of the assembly components can also be manipulated using the **Compass** tool. The **Compass** tool was covered in detail in Lesson 2. The same rules apply in the **Assembly Design Work Bench** the only difference is you have several components to select from. The following steps will show you how to move the **Swivel** using the **Compass** tool.

Figure 6.8

4.1   From the **Specification Tree**, select the **Swivel** branch as shown in Figure 6.8.

4.2   Place the **Compass** tool on the **Swivel** surface as shown in Figure 6.8. The **Compass** tool will turn green indicating that the selected component can be manipulated. For detailed instructions on how to manipulate the **Compass** tool refer back to Lesson 2.

4.3   Select the **Z axis** on the **Compass** tool and drag it in the positive direction. The **Swivel** will move along with the **Compass**. Practice manipulating the orientation of the **Swivel** using the **Compass** tool.

Figure 6.9

4.4   Move the **Compass** to the surface of the "**Top U-Joint**" as shown in Figure 6.9. Select the **Z axis** on the **Compass** and drag it in the positive direction. Notice you are still manipulating the **Swivels** location, not the "**Top U-Joint**". To move the "**Top U-Joint**" you must select the "**Top U-Joint**" branch from the **Specification Tree**.

The difference in using the **Compass** tool in the **Assembly Design Work Bench** and the **Part Design Work Bench** is that you must have the component you want to move highlighted in the **Specification Tree**. Step 5 shows you how to **Constrain** the assembly. You can use the **Compass** to move components even after they have been **Constrained**. To move the component back to the constrained position, you need to select the **Update** tool.

5 Assembling Existing Components

To assemble the components, **Constraints** will need to be created that define the relationships each object has with respect to the others. The steps below will show you how to create these **Constraints**.

5.1 Select the **Fix Component** tool ⚓ from the right side of the screen and then select the "**Bottom U-Joint**" part. It can be selected from the **Specification Tree** or by selecting the object on the screen. An **Anchor** symbol will appear on the part to show that it has been fixed as shown in Figure 6.10. A new branch will be added to the **Specification Tree**, the **Constraints** branch.

Figure 6.10

Figure 6.11

View B

View A (rotated)

select these surface

View B

View A

5.2   Select the **Contact Constraint** tool ⊞. This tool will place the selected
surfaces of one part, onto the selected surface of another part. Select the
surfaces shown in Figure 6.11, **Views A** and **B**. You may have to **Zoom**
in to select the surface shown in **View A**. The **Contact Constraint**
symbol will appear on each surface selected. A line connecting the two
surfaces will show that they share a common plane as shown in Figure
6.12. Figure 6.12 represents what the CATIA V5 screen will look like
when you have made the correct selection. The selection is complete, but
no parts have moved yet. To move the parts you have to select the
Update tool. Figure 6.13 shows that the "**Swivel**" was moved or updated
to the newest **Constraint** applied to it. What the **Contact Constraint** did
was place both surfaces selected in Figure 6.11 on the same plane.

Figure 6.12 (assembly with **Contact Constraint**)   **Figure 6.13**

Contact constraint

5.3   Select the **Coincidence Constraint**
      tool ✏. This command will align the   **Figure 6.14**
      centers of two holes or cylinders. This
      command will be used to place the shafts of
      the "**Swivel**" part through the holes in the
      "**Bottom U-Joint**".

5.4   Place the curser on the hole of the "**Bottom
      U-Joint**" part and move it around until the
      axis that runs through the center of the holes
      appears as shown in Figure 6.14. This can
      sometimes be tricky; the axis is hard to
      activate to make it visible. The pointer
      needs to be in just the right place in order
      for the **Axis Line** to appear. Moving the
      mouse around in the area of the axis should
      allow you to pick it up. When it appears,
      press down the left mouse button to select it.
      Once the **Axis Line** is selected it will show
      up as highlighted.

Center
Axis Line

place
pointer
here so axis
will show
up

NOTE: If you have trouble getting the **Axis Line** to appear, **Zoom In** on the area and try again.

Figure 6.15

place pointer here

center **Axis Line**

5.5   Repeat the same process to locate the **Axis Line** that passes through the center of the cylinder of the "**Swivel**" part as shown in Figure 6.15.

5.6   The "**Swivel**" should now be lined up with the "**Bottom U-Joint**" so that the shafts of the "**Swivel**" are inside the holes in the "**Bottom U-Joint**" as shown in Figure 6.16. Remember, you may have to manually select the **Update** tool, depending on your default setting.

Figure 6.16

Figure 6.17

5.7   Repeat Steps 5.2 thru 5.4 to constrain the "**Top U-Joint**" to the "**Swivel**"
       as shown in Figure 6.17. When you are done your assembly should look
       similar to the one shown in Figure 6.18. Notice in the **Specification Tree**
       an additional **Surface Contact Constraint** between the "**Top U-Joint**"
       and the "**Swivel**" was required to properly place the correct contact
       surfaces together.

Figure 6.18

5.8   Figure 6.18 shows the **U-Joint Assembly** fully assembled. You can use
       the **Compass** to position the individual parts for a better presentation. To
       reposition the parts complete the following steps.

   5.8.1.   Place the **Compass** on the surface of the "**Swivel**" as shown in
            Figure 6.19.

   5.8.2.   Make sure the "**Swivel**" branch of the **Specification Tree** is
            highlighted.

   5.8.3.   Using the **Compass** rotate the "**Swivel**" 90 degrees, as shown in
            Figure 6.20. Remember you may have to manually select the
            Update tool. You can lock the position of the assembly by
            pushing down the right mouse button when it is on the **Compass**.

   5.8.4.   If your "**U-Joint Assembly**" looks similar to what is shown in
            Figure 6.20 you are ready to move on to the next step.

Figure 6.19

Figure 6.20

6   Modifying A Component In The Assembly Design Work Bench

The individual components were created in the **Part Design Work Bench**. Each individual component can still be modified from the **Assembly Design Work Bench**. The component is actually modified in the **Part Design Work Bench**, but is accessed from the **Assembly Design Work Bench**. This step will have you modify the "**Top U-Joint**" shaft radius and length.

6.1   To enter the **Part Design Work Bench** from the **Assembly Design Work Bench**, double click on the component you want to modify. For this step, double click on the "**Top U-Joint**" branch as shown in Figure 6.21.

6.2   The next step is to find where, in the **Specification Tree**, the parameters for the shaft radius and length were created. This is one reason renaming the branches of the **Specification Tree** can be helpful. Another method of finding the particular branch is to select the entity itself. For this step, expand the branch labeled "**Top U-Joint**" as shown in Figure 6.21. Figure 6.21 shows the 'Top U-Joint" shaft highlighted. The shaft is **Pad.2** on the **Specification Tree**. The number assigned may differ depending on how and what order you created it. The important thing is that you select the correct **Pad** regardless of the number.

Figure 6.21

component being modified

6.3   Expand the **Pad** branch so that the **Sketch** branch is visible. Double click on the **Sketch**. This will take you to the **Sketch** where the shaft radius was first created.

6.4   Expand the **Sketch** branch so the **Radius** branch is visible. Double click on the **Radius** branch. This will bring up the **Constraint Definition** window as shown in Figure 6.22.

Figure 6.22

6.5   The **Radius** box currently is set at **.6in**. Replace the **.6in** with a **.75in**.

6.6   Select **Ok** to modify the radius.

6.7   Exit the **Sketcher Work Bench**. When you exit the **Sketcher Work Bench**, the shaft you just modified will turn **Red**. Be patient! The **Red** color is CATIA V5 signaling you that it is updating the solid. When CATIA V5 is done updating, the solid will go back to its default color and the shaft will now have a radius of **.75"**. If the update causes any problems an **Update Diagnosis : Sketch.8** window will appear as shown in Figure 6.23. Modifying the sketch radius from **.6"** to **.75"** will cause an update error. The fillet that joins the two bodies together (the shaft and U shaped body) is too large. The buttons on the right side of the window give you several options. For this step select the **Edit** button. This brings up the **Edge Fillet Definition** window so the value can be edited, also shown in Figure 6.23.

6.8   **Figure 6.23**

Fillet requires modification

6.9   Modify the **Fillet Radius** to **.05"**.

6.10 Select the **OK** button. The **Update Diagnosis** widow will disappear and the **Fillet** will be updated.

Figure 6.24

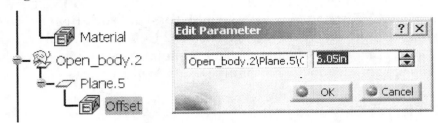

6.11   To modify the length of the shaft, expand the **Open_Body** branch of the **Specification Tree** (still in the "**Top U-Joint**" branch of the assembly). Double click on the **Offset** branch in the **Plane** branch as shown in Figure 6.24. This will bring up the **Edit Parameter** window also shown in Figure 6.24.

6.12   Modify the value of **6.05in** to **8.05in**. This is moving the **Plane** from 6.05 inches as it was originally created to 8.05 inches, 2 additional inches. The sketch that defines the shaft was created on this **Plane** and was extruded to the surface of the U-Shaped body. Modifying the location of the **Plane** also modifies the length of the **Pad**.

Figure 6.25

6.13   Select the **OK** button. The shaft will update, it will be 2 inches longer than before. Reference Figure 6.25:

NOTE: The **Circular Pattern** of the **Slot** was updated with the **Pad**. The automatic update of the **Slot** was determined by how the sketch making up the **Slot** was constrained. Figure 5.37 in Lesson 5 shows how the **Center Curve Sketch** was constrained. The **Center Curve** sketch was not constrained to an exact length but to entities that would update with the re-location of the sketch plane. Being more specific, the top endpoint of the line was constrained to 0 inches from the end of the shaft. The other end of the line was constrained 4.5 inches from the bottom of the part. This constraint method made the length of the line variable. The variable line defines the length of the **Slot**. Since that one **Slot** was used as a **Circular Pattern** all of the **Slots** were updated.

If your "**Top U-Joint**" looks similar to the one shown in Figure 6.26, you are ready to continue on to the next step. The changes were made in the **Part Design Work Bench** even though you started in the **Assembly Design Work Bench**. Getting back to where you started from is easy; double click on "**U-Joint Assembly**" in the **Specification Tree**. As you double click on "**U-Joint Assembly**", notice that the work bench changes back to the **Assembly Design Work Bench**.

Figure 6.26

7   Creating A Bill Of Materials

CATIA V5 offers a multitude of assembly tools to help you create, control and document your assembly. This step will introduce you to a few of the more common and/or required tools. These tools are **Bill Of Material**, **Compute Clash**, **Product Management**, **Analyzing Constrains** and **Measuring**.

7.1   Select the **Analyze** tool bar located in the top pull down menu. The **Analyze** tool menu is available only if you are in the **Assembly Design Work Bench**. This will bring up the menu shown in Figure 6.27.

Figure 6.27

7.2   Select the **Bill Of Material**. This will bring up the **Bill Of Material: U-Joint Assembly** window as shown in Figure 6.28. As the **Bill Of Material** window shows, CATIA V5 has been keeping a record of everything you have inserted and or created in the **Assembly Design Work Bench**.

Figure 6.28

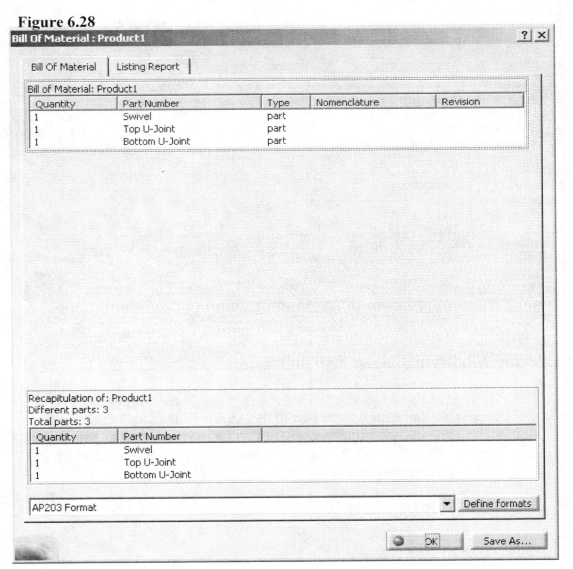

7.3   CATIA V5 allows you to export this information as a **.txt** file. Select the **Save As** button in the bottom right of the **Bill Of Material: U-Joint Assembly** window. Figure 6.29 shows an example of the **.txt** file from the **Bill Of Material: U-Joint Assembly** window.

Figure 6.29

Figure 6.30

8   Analyzing/Modifying Assembly Constraints

8.1   The next analysis tool CATIA V5 offers is the **Constraints Analysis**. Select the **Constraints** option from the **Analyze** menu, reference Figure 6.27. This will bring up the **Constraints Analysis** window as shown in Figure 6.30. This window supplies information on how many and what kind of **Constraints** were used in the assembly.

8.2   Take a minute to review the information contained in the **Constraints Analysis** window. Select the **OK** button to close out of the **Constraints Analysis** window. This method allows you to **Analyze** the **Constraints**. If you want to modify the **Constraints** complete the following steps.

    8.2.1   Make sure you are in the **Assembly Design Work Bench**.

    8.2.2   Double click on the selected **Constraint**. This will bring up the **Constraint Definition** window.

    8.2.3   Select the **More** button. This will expand the **Constraint Definition** window as shown in Figure 6.31. The **Constraint Definition** window gives you the name, the type and what entities the constraint is using.

    8.2.4   You can also get to this window by using the **Properties** window.

Figure 6.31

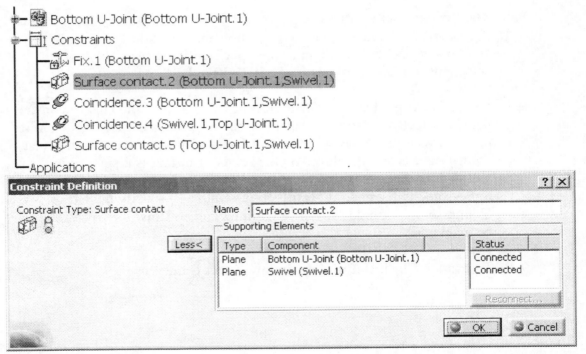

9   Clash Detection

9.1   Another handy tool located in the **Analyze** tool window is the **Compute Clash** option. Selecting the **Compute Clash** option will bring up the **Clash Detection** window as shown in Figure 6.32. The "**Bottom U-Joint**" has been placed in **Hide/Show** for clarification.

Figure 6.32

9.2   The **Prompt Zone** will prompt you to "**Select two components**". Select the "**Swivel**". Hold down the **Ctrl** button and select the "**Top U-Joint**". Both selections will highlight in the **Specification Tree**. The two selections will also show up in the **Definition** box.

9.3   Select the **Apply** button. The **Result** box will display the kind of contact the two selected components share. This particular assembly has **Contact** only between the "**Swivel**" and "**Top U-Joint**" components. Notice that the **Contact** is also displayed on the solids. **Contact** is displayed in yellow by default. If the two solids clashed, the **Clash** would be represented in red and the **Results** box would also specify the **Clash**. Your assembly should only have **Contact** and no **Clash** between components.

9.4   To exit the **Clash Definition** window, select **Cancel**.

10 Measuring Tools

10.1 Two other options in the **Analyze** tool bar are the **Measure Between** and **Measure Item**. Both tools are used the same as described in the **Introduction**. The two tools are the same as the **Measure** tools found on the bottom tool bar. **Measure Item** measures a single length of an entity. **Measure Between** measures the distance between entities you select.

10.2 The last tool in the **Analyze** tool bar is the **Measure Inertia**. Selecting **Measure Inertia** will bring up the **Measure Inertia** window as shown in Figure 6.33. You can measure the inertia of an individual component and/or the entire **Product**. You select the component you want the inertia information on and it will analyze it. Figure 6.33 shows the entire assembly inertia analysis. The centroid (center of mass) is displayed in the **Inertia Center** box as well as graphically on the assembly. You can customize the information displayed in the **Measure Inertia** window. You can also export the information as a **.txt** file.

Figure 6.33

To get the most out of this step you need to work through it, explore it and test it.

11 Assembly Dependencies

CATIA V5 gives you
many different ways to
view and analyze your
assembly. The
Dependencies tool is just
another way of analyzing
how your assembly is put
together. This tool is
found in the **Analyze** pull
down window. Figure
6.34 shows how the "**U-
Joint Assembly**"
Dependencies are linked
together. This tool is
particularly helpful when
you want to know which
parts were used to create a
particular **Constraint**.

Figure 6.34

12 Mechanical Structure

The **Mechanical Structure** tools is
another method of analyzing the
assembly. Figure 6.35 shows the
Mechanical Structure Tree for the "**U-
Joint Assembly**". This assembly is
relatively simple. As you get to larger and
more complex assemblies the value of this
tool will become more important.

Figure 6.35

13 Adding Annotation

CATIA V5 has supplied you with a method to communicate with written text right in
the assembly. You can do this by selecting the **Text With A Leader** tool from the
right tool bar. Then all you have to do is select the entity that you want the text
attached to. For this step select the .05 fillet radius as shown in Figure 6.36. This
will bring up the **Text Editor** window. You type in the note you want attached and
select the **OK** button. In this case make a note of the size of the radius fillet. Your
note should look similar to what is shown in Figure 6.36.

Figure 6.36

14 Saving A Specific View

The **Named Views** tool is a general tool available in most all of the CATIA V5 work benches. Even though this tool is not particular to the **Assembly Design** tool now is a good time to put it to use. This tool is particularly useful when you have zoomed and oriented the part and/or assembly to exactly how you want it. If you could not save this exact zoom value and orientation it might take a lot of extra time to get it close. Saving and naming the view

Figure 6.37

will take you exactly to the way it was saved. Another application is if you were working on a large part and/or assembly and you needed to view one end and then the other end, you would not want to have to **Pan** from one end to the other every time! Saving a view will allow you to go directly from one end to the other, as you saved it. To create, save and name a view complete, the following steps.

14.1   Zoom and orient the part/assembly or area of the part/assembly as you need it. For this step zoom in on the "**Swivel**" as shown in Figure 6.37, it does not have to be exact.

14.2   Select the **View** pull down window (top menu).

14.3   Select **Named Views…** . This will bring up the **Named Views** window, as shown in Figure 6.37.

14.4   Select the **Add** button. This will create the default view name "**Camera 1**". Delete "**Camera 1**" and replace with the name "**Zoom on Swivel**".

14.5   Select **Ok** to create the view.

14.6   Now you can rotate and zoom the assembly any way you want. If you want to get back to that exact view repeat the previous steps, except instead of creating a new view select the view you just created "**Zoom on Swivel**" and select apply. The screen will update to that particular view, just the way you saved it.

15 Exploding The Assembly

You spent a lot of time and effort in creating and constraining the "**U-Joint Assembly**". CATIA V5 has created a tool that can explode the assembly automatically in a matter of several mouse clicks. To create an exploded view of your "**U-Joint Assembly**" complete the following steps.

Figure 6.38

15.1 Select the **Explode** tool from the **Move** tool bar. This will bring up the **Explode** window as shown in Figure 6.38.

15.2 To view the default explode, select the **Apply** button. This will create the exploded assembly. Now you can select the **Play/Replay** button to re-assemble/explode the assembly. You can also use the mouse to manually control the explosion, by dragging the **Scroll Explode** button.

15.3 You can also customize the **Explode** tool by determining which entities will be fixed. For this step create a simple exploded assembly similar to the one shown in Figure 6.38.

16 Saving The Newly Created Assembly

Congratulations! You just completed your first assembly in CATIA V5. Save the file as "**U-Joint Assembly.CATProduct**". Notice CATIA V5 saves this as a separate file. The file has a "**CATProduct**" extension. This "**U-Joint Assembly.CATProduct**" file is directly linked to the "**CATPart**" file created in Lesson 5, the "**Bottom U-Joint.CATPart**".

To verify where all of the components are saved, select the **Tools, Product Management**. This will bring up the **Product Management** window. This window displays all of the assembly's components and where they are saved. If you are not in the **Assembly Design Work Bench** the **Product Management** option will not be accessible.

If you want to copy this assembly and all its linked components to another file, select **File, Send To**. This will allow you to copy it to another directory and/or mail.

Lesson 6 Summary

Though this was a simplified assembly, it did require you to go through the basic steps of inserting new and existing components (parts), re-orienting the components and bringing the components under specific restrictions, using **Constraints**. Even complex assemblies require these basic steps. Now that you have a basic idea of how to create an assembly, you are strongly encouraged to go back and try different variations of accomplishing the same thing. Try some of the unused tools.

Lesson 6 Review

After completing this lesson, you should be able to answer the questions and explain the concepts listed below.

1. How many standard tool bars are there in the **Assembly Design Work Bench**?
2. What file extension does CATIA V5 give to assembly files?
3. Is the assembly file directly linked to the "**CATPart**" files that are used in the assembly file?
4. What option under the **Start** pull down menu gives you access to the **Assembly Design Work Bench**?
5. What must be selected before components can be inserted into the **Assembly Design Work Bench**?
6. What tool inserts parts into the **Assembly Design Work Bench**?
7. What tool was used to move the parts after they were inserted into the **Assembly Design Work Bench**?
8. What tool is used to anchor a part to a fixed location?
9. What does the **Contact Constraint** tool do?
10. What does the **Contact Constraint** symbol look like once it has been applied the assembly?
11. What does the **Coincidence Constraint** tool do?
12. What does the **Coincidence Constraint** symbol look like once it has been applied to the assembly?
13. Why is it important to know how to move and orient parts after they have been inserted into the **Assembly Design Work Bench**?
14. **T** or **F** The **Axis Line** is always visible in the **Assembly Design Work Bench**.
15. If you want to find out how far apart two individual parts are, what tool would you use?
16. **T** or **F** The **Specification Tree** in the **Assembly Design Work Bench** not only shows the history of the assembly, but also the individual part that was inserted into the assembly.
17. List the two different methods of moving the individual parts around in the **Assembly Design Work Bench**.
18. If you move a component using the compass after it has been located using a **Constraint**, how would you restore it to its original **Constraint** location?
19. **T** or **F** CATIA V5 allows you to modify a component without leaving the **Assembly Design Work Bench**.
20. **T** or **F** The **Measure Inertia** tool and the **Bill Of Materials** tool are found in the same tool bar.

Lesson 6 Practice Exercises

Now that you have created one assembly in CATIA V5, you can strengthen your
newfound knowledge by completing the following practice exercises.

1   Insert the "**Lesson1 Exercise 1.CATPart**" and "**Lesson 1 Exercise 5.CATPart**".
    Assemble the two parts using the **Contact Constraint**. Your assembly should
    look similar to the one shown below. Save the assembly as "**Lesson 6 Exercise
    1.CATProduct**".

"Lesson 1 Exercise 5.CATPart"

"Lesson 1 Exercise 1.CATPart"

2   Insert the "**Lesson 1 Exercise 4.CATPart**" and "**Lesson 1 Exercise
     6.CATPart**". Assemble the two parts using the **Contact Constraint** and the
     Offset Constraint. Your assembly should look similar to the one shown below.
     Save the assembly as "**Lesson 6 Exercise 2.CATProduct**".

"**Lesson 1 Exercise 6.CATPart**"   "**Lesson 1 Exercise 4.CATPart**"

Offset Constraint

3   Insert the "**Lesson 5 Exercise 3.CATPart**" and "**Lesson 5 Exercise
    5.CATPart**". Assemble the two parts using the **Coincidence Constraint** and the
    Contact Constraint. Your assembly should look similar to the one shown below.
    Save the assembly as "**Lesson 6 Exercise 3.CATProduct**".

—"**Lesson 5 Exercise 3.CATPart**"

—"**Lesson 5 Exercise 5.CATPart**"

4   Insert the "**Lesson 5 Exercise 4.CATPart**" and "**Lesson 6 Exercise
     6.CATPart**". Assemble the two parts using the **Coincidence Constraint** and the
     Contact Constraint. Your assembly should look similar to the one shown below.
     Save the assembly as "**Lesson 6 Exercise 4.CATProduct**"

"**Lesson 5 Exercise 6.CATPart**"

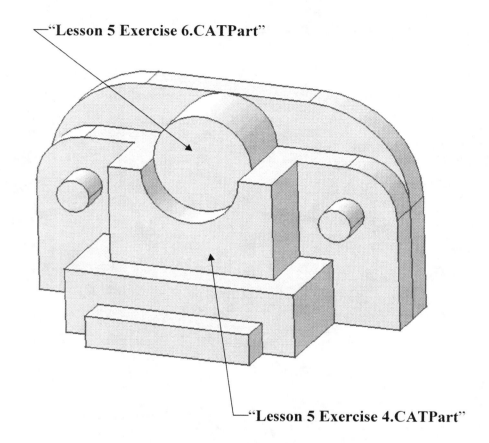

"**Lesson 5 Exercise 4.CATPart**"

Lesson 7   Generative Shape Design Work Bench

Introduction To Creating Wireframe And Surface Geometry Using The Generative Shape Design Work Bench

This lesson describes to you, step-by-step how to create a local axis and how to create wireframe geometry using lines, points and corners. This lesson will then show you how to create a surface from the existing wireframe. The end of the lesson shows you how to create a solid part from the wireframe and surfaces. This lesson does not cover all the tools found in the **Generative Shape Design Work Bench**. Each step lists which particular tool is used in the step. Lesson 8 is a continuation of the **Generative Shape Design Work Bench**.

Generative Shape Design

You will see a significant difference in the **Specification Tree**. So far all of the objects have been created under the **Part Body** branch of the **Specification Tree**. As you create the wireframe all of the lines will be created under the **Open_Body** branch, not the **Part Body** as in the previous lessons. The **Part Body** contains all of the solid geometry such as the **Pad** operations, **Fillets**, **Chamfers**, **Holes**, etc. The **Open_Body** contains everything that is not a solid such as **Lines**, **Curves**, **Points** and **Planes**. Since a wireframe is not a solid object, it will be listed under the **Open Body** branch in the **Specification Tree**.

The part that will be created in this lesson is shown in Figure 7.1. It will be called a "**Sheetmetal Bracket**" and will be saved as "**Sheetmetal Bracket.CATPart**".

Lesson 7 Objectives

This Lesson will show you how to do the following:

- Select the **Generative Shape Design Work Bench**
- Create **Local Axis System**
- Create 3D wireframe entities
- **Split** 3D entities
- Create a **Surfaces**
- Create a **Fillet** between two surfaces
- **Split** surfaces
- Give a surface a **Thickness**

Generative Shape Design Work Bench Tool Bars

There are five default tool bars found in the **Generative Shape Design Work Bench.** They are: **Surfaces, Wireframe, Operations, Replication** and **Law**. The five tool bars are shown below.

Just in case you forgot, the arrow at the bottom right of some of the tool icons is an indication of there being more than one variation of that particular type of tool. The **Select** tool bar is not mentioned because it is standard in all work benches.

The **Wireframe** Tool Bar

Tool Bar	Tool Name (default)	Tool Type Options

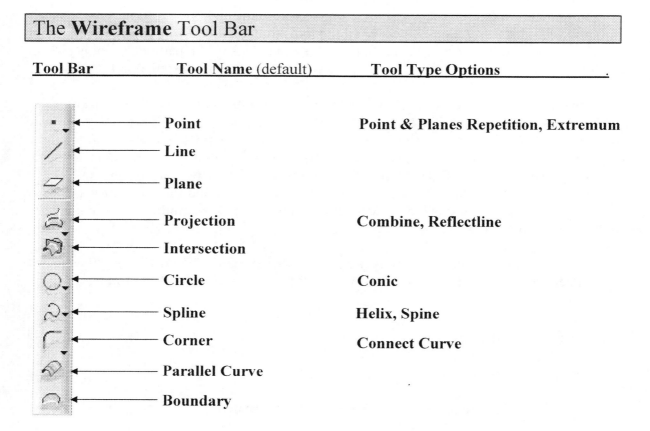

	Point	**Point & Planes Repetition, Extremum**
	Line	
	Plane	
	Projection	**Combine, Reflectline**
	Intersection	
	Circle	**Conic**
	Spline	**Helix, Spine**
	Corner	**Connect Curve**
	Parallel Curve	
	Boundary	

The **Operations** Tool Bar

Tool Bar	Tool Name (default)	Tool Type Options
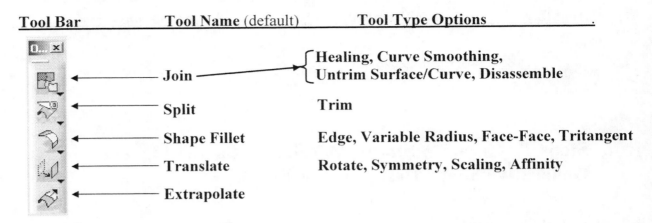	Join	Healing, Curve Smoothing, Untrim Surface/Curve, Disassemble
	Split	Trim
	Shape Fillet	Edge, Variable Radius, Face-Face, Tritangent
	Translate	Rotate, Symmetry, Scaling, Affinity
	Extrapolate	

The **Surfaces** Tool Bar

Tool Bar	Tool Name (default)	Tool Type Options
	Extrude	Revolve
	Offset	
	Sweep	Adaptive Sweep
	Fill	
	Loft	
	Blend	
	Extract	

The **Replication** Tool Bar

Tool Bar	Tool Name (default)	Tool Type Options
	Object Repetition	Points & Planes Repetition
	Rectangular Pattern	Circular Pattern
	Duplicate Open Body	
	Power copy Creation	Power Copy Instantiation, Power Copy In Catalog

The **Law** Tool Bar

Tool Bar	Tool Name (default)	Tool Type Options

Law ◄──────────── Law

Steps To Create A Simple Wireframe Part Using The Generative Shape Design Work Bench

1   Select The Generative Shape Design Work Bench

This step will use the **Generative Shape Design Work Bench** to create a "Sheetmetal Bracket" shown in Figure 7.1. Selecting the **Generative Shape Design Work Bench** is the same as selecting the **Sketcher Work Bench** and **Part Design Work Bench** as you did in Lessons 1 and 2. If the **Generative Shape Design Work Bench** does not appear in the "**Welcome To CATIA V5**" window you will have to select the **Generative Shape Design Work Bench** from the **Start** pull down menu. For reviewing this process reference Lesson 1 Step 2. Select the **Generative Shape Design Work Bench**. Your screen should look similar to the one shown in Figure 7.2 with the exception of the tool bars being two tool icons wide. By default the tool bars will be one tool icon wide. The screen in Figure 7.2 has been modified to two tool icons wide so all of the standard **Generative Shape Design Work Bench** tools can be represented. The bottom tool bar has also been modified to show all of the tools available. The process of moving the tool bars around on the screen is covered in detail in Lesson 2 Step 10.4.

Figure 7.1

Make sure the **Units** are set to inches and the grid is set to 1" **Primary Spacing** and 10 **Graduation**.

Notice the **Specification Tree**. The top of the tree is a **Part1** and under the **PartBody** branch you have an **Open_Body.1** branch. It is this branch that all of the wireframe geometry will be placed.

Figure 7.2

NOTE: The **Generative Shape Design Work Bench** screen looks similar to the
Part Design Work Bench screen. Notice that the tool bars on the right
side of the screen are different and the **Specification Tree** has an
Open_Body branch added to it.

2 Creating A Local Axis System

This step is not absolutely necessary for creating wireframe objects, but it is a useful
tool and will help you in your wireframe and surface creation. Creating a local axis
system can be applied in any of the CATIA V5's workbenches. This step will show
you how to create two different axis systems. The axis systems will be used later on
in the lesson. As you create and use the axis systems in this lesson, be thinking how
local axis systems might be used in past and future lessons and/or projects. This step
will have you create two local axis systems before creating the wireframe for the
"**Sheetmetal Bracket**".

The default 0,0,0 location for CATIA V5 is the intersection of the **XY**, **YZ**, and **ZX**
Planes. Since there is no coordinate system visible other than the representative
planes, create a point at the 0,0,0 location.

2.1   Create a point by completing the following steps.

Figure 7.3

2.1.1   Select the **Point** tool. This brings up the **Point Definition** window as shown in Figure 7.3.

2.1.2   Select the **Point Type** box. This displays all the different methods available for creating points.

2.1.3   Select the **Coordinates** option.

2.1.4   For the **X** value leave it at the default value of 0.

2.1.5   For the **Y** value leave it at the default value of 0.

2.1.6   For the **Z** value leave it at the default value of 0.

2.1.7   Select **OK**. This will create a point at the 0,0,0 location as shown in Figure 7.4.

Figure 7.4

point

2.1.8   Notice where the newly created point appears, the intersection of the three planes. Now that you have proven the location of the 0,0,0 location, lets move on.

2.2   The first axis system you will create is at the original 0,0,0 location, which is the intersection of the three planes and the location of the point you just created. To create an axis at the original 0,0,0 location, complete the following steps.

2.2.1   Select the **Axis** tool at the bottom of the screen. This will bring up the **Axis System Definition** window as shown in Figure 7.5.

2.2.2   Select the **Origin** box. With the box highlighted, select the point you just created at the 0,0,0 location. **Point.1** should now appear in the **Origin** box as shown in Figure 7.5. This locates the origin of the axis.

Figure 7.5

2.2.3   Leave **No Selection** as the default in the **X Axis** box.

2.2.4   Leave **No Selection** as the default in the **Y Axis** box.

2.2.5   Leave **No Selection** as the default in the **Z Axis** box.

shows what hand the axis is

2.2.6   Select the **OK** button to create the axis.

NOTE: You can reverse the direction of any of the axis by selecting that particular axis or by selecting the **Reverse** box to the right of each axis value box in the **Axis System Definition** window. It is important for you to know that changing the direction of a particular axis in relationship to one of the other two axis systems could change the axis system from a right hand axis system to a left hand axis system, reference Figure 7.6. The **Axis System Definition** window displays the type of axis being created.

Figure 7.6

Left-handed axis

Right-handed axis

If you want the X axis pointing in the direction of the Y axis, you must select the **X Axis** box and then select a geometrical entity that will indicate the direction of the axis. Since there are no other entities to select, you can select the plane that is normal to the direction you want the axis to point. If you define the direction of just one axis, CATIA V5 will rotate the other axis systems to create a right hand axis. To create a left hand axis, you must define the direction of the other two axis systems. Reference the **Axis System Definition** window. The bottom middle of the window will indicate **Right Hand** or **Left Hand** (reference Figure 7.5).

2.2.7   When you get the axis system oriented as shown in Figure 7.7, you are ready to go on to the next step.

Figure 7.7

2.3 The "**Sheetmetal Bracket**" you are going to create in this section of the lesson will start at the 10,0,10 location. Some of the points will be created using X,Y and Z coordinates. To make the point creation easier, you will need to create another local axis system at the 10,0,10 location. Having a local axis system will save you from having to calculate the points from the original 0,0,0 point. Create the local axis system by completing the following steps.

2.3.1 Create a point in the 10,0,10 location using the **Point** tool and the same process used in Step 2.1. The point will be used to locate the **Origin** of the new axis.

Figure 7.8   new point created

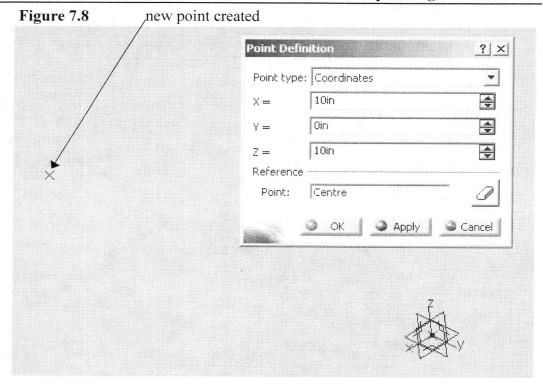

2.3.2   Complete Steps 2.2.1 through 2.2.7 to create a new axis system. The only difference in creating this axis system will be the **Origin**. Select the point created in Step 2.3.1 for the **Origin**.

2.3.3   Default values can be used for all of the other variables in the **Axis System Definition** window. Basically you are creating the same axis, the only difference is the **Origin**.

2.3.4   If your newly created axis system looks similar to Figure 7.9, you are ready to move on to the next step. (You may need to select the **Fit All In** tool to see the newly created axis.)

Figure 7.9

newly created axis (**Axis System.2**)

2.4   You now have two axis systems created. If you created a new point, the coordinates you assign to the point would be relative to the axis system that is current. In this context current means active. How do you tell what axis system is current? How do you make an axis system current? Double click on the axis you want to make current. This will bring up the **Axis System Definition** window. The bottom left of the **Axis System Definition** window has a toggle box labeled **Current**. By selecting this box, you make that particular axis system current. This means, if you create a point at the 0,0,0 location, it will be created in relation to that axis system. If you unselect it, it will be an inactive axis system. If you leave this box blank, it will default to the previous axis. For this section of the lesson, make the newly created axis system current (**Axis System.2**).

Figure 7.10

designates the current axis system

Figure 7.11

2.5   You can verify which axis system is
       current by using the **Specification Tree**.
       Figure 7.11 shows **Axis System.1** and
       Axis System.2 in the **Specification Tree**.
       Notice the difference between the two axis
       system icons. One is thin and dark while
       the other is thick and orange in color. The
       thick orange axis system icon is the current
       axis system. Double clicking on the axis
       system in the **Specification Tree** or on the
       Axis its self can change this. This will
       bring up the **Axis System Definition**
       window where you can toggle on or off the
       Current box as described in Step 2.4.

2.6   Your **Specification Tree** now has a branch labeled **Axis System.1** and a
       branch labeled **Axis System.2**. It will not take long to forget which axis is
       which. It would be a good idea at this point to rename the two axis
       systems so that they retain some logical meaning. This is done the same
       as renaming any other entity in the **Specification Tree**. Complete the
       following steps to rename **Axis System.1** and **Axis System.2**.

2.6.1   Highlight **Axis System.1** in
        the **Specification Tree**.

2.6.2   Push the right mouse button.
        This brings up the **Edit**
        window (Figure 7.12).

2.6.3   Select the **Properties** option.

2.6.4   In the **Properties** window
        select the **Feature Properties**
        tab (Figure 7.13).

2.6.5   Edit the **Name** box. Change
        the name from **Axis System.1**
        to **Main Axis**.

Figure 7.12

Figure 7.13

2.6.6   Select the **OK** button to complete the task.

2.6.7   Complete the same steps as described above to change **Axis System.2** to **Sheetmetal Bracket Axis**.

With the two axis systems created and renamed and the **Sheetmetal Bracket Axis** selected as the current axis system, you are ready to start creating wireframe geometry.

3 Creating Points ▪

You must first determine where the part will be created in relationship to the 0,0,0 point and how it will be oriented. After the location and orientation has been decided you can start creating wireframe geometry. For this section of the lesson you will need to create three points. Create the points by completing following steps.

3.1   First, verify that the **Sheetmetal Bracket Axis** is the current axis, reference Step 2.

3.2   Using the **Point** tool, create the three points using the coordinates below. Instructions to creating points are covered in detail in Step 2.1.

      Point 1 (0,0,0)
      Point 2 (1,0,0)
      Point 3 (0,0,2)

NOTE: The newly created points are added to the **Specification Tree**. They will be labeled as **Point.3**, **Point.4** and **Point.5**. You have already created **Point.1** and **Point.2** in the previous steps. If the points are not visible in the **Specification Tree**, you may need to select the plus sign to the left of the branch. This should expand the **Specification Tree** so all of the points are visible. Rotate the screen to get a better view of the points. Your screen should look similar to the one shown in Figure 7.14.

Figure 7.14

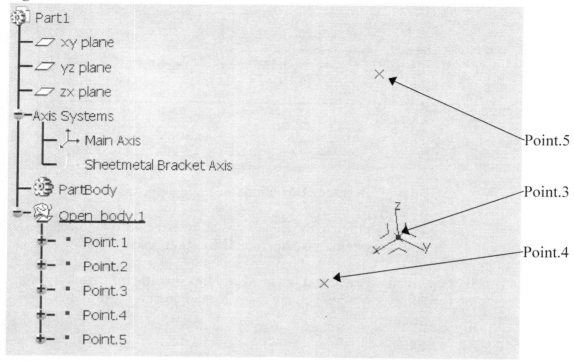

3.3 Rename the three points using the same process described in Step 2.6. Name the points accordingly.

Point at 0,0,0 = **First Point**
Point at 1,0,0 = **Second Point**
Point at 0,0,2 = **Third Point**

After renaming the points, the **Specification Tree** should look similar to Figure 7.15.

3.4 The point location can be modified by double clicking on any one of the points in the **Specification Tree**. This will bring up the **Point Definition** window for that particular point. The **Point Definition** window shows the point X, Y and Z values. It is in this

Figure 7.15

window that you can edit the X, Y and Z values or you can expand the **Point** branch out to the individual X, Y and Z values. Double clicking on the individual branches will bring up the **Edit Parameter** window. You can change the individual value in this window also.

4 Creating Lines Using the Point–Point Method

Now you will use the points created in Step 3 to define the lines that make up the wireframe of the "**Sheetmetal Bracket**". Remember, the points and lines you are creating are three-dimensional, they are not **Sketcher** entities.

4.1 Select the **Line** tool. This will bring up the **Line Definition** window as shown in Figure 7.16.

4.2 The first box in the **Line Definition** window is the **Line Type** box. Select the down arrow to the far right of the **Line Type** box. This will display the five different options (methods) for creating a line.

4.3 Select the **Point-Point** method. This selection requires only two other inputs by you the user, **Point 1** and **Point 2**. The starting point of the line and the ending point of the line.

4.4 For **Point.1** select the point you created and renamed as **First Point** in Step 3. The point may be selected graphically or by selecting it from the **Specification Tree**.

4.5 For **Point 2** select the point you created and renamed as **Second Point** in Step 3.

4.6   Select the **OK** button to create **Line.1**. The **Geometry On Support** box in the **Line Definition** window is optional and not required to create a **Point-Point** type line.

4.7   Create **Line.2** using the **Point-Point** method. Use the **First Point** and **Third Point** for the **Point 1** and **Point 2** input boxes.

If your wireframe looks similar to the one shown in Figure 7.17 you are ready to move on to the next step.

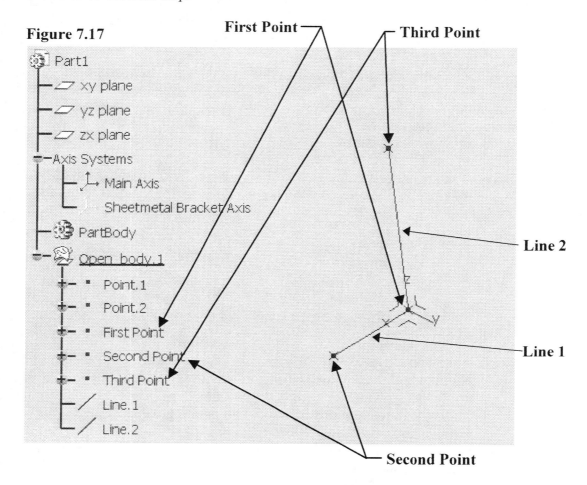

Figure 7.17

5   Creating Line 3 Using the Point–Direction Method ⟋

The **Point-Point** method in Step 4 required predefined points; points created using the **Point** tool. Points created using the **Point** tool are represented by an **X**. These points have there own branch in the **Specification Tree** and are labeled as **Points** sequentially. As you created lines using these points, you noticed that CATIA V5 added dots to both ends of the lines you created. These dots can also be used as points. You could select them as points when using the **Point-Point** line creation method. You can analyze their location in reference to the X, Y and Z coordinates. When creating points with the **Point-Direction** method, the points (dots) are found under the **Line** branch of the **Specification Tree** and labeled **Start** and **End**. Figure 7.14 shows points (X's) created using the **Point** tool, Figure 7.17 shows points (dots) created at the start and end of each line. In this step you will create **Line.3** using the **Point–Direction** method. The point you use will be the point at the end of **Line.1**. Completing the following steps.

5.1   Select the **Line** tool.

5.2   From the **Line Definition** window, select the down arrow to the right side of the **Line Type** box. This will expand the box so it will list all five methods of creating lines.

5.3   Select the **Point–Direction** method. Notice, as you select a different method, the other boxes within the **Line Definition** window change. The **Point–Point** method only required you to select **Point 1** and **Point 2**. The **Point–Direction** method requires a **Point** (anchor point), a **Direction**, a **Start** and an **End**. It also gives you an option to **Reverse Direction** of the line. Another option is to specify **Support** geometry. Reference Figure 7.18 for the **Line Definition** window with the **Point–Direction** line type selected.

5.4   With the **Point–Direction** line type selected make sure the **Point** box is highlighted. Select **Second Point**. **Second Point** will show up in the **Point** box.

5.5   The **Direction** box will highlight as soon as the **Point** box has an entity selected. For the **Direction** box, select **Line.2**. All **Line.2** does is give a direction for the line you are creating. As Figure 7.19 shows **Line.3** is parallel to **Line.2**.

Figure 7.18

5.6   When you select the direction, CATIA V5 provides a preview of the line you are creating. Figure 7.19 shows the default **Start** point and the default **End** point. The default **Start** point is the same point you select for the **Point** box. For this section of the lesson the default **Start** point will suffice. Tab or use the mouse to move the cursor over the **End** box.

5.7   For the **End** box type in **.75 in**. This gives the length of the line.

Figure 7.19

5.8   Hit **Enter** or select **OK** to create the line. **Line.3** is now complete. Your wireframe so far should look similar to the one shown in Figure 7.19.

5.9   Use the same process to create **Lines 4, 5, 6** and **7**. Apply the following information to the **Line Definition** window using the **Point-Direction** method. For the **Point** box select the point at the end of the line just created. For example to create **Line.4** you will select the point at the end of **Line.3** as shown in Figure 7.19. Reference Figure 7.20 for all of the lines called out in the following table.

Point at the
end of **Line.3**

Line	Point	Direction	End (length)
Line.4	Point at the end of **Line.3**	**Line.1**	1"
Line.5	Point at the end of **Line.4**	**Line.3**	.75"
Line.6	Point at the end of **Line.5**	**Line.4**	1"
Line.7	Point at the end of **Line.6**	**Line.2**	2"

6   Creating Line 8 Using the Same Point–Direction Method

The process to create **Line.8** using the **Point–Direction** method is almost identical to Step 5, except that the **Direction** box will use a third-dimension. Step 5 **Directions** were all on the same two-dimensional plane. There is no reference line pointing in the same direction as **Line.8**. This step will show you that other reference elements can be used in the place of a line. You will be expected to create the remaining lines for the "**Sheetmetal Bracket**" using the methods described so far. Create **Line.8** by completing the following steps.

6.1   Select the **Line** tool.

6.2   From **Line Type** box (in the **Line Definition** window), select the **Point–Direction** method as shown in Figure 7.18.

6.3   For the **Point** box, select the point at the top of **Line.7**. If it is unclear which line is **Line.7** reference Figure 7.21.

6.4   For the **Direction** box, select the **Y Axis**. In Step 5 you had lines (existing geometry) to select from. The **Y Axis** is the only geometry that defines the direction of **Line.8**.

NOTE: This is the difference between Step 5 and Step 6. You can use almost any CATIA 5V geometry to define the direction of a line.

6.5   Reference Figure 7.20 to make sure **Line.8** is being created in the correct direction. If the default direction is opposite of what is shown in Figure 7.20, select the **Reverse Direction** button in the **Line Definition** window.

6.6   For the **End** box value type in **2in**.

6.7   If the wireframe looks similar to what is shown in Figure 7.20 select **OK** to create **Line.8**.

Figure 7.20

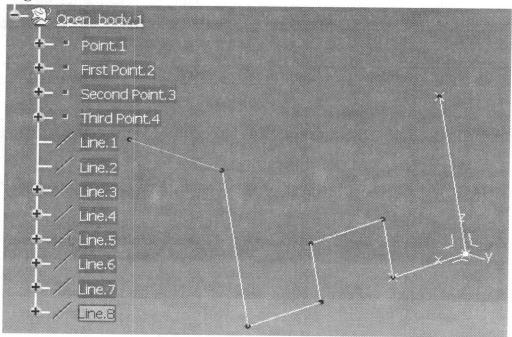

6.8   If there are any questions on the lengths of the lines created thus far use the **Measure** tool located at the bottom of the screen to verify line length.

7   Completing The Wireframe By Creating Lines 9, 10 and 11 Using The Point-Direction Method

Now that you have some experience using several variations of the **Line** tool, complete the wireframe by creating **Lines 9, 10** and **11**. There are other methods available to create the remaining lines. You are encouraged to explore the other methods. This step supplies the basic information to complete the wireframe using **Point-Direction** method.

7.1   Use the **Point-Direction** method and the information supplied below to complete the "**Sheetmetal Bracket**" wireframe.

Line	Point	Direction	End (length)
Line.9	Point at the end of **Line.8**	**Line.2**	3"
Line.10	Point at the end of **Line.9**	**Line.8**	2"
Line.11	Point at the end of **Line.10**	**Line.9**	3"

7.2   If your "**Sheetmetal Bracket**" wireframe looks similar to the one shown in Figure 7.21 you are ready to continue to the next step.

        NOTE: You could have created both **Line 10** and **11** using the **Point-Point** method.

        NOTE: Be sure that your completed "**Sheetmetal Bracket**" wireframe looks similar to the one shown in Figure 7.1. If your completed "**Sheetmetal Bracket**" wireframe does not look similar to the one shown in Figure 7.1 the remaining steps may not work as described.

Figure 7.21

8 Creating Planes

The basic wireframe is complete, but before you apply a surface to the wireframe you will need to touch it up. Planes are required for the **Corner** tool. It is more efficient to create the support entity prior to getting half way through the **Corner** process and realizing you do not have a support entity. The support entity that is best suited for the **Corner** process is the **Plane**. The **Corner** tool will be covered in Step 9. To create the **Planes** complete the following steps.

    8.1   Select the **Plane** tool.

    8.2   The **Plane Definition** window will appear. If you select the down arrow to the far right of the **Plane Type** box, CATIA V5 will display all of the different methods to create a plane. The method you will use in this step is the **Through Two Lines** method. Figure 7.22 displays the **Plane Definition** window along with the many different methods of creating planes.

Figure 7.22

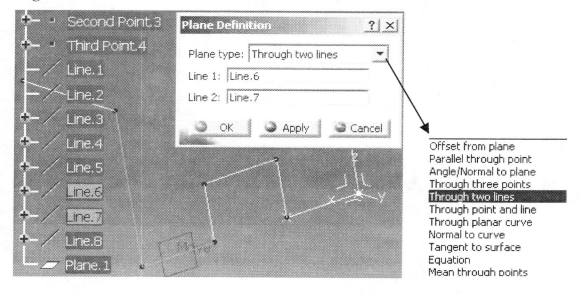

8.3 Select the **Through Two Lines** method. CATIA V5 does not require you to select the option. If you selected the **Plane** tool and then just selected the first line, CATIA V5 will automatically select the **Through Two Lines** method.

8.4 To create the first plane select **Line.6** and **Line.7** as shown in Figure 7.22. CATIA V5 will then place a plane in the window. Attached to the plane will be the word **Move**. This is prompting you to move the plane to another location. To move the plane, move mouse over the **Plane** until it turns to an orange color. Select the plane and drag it to the desired screen location. Once you have the plane placed where you want it, select the **OK** button to create the plane. The **OK** button has to be selected to complete the **Plane** creation.

8.5 CATIA V5 numerically names the planes you create i.e. **Plane.1**, **Plane.2** ...and so on. When you have multiple planes on the screen, it can be difficult to know what each plane represents. It is a good idea to rename the planes so that you can readily select the correct plane. This would be a good time to rename the plane you created in Step 8.4. The name should help you understand what the plane represents. Rename the plane to **Cutout Flange**. If you do not remember how to rename an element in the **Specification Tree,** refer back to Step 2.6.

8.6   The next required plane represents the **Top Flange** of the wireframe.
       Create a plane using the same process as the steps described above, except
       select **Line.8** and **Line.9**. Rename this plane as **Top Flange**. Your
       "**Sheetmetal Bracket**" wireframe and **Specification Tree** should look
       similar to Figure 7.23.

Figure 7.23

9   Creating Corners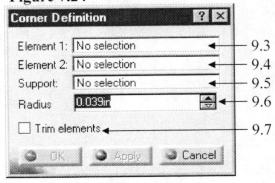

Creating the **Corners**. Now that the **Support** entities (the **Planes**) have been created,
you can add the **Corner** to the "**Sheetmetal Bracket**" wireframe. To create the
Corners complete the following steps.

9.1   Select the **Corner** tool.

9.2   This will bring up the **Corner Definition** window as shown in Figure
       7.24. The **Corner Definition** window has four boxes that will need to be
       filled in before the **Corner** can be created.

9.3   The first **Corner** you are going to
       create is between **Line.8** and **Line.9**.
       Highlight the **Element 1** box and
       select **Line.8**.

9.4   The **Element 2** box will
       automatically highlight. Verify that
       it is highlighted and select **Line.9**.

Figure 7.24

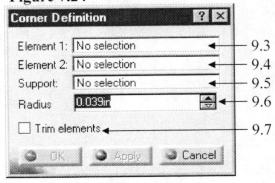

9.5   Make sure the **Support** box is highlighted and then select the **Plane** you renamed as **Top Flange**.

NOTE: The lines selected for **Element 1** and **Element 2** must be on the same **Plane**.

9.6   For the **Radius** box type **.6in**.

9.7   For this particular operation you will want to trim the excess lines. Select the **Trim Elements** box. Select **OK** to create the **Corner**. This will complete your first **Corner** operation. If your "**Sheetmetal Bracket**" wireframe looks similar to the one in Figure 7.25, you are ready to create the other three **Corners**. Notice that a **Corner** branch has been added to the **Specification Tree** and that **Line.8** and **Line.9** are now part of that **Corner** branch. **Line.8** and **Line.9** are the parents of the **Corner**.

Figure 7.25

9.8   In this step you will create a **Corner** using **Line 3** and **Line 4**. Complete the same steps used in Steps 9.1 – 9.7 except select the entities listed below.

       9.8.1   **Element 1** = **Line.3**
       9.8.2   **Element 2** = **Line.4**
       9.8.3   **Support**   = **Plane** labeled Cutout **Flange**
       9.8.4   **Radius**   = **.25in**
       9.8.5   **Trim Elements** = Check the box
       9.8.6   Select **OK** to create the **Corner**

9.9 In this step you will create a **Corner** using **Line.4** and **Line.5**. Complete the **Corner** using the entities listed below.

       9.9.1 **Element 1 = Corner.2**
       9.9.2 **Element 2 = Line.5**
       9.9.3 **Support** = **Plane** labeled **Cutout Flange**
       9.9.4 **Radius** = .25in
       9.9.5 **Trim Elements** = Check the box
       9.9.6 Select **OK** to create the **Corner**

9.10 In this step you will create a **Corner** using **Line.9** and **Line.10**. Complete the **Corner** using the entities listed below.

       9.10.1 **Element 1 = Line.9**
       9.10.2 **Element 2 = Line.10**
       9.10.3 **Support** = **Plane** labeled **Top Flange**
       9.10.4 **Radius** = .6in
       9.10.5 **Trim Elements** = This time **Do Not** check the box
       9.10.6 Select **OK** to create the **Corner.**

9.11 If your "**Sheetmetal Bracket**" wireframe looks similar to Figure 7.26 you are ready for Step 10.

NOTE: When you created a **Corner** using **Lines 8** and **9** both lines became **Corner.1**. You can prove this by selecting what was formally known as **Line.8** and see that **Corner.1** will highlight on the **Specification Tree**.

Figure 7.26

10 Using The Split Tool

In the previous step you did not trim **Lines 9 & 10**. In this step you will manually trim the lines using the **Spilt** tool. To **Split** the **Corner** and **Lines 9 & 10,** complete the following steps.

  10.1 Select the **Split** tool.

  10.2 This will bring up the **Split Definition** window. Select **Corner.1** for the **Element To Cut** box. Reference Figure 7.27 for **Corner** selection and **Split Definition** window.

Figure 7.27

  10.3 Select **Corner.4** for the **Cutting Element:**.

NOTE: The line that is highlighted during the **Split** process is the line that will remain. The line on the other side of the **Cutting Element** will be trimmed (deleted) unless you select the **Other Side** button that will swap the selection of line to keep and line to trim.

  10.4 Select **OK** to complete the **Split**.

NOTE: The **Split** tool trimmed off the excess lines.

  10.5 Now you need to **Split Line.10**. To **Split Line.10,** repeat the previous step except change the **Element To Cut** to **Line.10** and the **Cutting Elements** to **Corner.4**.

10.6 Select **OK** to complete the **Split**. If your "**Sheetmetal Bracket**" wireframe looks similar to the one shown in Figure 7.28 you are ready to move on to Step 11.

Figure 7.28

11 Adding An Elliptical Wireframe Using The Sketcher Work Bench

You may not have noticed, but the **Tool Bar** section of this lesson listed the **Sketcher Work Bench** as one of the tools available in the **Generative Shape Design Work Bench**. This step will demonstrate how useful it can be in creating wireframe geometry. The part in Figure 7.1 shows the "**Sheetmetal Bracket**" has an elliptical cut out on the top flange. This is the step that will define the ellipse. Since the **Sketcher Work Bench** has been covered in **Lesson 1**, instructions related to the **Sketcher Work Bench** will be less detailed. To create the ellipse, complete the following steps. Use Figure 7.30 as a reference.

11.1 Select the **Sketcher Work Bench** icon.

11.2 Select the **Plane** labeled **Top of Wireframe**.

11.3 Select the **Ellipse** ⬭ tool.

11.4 The **Prompt Zone** will prompt you to "**Click To Define The Ellipse Center**". For this step, select near the center of the flange. An exact location is not required at this time. The exact location along with the exact ellipse size can be modified and constrained later.

11.5 The next prompt is "**Click To Define The Major Axis And Ellipse Orientation**". The major axis is parallel with **Line.9**, so select an approximate location near **Line.9**.

11.6 The next prompt is "**Click To Define A Point on the Ellipse**". Select a point somewhere between **Line.10** and the center of the ellipse. Your ellipse is now created.

11.7 To modify the ellipse, double click on it. This will bring up the **Ellipse Definition** window. Modify the **Major Radius** to **1.125in**.

11.8 Modify the **Minor Radius** to **.563in**.

11.9 Leave the **Angle** at **0**.

11.10 If you know or want to calculate the exact center of the top flange, you can modify the center point of the ellipse using **Cartesian** or **Polar** coordinates. Figure 7.29 shows the center point of the ellipse as located using the **Constraint** tool. You know the dimensions of the top flange, so constrain them accordingly. If the **Constraint Definition** window shows the constraint value as a reference, toggle the **Reference** box off. If your sketch looks similar to the one shown in Figure 7.29 you are ready to continue on to the next step.

NOTE: Remember, when entering values, you can use math operators. For example, if you know the diameter is 1.125in, but you were prompted for a radius value, you could use a calculator to figure the radius value or you could enter "1.125/2" and CATIA V5 will calculate and enter it for you.

Figure 7.29

12 Appling A Surface To The Wireframe Using The Fill Tool

Creating the wireframe geometry was the difficult part of this lesson. If the wireframe was created correctly, applying the surface will be simple and fun. Complete the following steps to apply a surface to the "**Sheetmetal Bracket**" wireframe.

12.1   Select the **Fill** tool in the **Generative Shape Design Work Bench**.

12.2   This will bring up the **Fill Surface Definition** window as shown in Figure 7.30.

12.3   Select all of the wireframe entities that define the boundary of the top part of the "**Sheetmetal Bracket**" as shown in Figure 7.30. If you followed this lesson closely, the entities should be identified the same as the selected entities in the **Fill Surface Definition** window in Figure 7.30. If you have explored beyond what this lesson covers, your geometry may be identified a little bit differently. For example, if you created additional lines, your wireframe may be using a **Line.21** or so. The important thing in this step is to select the geometry that defines the boundary of the top flange of the "**Sheetmetal Bracket**" wireframe similar to what is shown in Figure 7.30.

NOTE: The geometry listed in **Boundary** section of the **Fill Surface Definition** window is also highlighted in the **Specification Tree** and the wireframe geometry its self.

NOTE: The geometry defining the boundary cannot have any gaps. If the boundary has gaps you will get a **Boundary Definition Error**. All boundary geometry must be connected with the previous selection. You cannot select a line, skip a line, and then select another line or you will get a **Boundary Definition Error**.

Figure 7.30

12.4 For this particular step no **Support** elements are required.

12.5 Leave the **Continuity** box at **Point**.

12.6 When you have defined the boundary as shown in Figure 7.30 select **OK**
      to create a surface. Notice that a **Fill.1** branch has been added to the
      Specification Tree. If your newly created surface looks similar to the one
      shown in Figure 7.31 you are ready to apply a surface to the **Cutout
      Flange**.

Figure 7.31

12.7 Use the **Fill** tool to apply a surface to the **Cutout Flange**. The **Boundary** should consist of **Line.1**, **2**, **11**, **7**, **6** and **Corner.3**. **Line.11** is also a shared boundary for **Fill.1**, the surface on the **Top Flange**.

12.8 If your "**Sheetmetal Bracket**" looks similar to the one shown in Figure 7.32, you are ready to move on to Step 13.

Figure 7.32

13 Creating A Fillet Between Two Surfaces

The two **Fill** surfaces you created in Step 12 are at a right angle to each other. CATIA V5 represents this with no problem, but in the manufacturing world this is not a true representation of an actual part. By adding a **Fillet** (radius) between the **Fill.1** surface and the **Fill.2** surface, your wireframe will be accurately represented. To create the **Fillet**, complete the following steps.

13.1 Select the **Shape Fillet** tool.

13.2 This will bring up the **Fillet Definition** window as shown in Figure 7.33.

13.3 Select **Fill.1** for the **Support 1** box.

13.4 Select **Fill.2** for the **Support 2** box.

13.5 Type in **.5** for the **Radius** box.

13.6 Keep the default **Smooth** for the **Extremities** box.

13.7 Verify the **Trim Support Elements** box is selected.

13.8 Red directional arrows will appear out of the two **Support** surfaces you selected. Make sure they are pointed in the direction shown in Figure 7.33. If the arrows are pointed in the opposite direction, select the arrow to reverse the direction.

13.9 When the **Fillet Definition** window is set up as shown in Figure 7.33, select **OK** to create the **Fillet**.

13.10 The excess surfaces are trimmed, but the lines that were used to create the initial surface are not. **Line.11**, the line that shared the boundary of both **Fill.1** and **Fill.2**, and others are still visible. You **cannot** delete these elements because they help to define **Fill.1** and **Fill.2**. Since you cannot delete the supporting elements, place them in **No Show** You will need to select the **Hide/Show** tool between each element selected.

Figure 7.33

13.11 If your "**Sheetmetal Bracket**" looks similar to the one shown in Figure 7.34, you are ready to move on to Step 14. Figure 7.34 shows the "**Sheetmetal Bracket**" right after the **Fillet** operation. Figure 7.35 shows the "**Sheetmetal Bracket**" after **No Showing** the supporting elements.

Figure 7.34

Figure 7.35

14 Creating The Elliptical Cutout Using the Split Tool

In this step you will use the sketch you created in Step 11 to remove the surface inside of the **Ellipse**. The tool required to complete this task is the **Split** tool. To remove the surface from inside of the ellipse, complete the following steps.

14.1 Select the **Split tool**. Notice this tool is a variation of the **Trim** tool. Do not confuse them: they are similar but produce different results.

14.2 This will bring up the **Split Definition** window. Select **Fillet.1** for the **Element To Cut** box.

14.3 Select **Sketch.1** (ellipse) for the **Cutting Element** box.

14.4 In this case you want to remove the surface inside of the ellipse, so do not select the **Keep Both Sides** box.

14.5 If the dimmed surface is the same as shown in Figure 7.36, you will not have to select the **Other Side** button. If the dimmed surface is on the outside of the ellipse then you will have to select the **Other Side** button.

14.6 If you have everything selected as shown in Figure 7.36, you can select the **OK** button to create the **Split**.

Figure 7.36

14.7 If your "**Sheetmetal Bracket**" looks similar to the one shown in Figure 7.37, you are ready to move on to the next step.

Figure 7.37

15 Creating Surface Thickness Using The Thick Surface Tool

CATIA V5 has made this powerful tool simple to complete. CATIA V5 takes the selected surface and gives it thickness. You as the user define the **Surface**, the **Direction** and the **Thickness**. To complete the "**Sheetmetal Bracket**" part complete the following steps.

15.1 In this step you will be switching from the **Generative Surface Design Work Bench** to the **Part Design Work Bench**. The **Thick Surface** tool is found in the **Part Design Work Bench**. Highlight he **Part.1** on the **Specification Tree**.

15.2 With the **Part.1** (base of the **Specification Tree**) highlighted select the **Part Design Work Bench**. Your "Sheetmetal Bracket" in the work area will not change, but the workbench and workbench tools will.

15.3 Select the object to thicken: **Split.3**.

15.4 Select the **Thick Surface** tool. There will only be a few tools available for you to choose from. The tools that don't apply to surfaces will be dimmed meaning it is not selectable. Do not confuse the **Thick Surface** tool with the **Thickness** tool.

15.5 This will bring up the **ThickSurface Definition** window as shown in Figure 7.38.

15.6 Type in **.05in** for the **First Offset** box. This offset value is the part thickness.

15.7 You can leave the **Second Offset** box set at **0**. This part requires you to offset the thickness in only one direction.

15.8 For the **Object To Offset** select the " **Sheetmetal Bracket**" currently represented in the **Specification Tree** as **Split.3**.

15.9 Verify the arrows are pointing inward of the part as shown in Figure 7.38. If the arrows are pointing in the opposite direction, select the **Reverse Direction** button.

15.10 When all of the variables are defined as they are shown in Figure 7.38, select the **OK** button to create the **Surface Thickness** (solid).

Figure 7.38

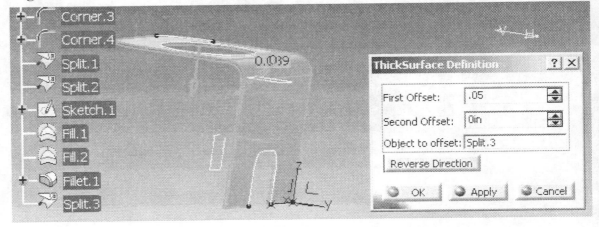

15.11 At this point, both the solid and the surface share the same space. It may be difficult to differentiate between the two entities. To simplify the work space, select **Split.3** (the surface) from the **Specification Tree** and put it in **No Show**. The solid will be the only thing left on the screen.

NOTE: The **Specification Tree** will now have a new branch on it. It will not be found under the **Open_Body** branch, but the **PartBody** branch. The solid will exist under the **PartBody** branch as did the other solids created in the **Part Design Work Bench**. The only branch under the **PartBody** branch will be the **Thickness** branch.

15.12 Apply **Aluminum** material to the "**Sheetmetal Bracket**". Reference **Lesson 2** for instructions.

15.13 Change the **View Applications** to show the **Material.** If your "**Sheetmetal Bracket**" looks similar to what is shown in Figure 7.39 you have successfully completed the "**Sheetmetal Bracket**".

15.14 Save your part as "**Sheetmetal Bracket.CATPart**".

NOTE: Geometry created in the **Generative Shape Design Work Bench** is saved with the same extension as geometry created in the **Part Design Work Bench.** The extension is "***.CATPart**".

Figure 7.39

Lesson 7 Summary

There are other possible methods of creating this part; this lesson only covers a few of the possibilities. This lesson is designed to give you enough basic information so that you can explore the other possibilities on your own. You are strongly encouraged to explore the other methods. Lesson 8 will cover additional **Generative Shape Design** tools and applications. Congratulations and good luck on the **Lesson Review** and **Practice Exercises**.

Lesson 7 Review

After completing this lesson, you should be able to answer the questions and explain the concepts listed below:

1. What two **Work Benches** are used in this lesson?
2. How many standard toolbars are there in the **Generative Shape Design Work Bench**?
3. What are the 5 options available in CATIA V5 for creating a line?
4. What is the difference between a **Part Body** and an **Open_Body**?
5. Which tool may be selected to trim a line that is too long?
6. When trimming a line, what color is the part of the line that will be deleted?
7. When trimming a line, what color is the part of the line that will be kept?
8. Which tool should be selected to see the objects that have been hidden?
9. What are the six options available in CATIA V5 for creating a plane?
10. Which plane creation methods were used in this lesson?
11. Why did planes have to be created before the **Corner** tool could be used in this lesson?
12. How many different ways can you create a point in CATIA V5?
13. What is the difference between the **Spit** tool and the **Trim** tool?
14. **T** or **F** The **Fill** tool is used to create a solid from an existing surface.
15. **T** or **F** You can create a **Left Hand Axis** in CATIA V5.
16. When creating an axis, how do you define the direction of the **X Axis**?
17. **T** or **F** In CATIA V5 the trimmed elements are deleted.
18. Explain the relationship of parent and children geometry.
19. What tool is used to create a solid (**PartBody**) from a surface (**Open_Body**)?
20. What workbench is the tool in question 19 found in?

Lesson 7 Practice Exercises

Now that your CATIA V5 tool box has more tools in it, put these tools to use on the following practice exercises. Each of the practice exercises will need to be done in the **Generative Shape Design Work Bench** and created as a wireframe.

1. You may recognize the part below; it was a practice exercise in Lesson 1. This part is much easier to create in the **Sketcher Work Bench**. Completing this part as a wireframe will give you the opportunity to compare methods (sketcher vs. wireframe).

   1.1 Create a wireframe of the front surface using the **Point**s and **Lines** tools.
   1.2 Create a surface over the wireframe using the **Fill** tool.
   1.3 Create a solid from the surface using the **Thick Surface** tool.
   1.4 Apply a material of your choice to the solid.
   1.5 Set the **Visualization** to display the material applied.
   1.6 Save the completed part as "**Lesson 7 Exercise 1.CATPart**".

   NOTE: You could copy the exercise from Lesson 1, but the **Specification Tree** shows the history of how the part was created.

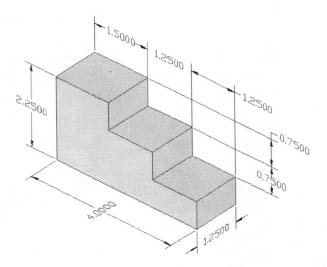

2   This exercise is also from Lesson 1. The geometry is getting a little more
    complex. This part has the same requirements as stated in Exercise 1. When
    you are done, save the part as "**Lesson 7 Exercise 2.CATPart**".

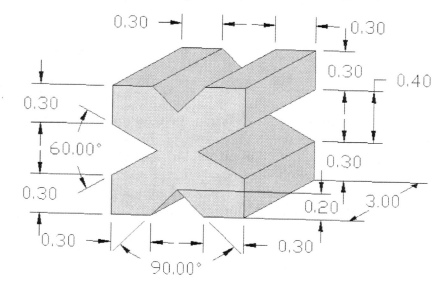

3   This part is taken from Lesson 2 Practice Exercises. It is not difficult but does
    offer a few new geometrical challenges. When you are done, save the part as
    "**Lesson 7 Exercise 3.CATPart**".

4   This part is more of a challenge than the first three. This part requires
     drawing lines, offsetting them and then rotating them. There are several
     possible methods of creating this part. You can use any method that works for
     you. When you are done, save the part as "**Lesson 7 Exercise 4.CATPart**".

HINT: Create everything on the same surface. Then use the **Translate** and
        Rotate tools from the **Operations** toolbar to offset and rotate the lines.
        Use the dimensioned drawing above.

5   This part requires you to use tools and processes that were not fully covered in this lesson. This exercise is for those who thrive on exploring and trying new things. When you are done save the part as "**Lesson 7 Exercise 5.CATPart**".

HINT: To create the 20 deg. line, use the **Angle/Normal to curve** option in the **Line Type** box of the **Line Definition** window. Another hint is that you may have to use tools in the **Part Design Work Bench** prior to using the **Thick Surface** tool.

6   The dimensions give the information you need to create the point locations for this part. You could also create the lines using the coordinates, skipping the need for points. Create the wireframe for the part shown below. You can use the methods covered in this lesson and/or you can explore and try your own method. The thickness of the part shown below is .125 inches. When you are done, save the part as "**Lesson 7 Exercise 6.CATPart**".

Notes:

Lesson 8   G̲enerative S̲hape D̲esign W̲ork B̲ench

Creating Wireframe And Surface Geometry Using The Sweep Tool

This lesson gives step-by-step instructions on how to create the
wireframe geometry required to create a **Swept** surface, using the
Sweep tool. There are other **Generative Shape Design** tools
used in this process, but the main focus will be the **Sweep** tool.
Some of the processes and tools used in Lesson 7 could be
applied in this lesson. There are many different methods that
could be used to create the part used in this lesson. The purpose of this lesson is to show
you how to create a part using the **Sweep** tool. An additional purpose of this lesson is to
show you several different methods of accomplishing the same and/or similar tasks.
Once you have completed the different methods, you can choose which method is best
for you.

Generative Shape Design

As in Lesson 7, you will convert the wireframe/surface into a solid part. When you save
your **CATPart,** save it as the "**Joggled Extrusion.CATPart**". The "**Joggled
Extrusion**" is shown in Figure 8.1.

Figure 8.1 (Dimensions for the "**Joggled Extrusion**" that will be created)

Lesson 8 Objectives

This Lesson will show you how to do the following:

- Create a **Profile** Sketch
- Create a **Guided Curve** Sketch
- **Join** curve entities
- Create surfaces using the **Sweep** tool
- Create a **Trim** sketch
- **Extrude** a sketch into a surface
- **Split** surfaces
- Create surface **Offset**
- Create surface with the **Fill** tool
- **Join** surfaces
- **Close** Surfaces to create a solid
- Modify entities using the **Pocket** tool (Part Design Work Bench)
- Create surface **Fillet**
- **Apply Material**

Generative Shape Design Work Bench Tools Bars

There are five standard tool bars found in the **Generative Shape Design Work Bench**. They are **Surfaces**, **Wireframe**, **Operations**, **Replication** and **Law**. The five tool bars are shown in Lesson 7.

Steps To Creating A Part Surface Using The Sweep Tool

This lesson uses the **Generative Shape Design Work Bench** as well as the **Sketcher** and **Part Design Work Benches**. The main focus will be in the **Generative Shape Design Work Bench**. It is in the **Generative Shape Design Work Bench** that the **Sweep** tool is found. In this lesson you will be creating the "**Joggled Extrusion**" which is shown in Figure 8.1.

It is important for you to understand what you are going to create prior to starting. What is required will determine the method you use to create the part. Requirements for this lesson are shown in Figure 8.1. A basic outline of the processes used in this lesson is listed below.

a. Create an open profile of the "**Joggled Extrusion**" using the inside surface dimensions (inside mold line). Create the open profile in the **Sketcher Work Bench**.

b. Create a path to extrude the open profile along (**Sweep**). This path is not a straight line; it will include the joggle as shown in Figure 8.1.

c. Trim the top flange as defined in Figure 8.1 using the **Plane** tool, **Sketcher Work Bench**, **Extrude** tool and the **Split** tool.

d. Create the surface thickness (the outside mold line dimensions) using the **Offset** tool.

e. Complete the surface using the **Fill** and **Join** tools.

f. Switch to the **Part Design Work Bench,** close the surface and create a solid using the **Close** tool.

g. Clean up the **CATPart**.

There are similarities and significant differences between the "**Joggled Extrusion**" and the part you created in Lesson 1 and Lesson 2: the "**L Shaped Extrusion**". Figure 8.2 shows the comparison between the two parts.

Figure 8.2

L Shaped Extrusion	Joggled Extrusion
required a closed profile in the **Sketcher Work Bench**	required a open profile in the **Sketcher Work Bench** or wireframe in the **Generative Design Work Bench**
extruded with the **Pad** tool in **the Part Design Work Bench**	requires geometry to define the path the profile will be extruded along (**Sweep**)
extrusion direction limited, normal to the sketch plane only	extrusion direction limited only by the path selected
result of the extrusion is a solid	the result of the **Sweep** is a surface, additional steps are required to create a complete solid

There are advantages and disadvantages to both. The **Pad** tool is faster for creating a complete solid, but it is also limited. The "**Joggled Extrusion**" could not be created in the **Part Design Work Bench** because of the joggle.

1   Select The Generative Shape Design Work Bench

Make sure the **Units** are set to inches and the grid is set to 1" **Primary Spacing** and 10 **Graduation**.

Select the **Generative Shape Design Work Bench**

2   Creating The Profile In The Sketcher Work Bench

In this step you will create the profile required by the **Sweep** tool. The profile is similar to the profile you created in the **Part Design Work Bench**. Reference Figure 8.2 for the similarities and the differences. The profile could be created in the **Generative Shape Design** workspace using the tools in the **Wireframe Tool Bar**. This lesson will have you create the profile in the **Sketcher Work Bench** because a planner sketch/wireframe is quicker and easier in the **Sketcher Work Bench**.   Use the dimensions given in Figure 8.1 and the sketch in Figure 8.3. When using the dimensions, remember that the part is .10 of an inch thick. This means that when you create the overall height of the part (2.13"), you will need to subtract .10". The .10" is the thickness of the "**Joggled Extrusion**". Creating the part thickness will be one of the last steps in creating the "**Joggled Extrusion** ". CATIA V5 makes it easy to modify your sketch, but it is still easier to do it right the first time. Create the profile by completing the following steps.

2.1   Create the sketch on the **ZX Plane**.

2.2   Create the basic outline of the cross section as shown in Figure 8.3.

2.3   **Constrain** the cross section as shown in Figure 8.3. Remember, when adding constraint values you can enter algebraic formulas. A simple example is typing in the part height dimension 2.13" minus the part thickness .10" and CATIA V5 will calculate the resulting value, 2.03".

Figure 8.3

2.4 After you have your sketch constrained similar to what is shown in Figure 8.3, add the radii using the **Corner** tool. When you create the radii, if you will get a message as shown in Figure 8.4, select **Yes**. All this does is convert your constraint to a distance constraint.

Figure 8.4

2.5 Add the radii as shown in Figure 8.5 using the **Corner** tool. The .19" radii will be the outside mold line of the surface, while the .09" radii will be the inside mold line of the surface. When you get your sketch to look similar to the one shown in Figure 8.5, exit the **Sketcher Work Bench**.

2.6 CATIA V5 will automatically name this sketch **Sketch.1**. **Sketch.1** does not really give you any information. Rename **Sketch.1** to **Profile Sketch**. **Profile Sketch** contains more information. At the very minimum, it gives you an idea of what is contained in the sketch.

Figure 8.5

3   Creating The Guided Curve In The Sketcher Work Bench

In this step you will create the **Guided Curve** required for the **Sweep** tool. The **Guided Curve** will be created using the dimensions shown in Figure 8.1. To create the **Guided Curve,** complete the following steps.

   3.1   Create a sketch on the **YZ Plane**.

   3.2   Create the basic outline of the **Guided Curve** as shown in Figure 8.6. Creating the **Guided Curve** and constraining it as shown can be tricky. The following steps might be helpful, refer to Figure 8.6.

      3.2.1   Create a rough sketch of the three lines similar to Figure 8.6.

      3.2.2   Constrain **Line.1** to 2.03" from the **H Axis**.

      3.2.3   Constrain the starting point of **Line.1** (use **Point.1**) from the **V Axis** to 0.0". Anchoring this point will over constrain the sketch. Setting the Constraint to 0.0" will accomplish the same thing without over constraining the sketch.

      3.2.4   Constrain the length of **Line.1** to 5.5".

      3.2.5   Constrain the starting point of **Line.3** to 6.25" from the **V Axis**.

      3.2.6   Constrain **Line.3** to 1.93" from the **H Axis**.

      3.2.7   Constrain the ending point of **Line.3** to 10.0" from the **V Axis**.

    3.3   When you get the sketch to look similar to what is shown in Figure 8.6, exit the **Sketcher Work Bench**.

    3.4   Rename the sketch "**Guided Curve Sketch**".

Figure 8.6

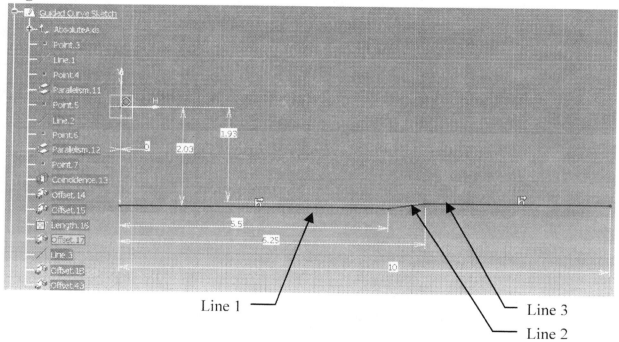

Line 1

Line 3

Line 2

4 Joining The Guided Curve Entities Using The Join 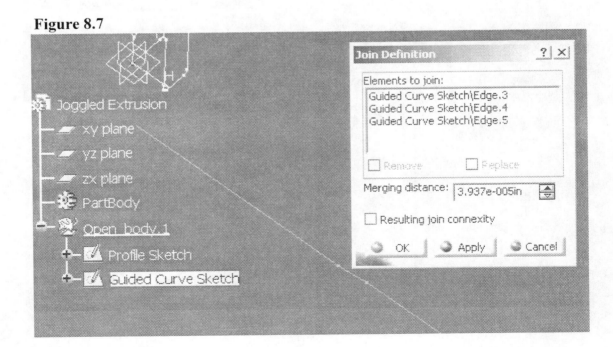 Tool

The path you are going to sweep (extrude) the **Profile Sketch** along is now complete. If you attempted to sweep the profile now you would only sweep it along **Line.1**. The **Guided Curve Sketch** must be joined into one entity so the profile can be swept along the entire length of the **Guided Curve Sketch**. To **Join** the **Guided Curve Sketch** entities, complete the following steps.

4.1 Select the **Join** tool icon.

4.2 This will bring up the **Join Definition** window as shown in Figure 8.7.

4.3 Select all three sketch lines that make up the **Guided Curve Sketch**. (Depending on how the lines were created, the selectable elements may change. You may only be able to select the **Guided Curve Sketch**; therefore, having only one element in the **Elements To Join** box. The three lines selected will be listed in the **Elements To Join** box as shown in Figure 8.7.

4.4 Leave the default value in the **Merging Distance** box.

4.5 Select **OK** to join the sketch entities.

4.6 A **Join** branch will appear on the **Specification Tree**.

Figure 8.7

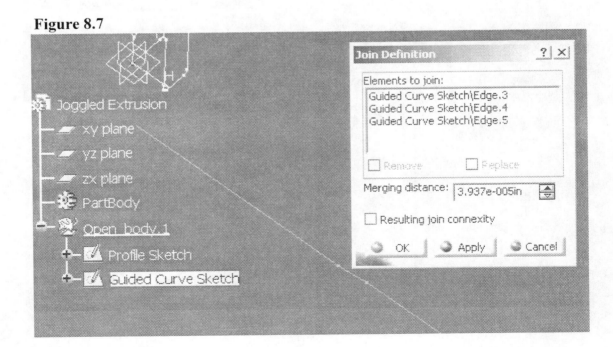

5   Creating A Surface Using The Sweep 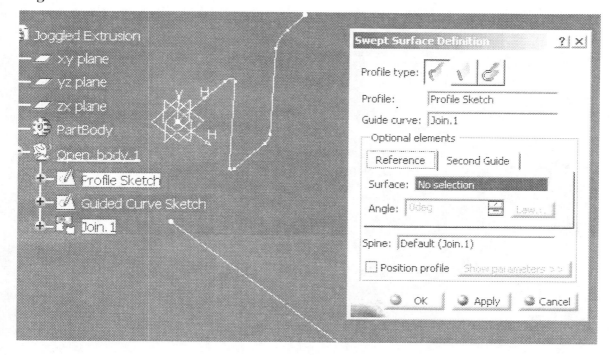 Tool

You are now ready to **Sweep** the **Profile Sketch** along the **Guided Curve Sketch**. To complete this task, perform the following steps.

5.1   Select the **Sweep** tool icon.

5.2   This will bring up the **Swept Surface Definition** window as shown in Figure 8.8.

5.3   Select the **Explicit** icon for the **Profile Type**. It is the first of the three icons.

5.4   Select the **Profile Sketch** for the **Profile** box.

5.5   Select **Join.1** for the **Guided Curve** box. Remember, the **Guided Curve Sketch** is the parent entity of **Join.1**.

5.6   The remaining options can be left at their default values. This step does not require any **Optional Elements**.

5.7   When your selection looks similar to Figure 8.8, select the **OK** button to create the **Swept Surface**.

Figure 8.8

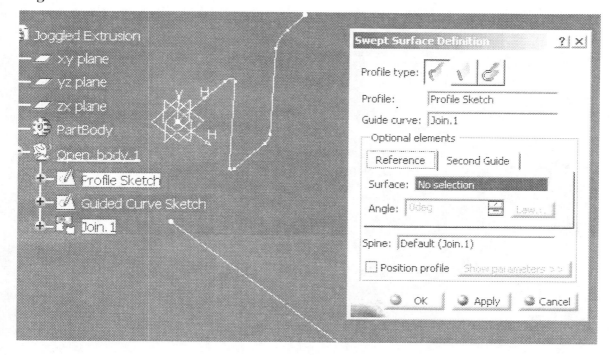

5.8   The resulting **Swept Surface** should look similar to the one shown in Figure 8.9. Notice the **Sweep.1** branch was added to the **Specification Tree**.

5.9   Before you continue on to the next section, **No Show** the **Profile Sketch** and **Guided Curve Sketch**. This lesson will require you to create additional sketches. **No Showing** the existing sketches will make the working space less confusing.

Figure 8.9

6   Creating The Trimmed Profile For The Top Flange Using The Sketcher Work Bench

The part surface for the "**Joggled Extrusion**" has now been created, but the part is not complete. If you reference Figure 8.1 you will notice that the top 1" wide flange has two different angles on it. In this step you will create a sketch that defines the trimmed flange, extrude the sketch and trim the extruded surface. The following steps are to help guide you through this process.

6.1   Create a **Plane** that represents the top flange surface as shown in Figure 8.10.

Figure 8.10

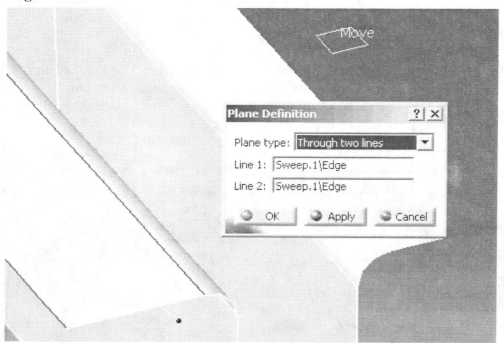

6.2   Create a sketch using the plane you created in Step 6.1. Use the
dimensions in Figure 8.1 and the constraints in Figure 8.11 to create the
flange profile. Constrain the sketch as shown in Figure 8.11. The .5"
constraint located at the bottom right of Figure 8.11 is not located at the
bottom of the part, but .3" up from the bottom of the part. The reason for
this is, that end of the part has an angle cut into it a total length of .3" at
the top of the part, reference the front view of Figure 8.1. The angle will
be trimmed off in the **Part Design Work Bench**.

Figure 8.11

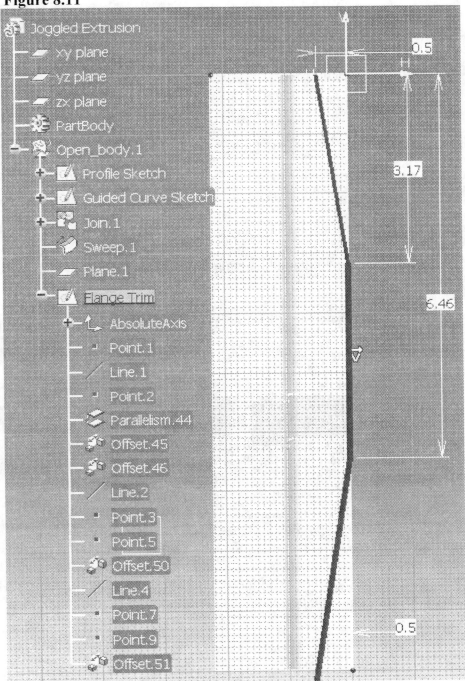

6.3 Exit the **Sketcher Work Bench**.

6.4 **No Show Line.1**.

6.5 Rename the newly created sketch to "**Flange Trim**".

6.6   Change the color of the "**Joggled Extrusion**" surface (**Sweep.1**). You can determine the color. When all of the surfaces have the same properties (color), they can be confusing and/or hard to differentiate. Remember, this is done through **Properties**, **Graphic** and then **Color**.

7   Extruding The "Flange Trim" Sketch Using The Extrude Tool

In this step you will extrude the sketch created in Step 6. To extrude the "**Flange Trim**" sketch, complete the following steps.

7.1   Select the **Extrude** tool.

7.2   This will bring up the **Extruded Surface Definition** window as shown in Figure 8.12.

7.3   For the **Profile** box, select the "**Flange Trim**" sketch.

7.4   The **Direction** box will default to **Plane.1**, the plane the sketch was created on.

7.5   The **Extrusion Limits** box allows you to type in values for both directions, **Limit 1** and **Limit 2**. Another method of defining **Limit 1** and **Limit 2** is moving the mouse over the green arrow, selecting the arrow and then dragging the arrow in the direction and distance you want the sketch extruded. For this step you can extrude the sketch using either method. Extrude the sketch to the approximate distances shown in Figure 8.12. An exact distance is not necessary for this step. The only requirement is that the extruded surface passes through the "**Joggled Extrusion**" surface.

7.6   If your extruded surface looks similar to what is shown in Figure 8.12, you are ready for the next step, trimming the surfaces.

Figure 8.12

8   Trimming The Surfaces Using The Split Tool

In this step you will trim the flange of the "**Joggled Extrusion**" by splitting the "**Joggled Extrusion**" surface with the surface you extruded in Step 7. This will be done using the **Split** tool. A similar tool is the **Trim** tool. You could complete this process using either tool. The **Split** tool in this situation is the quicker tool. To split the two surfaces, complete the following steps.

    8.8   Select the **Split** tool.

Figure 8.13

Excess surface to be **Split**

8.9   This will bring up the **Split Definition** window as shown in Figure 8.13.

8.10   Select the **Sweep.1** branch of the **Specification Tree** for the **Element To Cut** box. Remember, **Sweep.1** is the "**Joggled Extrusion**" surface.

8.11   Select the **Extrude.1** branch of the **Specification Tree** for the **Cutting Element** box. The excess surface on the "**Joggled Extrusion**" will dim.

The dimmed surface is the surface that will be trimmed away. Make sure the correct surface is dimmed prior to completing the **Spit** process. If the wrong surface is dimmed, select the **Other Side** button in the **Split Definition** window. For the correct surface, reference Figure 8.13.

8.12 After verifying you have the correct surface being **Split**, select **OK** to complete the process.

NOTE: The **Extrude.1** surface is still there and the remaining "**Joggled Extrusion**" has turned back to its default color. The flange should have been trimmed as shown in Figure 8.14. The surface that you changed colors is now in **No Show**. The current "**Joggled Extrusion**" surface is represented in the **Specification Tree** as the **Split.1** branch. If you select the **Split.1** branch, the "**Joggled Extrusion**" part will also highlight.

8.13 You cannot delete the **Extrude.1** surface. **Extrude.1** is a parent of your current "**Joggled Extrusion**" surface. Although you cannot delete it, you can get it out of the way by placing it in **No Show**. Also, **No Show** your "**Flange Trim**" sketch.

8.14 If your "**Joggled Extrusion**" looks similar to the one shown in Figure 8.14, you are ready to continue to the next step.

Figure 8.14

9 Creating Surface Thickness Using The Offset Tool

Using the **Offset** tool to create an additional surface is the first step in giving the "**Joggled Extrusion**" part actual part thickness. Remember, the original surface you created was the **Inside Mold Line** of the part. This determination made a significant difference in applying dimensions to the **Profile Sketch**. The surface you create in this step will be the **Outside Mold Line** of the "**Joggled Extrusion**". When you are done with Step 9 you will have a surface that represents both inside and outside surfaces of the "**Joggled Extrusion**". To create an offset surface, complete the following steps.

9.1   To help you visualize the different surfaces, change the color of the **Split.1** surface ("**Joggled Extrusion**").

9.2   Select the **Offset** tool.

9.3   This will bring up the **Offset Surface Definition** window as shown in Figure 8.15.

9.4   For the **Surface** box, select the **Split.1** surface.

9.5   CATIA V5 gives you the two methods of defining the offset distance. One method is moving your mouse over the green arrow labeled **Dist** and dragging the arrow to the desired value and in the desired direction. The other method, a more precise method, is to type the exact value in the **Offset** box in the **Offset Surface Definition** window. For this step, type **.1in.** for the **Offset** value.

9.6   If your offset surface looks similar to what is shown in Figure 8.15, select **OK** to create the offset surface. You are ready to continue on.

NOTE: The new offset surface is created in the default surface color. The **Specification Tree** has added an **Offset.1** branch.

Figure 8.15

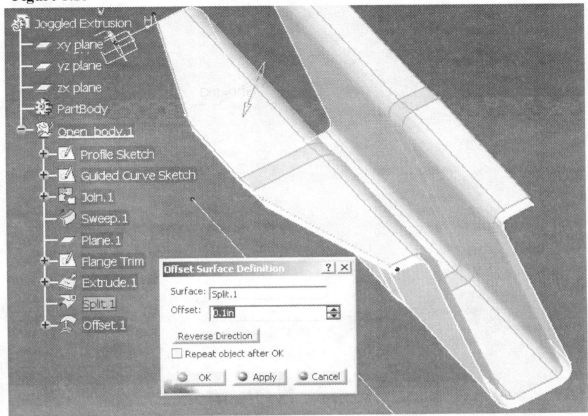

10 Closing The Surfaces Using The Fill 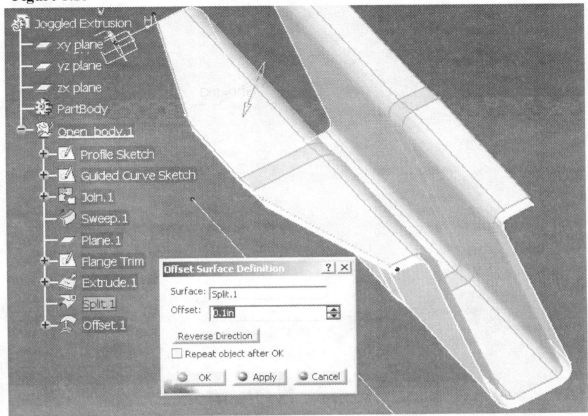 Tool

Your "**Joggled Extrusion**" now has a surface representing both the inside and outside of the part. To create a solid part (**PartBody**), the surface must be completely closed by surfaces. For detailed instructions on how to use the **Fill** tool, refer to Step 12 in Lesson 7. The following instructions are general steps to close the part with surfaces.

10.1   This step requires you to create six small surfaces. Change the color of the **Offset.1** surface. This will help you differentiate between the existing surfaces and the new small surfaces. The color is not important, as long it contrasts the existing and default surface colors.

10.2   Before you use the **Fill** tool, you will have to create the boundaries for the surfaces. The **Line** tool can be used to create the boundaries. Create lines between the inner surface (**Split.1**) and the outer surface (**Offset.1**) as shown in Figure 8.16. Use the **Point-to-Point** method of creating lines.

Figure 8.16

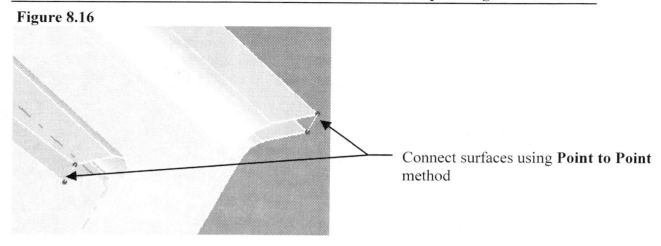

Connect surfaces using **Point to Point** method

10.3   Create lines 1 through 10 in the locations shown in Figure 8.17.

Figure 8.17

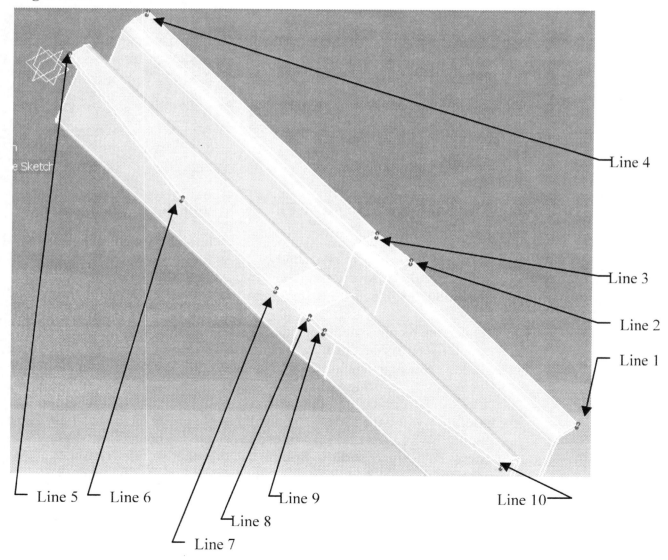

Line 4

Line 3

Line 2

Line 1

Line 5   Line 6   Line 9   Line 10

Line 8

Line 7

10.4 When all ten lines are created, you are ready to create surfaces. Select the **Fill** tool.

10.5 This will bring up the **Fill Surface Definition** window. As an example, select the boundaries as shown in Figure 8.18 to create one of the surfaces. Use the same process to create surfaces for all eight planner boundaries shown in Figure 8.19. Remember, when repetitive tool selection is required, double clicking on the particular tool will automatically reselect the tool after each completion.

NOTE: You may be required to add an additional boundary depending on how you created your **Sweep.1** sketch. The requirement for this step is to create surfaces that totally enclose the thickness of the part. You are creating an enclosed volume. The volume must not have any open surfaces. Another way of looking at it is the surfaces must hold air, you must patch all air leaks using the **Fill** tool.

10.6 Do not create surfaces on either end of the "**Joggled Extrusion**" part, only the side that represents the thickness of the part.

Figure 8.18

10.7 When all eight surfaces defined in Figure 8.19 have been created, you can go on to Step 11. It is critical that all eight surfaces have been created correctly or the process used in Step 11 will not work. **No Show** the 10 lines that were created. They could cause problems in later steps.

Figure 8.19

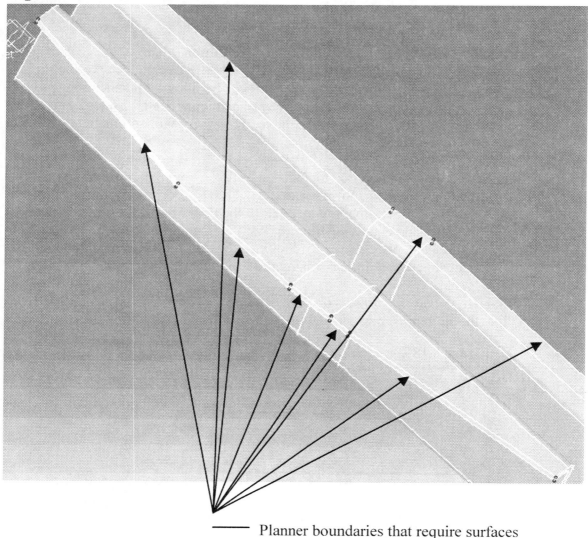

——— Planner boundaries that require surfaces

11 Joining The Surfaces Using The Join 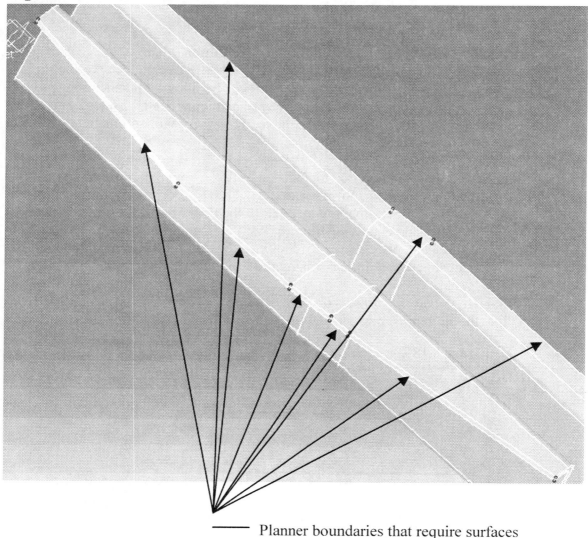 Tool

Before the surfaces can be converted to a solid, the surfaces must be joined into one complete surface. This step will have you join all the surfaces into a **Join.2** surface. The following instructions are a basic guideline to completing this step. If you need detailed instruction on using this tool, refer back to Step 4.

11.1 Select the **Join** tool.

11.2 This will bring up the **Join Definition** window.

11.3 Select the **Split.1** surface, **Offset.1** surface and **Fill.1** through **Fill.8** surfaces. Make sure the selected surfaces show up in the **Elements To**

Join box. Selecting each individual surface could be difficult. In this case it is easier to select the surfaces from the **Specification Tree** as shown in Figure 8.20.

11.4 If you have all ten surfaces selected, hit the **OK** button to join the surfaces.

Figure 8.20

NOTE: You modified the colors of the **Split.1** and **Offset.1** surfaces. Those surfaces are no longer visible, but not deleted. CATIA V5 moved the **Split.1** and **Offset.1** surfaces to the **No Show** workspace. If they were deleted, all of the surfaces that were built using them would also be deleted. In this case, it would be the **Join.2** surface. The result of the **Join** tool is the new resulting surface. The **Join.2** surface shows up in the default colors.

11.5 If your **Join.2** surface looks similar to what is shown in Figure 8.21, you are ready for Step 12.

Figure 8.21

12 Closing The Surfaces Using The Close Surface Tool

At this point your "**Joggled Extrusion**" represented by the **Join.2** surface is completely enclosed except for the two ends of the part. You could have completely enclosed the surface using the process defined in Step 11, but that would have required more detailed and time consuming work. It would have required 6 additional lines for boundaries and 18 additional surfaces. The **Close Surface** tool combines all that work into several easy steps. To use this tool you must bring up the **Part Design Work Bench**. Close the "**Joggled Extrusion**" surface by completing the following steps.

12.1 The first step is to bring up the **Part Design Work Bench**. Select the "**Joggled Extrusion**" at the top of the **Specification Tree**. With the "**Joggled Extrusion**" highlighted, select the **Part Design Work Bench**.

12.2 The tool bars will change from the **Generative Shape Design Work Bench** to the **Part Design Work Bench**.

12.3 From the **Part Design Work Bench** select the **Close Surface** tool. This tool is in the **Surface Based Features** tool bar. The default tool that shows up under that tool bar is the **Split** tool. Select the arrow at the bottom right of the icon to access the **Close Surface** tool.

12.4 CATIA V5 will prompt you in the prompt zone to "**Select the surface to close**". Select the **Join.2** surface.

12.5 This will bring up the **CloseSurface Definition** window as shown in Figure 8.22. Make sure that the **Join.2** surface is entered in the **Object To Close** box and the geometry is highlighted as shown in Figure 8.22.

Figure 8.22

12.6 Select the **OK** button to close the surface and create a solid.

NOTE: The **CloseSurface.1** branch was added to the **PartBody** branch of the **Specification Tree** not the **Open_Body.1** branch. The reason is, that it was created in the **Part Design Work Bench**. Your "**Joggled Extrusion**" now has a surface and a solid visible on the screen.

12.7 At this point you are done working with the surface, so place the **Join.2** surface in the **No Show**.

12.8 At this point the "**Joggled Extrusion**" solid should be the only geometry visible. If your "**Joggled Extrusion**" solid looks similar to what is shown in Figure 8.23, you are ready to proceed to the next step. Just a few more steps and you will be done with the "**Joggled Extrusion**". Figure 8.23 shows the **CloseSurface.1** surfaces highlighted.

Figure 8.23

13 Adding The 8-Degree Angle Using The Plane And Pocket Tools

If you reference Figure 8.1, you will notice the right side of the **Front View** shows that the "**Joggled Extrusion**" has an 8-degree angle on it. This angle could have been created in the **Generative Shape Design Work Bench,** but would have added additional steps. This step uses the **Generative Shape Design Work Bench** to define the **Plane** that will create the 8-degree angle. This step uses the **Pocket** tool found in the **Part Design Work Bench**. To create the required angle, complete the following steps.

13.1 The **Plane** tool is found in the **Generative Shape Design Work Bench,** so bring up the **Generative Shape Design Work Bench** up.

13.2 Select the **Plane** tool.

13.3 This will bring up the **Plane Definition** window. For the **Plane Type** box, select the **Angle/Normal To Plane** option.

13.4 For the **Rotation Axis** box, select the bottom horizontal edge of the "**Joggled Extrusion**". Reference Figure 8.24.

13.5 For the **Reference** box, select the edge surface as shown in Figure 8.24.

13.6 For the **Angle** box, type in **-8deg**. Verify that the **Plane** is rotated 8 deg in the correct direction. If it is not, type in **8deg** and select the **Plane**. The represented **Plane** will be updated to show the revised angle.

13.7 When you get the **Plane** to look similar to what is shown in Figure 8.24, select the **OK** button to create the **Plane**. If you want to move the **Plane** away from the part, you need to select it prior to selecting the **OK** button.

Figure 8.24   Select this edge surface for the **Reference**

Select this line for the **Rotation Axis**

13.8 Now that you created the geometry that will be used to define the 8-degree angle, you can bring up the **Part Design Work Bench**.

13.9 In the **Part Design Work Bench,** select the **Sketcher Work Bench**.

13.10 Select the **Plane** you created in the previous steps.

13.11 All that is required in this step, is to create a rectangular sketch that encompasses the end of the "**Joggled Extrusion**". Create a sketch similar to the one shown in Figure 8.25.

13.12 Exit the **Sketcher Work Bench**.

Figure 8.25

13.13 With the **Sketch** highlighted, select the **Pocket** tool.

13.14 This will bring up the **Pocket Definition** window as shown in Figure 8.26. The exact values are not critical as long as the direction is correct and the **Depth** is enough to encompass the part of the angle that is being trimmed. The values shown in Figure 8.26 are sufficient.

13.15 If your "**Joggled Extrusion**" looks similar to the one shown in Figure 8.26, select the **OK** button the create the **Pocket**.

NOTE: No pocket was created! The 8-degree angle was trimmed off. You could have created a **Pad** and then used a **Boolean Operation** to subtract it out, but that would have required additional steps. As this demonstrates the **Pocket** tool can be a handy tool.

Figure 8.26

13.16 If your "**Joggled Extrusion**" looks similar to what is shown Figure 8.27, you are ready to create the **Fillets**, Step 14.

NOTE: It is important for you to know that there is a quicker way to trim off the 8-degree angle. The quicker method is to use the **Split** tool in the **Part Design Work Bench**. You are encouraged to try this method. It is a quicker method; no **Sketch** or **Pocket** selection is needed. Even though it is a quicker method in some situations, the trim operation will extend the edge curve representation. For the "**Joggled Extrusion**", the **Pocket** method was a cleaner method. You are encouraged to try trimming the 8-degree angle using the **Split** tool or try one of the many other possible methods. Trying the different variations will give you a chance to compare the different options.

Figure 8.27

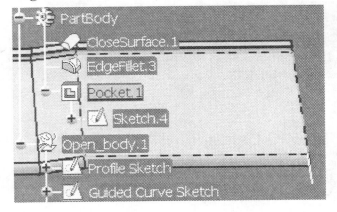

14 Dressing Up The "Joggled Extrusion" Solid Using The Fillet Tool

The **Fillet** tool was covered in detail in Lesson 2. This process should be a review. The four fillets you will be creating in this step could have been created as surfaces in the **Generative Shape Design Work Bench**, but would have required additional sketches, extruded surfaces, split surfaces, lines defining boundaries, filling surfaces and adding them to the join step. Creating the fillets in the **Part Design Work Bench** requires only a few simple steps. The steps are listed below.

14.1 Select the line defining the corner of the flange as shown in Figure 8.28.

14.2 Select the **EdgeFillet** tool.

14.3 This will bring up the **Edge Fillet Definition** window. For the **Radius:** box, type in **.18in**. Reference Figure 8.1 for part dimensions.

14.4 The edge you selected in Step 13.1 will show up in the **Object(s) To Fillet** box.

14.5 Leave the **Propagation** box on **Tangency**.

14.6 Select **OK** to create the **Edge Fillet**.

Figure 8.28

14.7 Select the **EdgeFillet.1** you just created.

14.8 Press the **Ctrl C** keys simultaneously. This copies the **EdgeFillet.1** to the **Windows Clip Board**.

14.9 Select one of the other edges that require a .18" edge fillet. The dimensioned **Top View** in Figure 8.1 displays the corners that require a .18" radius edge fillet.

14.10 With one of the other edges highlighted, press the **Ctrl V** keys simultaneously. This pastes the **EdgeFillet.1** properties copied in Step 13.8 to the selected edge. You should now have two .18" radius edge fillets.

14.11 Repeat the process described in Step 14.10 to the remaining two edges. When you have completed creating the four edge fillets, your "**Joggled Extrusion**" should look similar to the one shown in Figure 8.29

Figure 8.29

15 The Finishing Touch: Appling Material

As you complete the lessons, you can see how important it is to have a good understanding of the **Sketcher** and **Part Design Work Benches**. Even though the majority of this lesson discussed **Generative Shape Design Work Bench** tools, a good portion of the tools was covered in previous chapters. Lessons 7 and 8 should have given you ideas on new and different ways to create and design three-dimensional geometry. The last step in completing the "**Joggled Extrusion**" is to apply **Aluminum** material and change the **View Parameters** to show the material. If your "**Joggled Extrusion**" looks similar to the one shown in Figure 8.30, you are officially done with the Lesson 8 instruction exercise. You are now ready to tackle the **Lesson 8 Review** questions and **Lesson 8 Practice Exercises.** Congratulations! Don't forget to save your "**Joggled Extrusion.CATPart**".

Figure 8.30

Lesson 8 Summary

As in Lesson 7 there are other possible methods of creating this part. This lesson only covers a few of the possibilities. The **Generative Shape Design Work Bench** is a work bench with a wide variety of applications and possibilities, the last two lessons only scratched the surface. This lesson is designed to give you enough basic information so that you can explore the other possibilities on your own. You are strongly encouraged to explore the other methods.

Lesson 8 Review

After completing this lesson you should be able to answer the questions and explain the concepts listed below.

1. **T** or **F** In the **Generative Shape Design Work Bench,** a sketch can be extruded into a surface.
2. **T** or **F** Geometry created in the **Generative Shape Design Work Bench** is placed under the **Open_Body** branch of the **Specification Tree.**
3. In relationship to the **Sweep** tool, what is the **Profile**?
4. In relationship to the **Sweep** tool, what is the **Guided Curve**?
5. Explain the relationship between the **Profile** and the **Guided Curve**.
6. Why wasn't the "**Joggled Extrusion**" created in the **Part Design Work Bench** like the "**L Shaped Extrusion**" was?
7. **T** or **F** The **Join** tool can join surfaces only.
8. **T** or **F** There is a **Split** tool in the **Generative Shape Design Work Bench**.
9. **T** or **F** There is a **Split** tool in the **Part Design Work Bench**.
10. In this lesson, what tool was used to create a solid (**PartBody**) from a surface (**Open_Body**)?
11. What work bench is the tool in question 19 found in?
12. Most radii and/or fillets can be created at what stage of the design process?
    a. In the **Sketcher Work Bench**.
    b. During the surface creation; in the **Generative Design Work Bench**.
    c. During the solid creation; in the **Part Design Work Bench**.
    d. Both a and b.
    e. All the above.
13. When a surface is trimmed away, is it deleted?
14. Explain your answer to question 13.
15. When extruding a surface, CATIA V5 allows you which methods of determining the length (limit) of the extrusion.
    a. Typing in the **Limit 1** value in the **Extruded Surface Definition** window.
    b. Typing in the **Limit 2** value in the **Extruded Surface Definition** window.
    c. Selecting the green arrow and dragging it to the desired extrusion length value.
    d. Both a and b.
    e. All of the above.
16. **T** or **F** The result of using the **Split** tool in the **Generative Surface Design Work Bench,** is one combined surface.
17. **T** or **F** In this lesson, when you used the **Sweep** tool, a **Plane** was required to complete the process.
18. What **Generative Shape Design Work Bench** tool was used to create and define the part thickness?

19. When creating several sketches or other similar entities, why is it a good idea to rename them instead of leaving them at the default name? For example Sketch.1, Sketch.2 and so on.

20. What workbench is the **Close Surface** tool located in?

Lesson 8 Practice Exercises

Now that your CATIA V5 tool box has more tools in it, put them to use on the following practice exercises. Each of the practice exercises will require the **Generative Shape Design Work Bench** and the **Part Design Work Bench**.

1. Create a sketch on the **ZX Plane** as shown in Figure 8.31. Name the sketch, "**Guided Path**".

2. Create a sketch on the **YZ Plane** as shown in Figure 8.32. Name the sketch, "**Profile**". Notice where the 0,0 point is on both sketches. It is important that the sketches are in correct relationship to each other, reference Figure 8.33.

Figure 8.31

Figure 8.32

Figure 8.32

3. Use the **Sweep** tool to create a swept surface. Select the **Profile** sketch for the **Profile** box and the **Guided Path** sketch for the **Guided Path** box. Rename the **Sweep** branch to "**Pipe Surface**".

4. **No Show** the "**Pipe Surface**" surface created in Exercise 3. Create another surface using the **Sweep** tool. This time select the **Guided Path** sketch for the **Profile** box and the **Profile** sketch for the **Guided Path** box. Rename this surface to "**Flange Surface**".

5. Select the **Part Design Work Bench**. Give the **Flange Surface** a **.075in** thickness. The **Flange Surface** is the inside surface. **Hint:** Use the **Thick Surface** tool. After **No Showing** the **Open_Body** entities, your part should look similar to the one shown in Figure 8.33.

6. **No Show** the **ThickSurf** branch created in the **PartBody** in Exercise 5. Use the **Offset** tool and **Close** tool in the **Part Design Work Bench** to accomplish the same thing. Save your completed part as "**Lesson 8 Exercise 6.CATPart**".

7. Go back into the **Guided Path** sketch and modify the **2"** radius to **1"**. Then modify the **ThickSurf** value from **.075"** to **.125"**. Notice how CATIA V5 automatically updates the surfaces and solids to the new values. Save your completed part as "**Lesson 8 Exercise 7.CATPart**".

8. Observe the differences between the two processes. What extra steps were required to complete the exercise using the process required in Exercise 7?

Figure 8.33

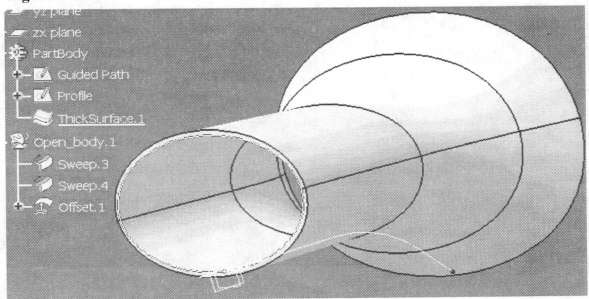

NOTES:

Introduction To The DMU Navigator Work Bench Using The Fly Mode

In order for you to complete this lesson, you must download a zipped file (**SuperMileage.zip**) from the SDC Publications website. This lesson uses twelve **CATPart** files and one **CATProduct** file that make up a concept car known as the **SuperMileage.CATProduct** as shown in Figure 9.1. Using this larger assembly within the **DMU Navigator** will allow you to better understand how the **DMU** fits into the product review process.

Figure 9.1 SuperMileage.CATProduct

Lesson 9 Objectives

This Lesson will show you how to do the following:

- Down load the **SuperMileage.Zip** file
- Unzip the **SuperMilage.Zip** file
- Enter the **DMU Navigator Work Bench**
- How to insert components into the **DMU Navigator Work Bench**
- How to use the **Fly Mode**

DMU Navigator Work Bench Tool Bars

There are seven standard tool bars found in the **DMU Navigator Work Bench**. Six of the seven tool bars are shown below. The individual tools found in each of the six tool bars are labeled to the right of the tool icon. This chapter will not cover every tool found in the **DMU Navigator Work Bench**.

The **Navigator** Tool Bar

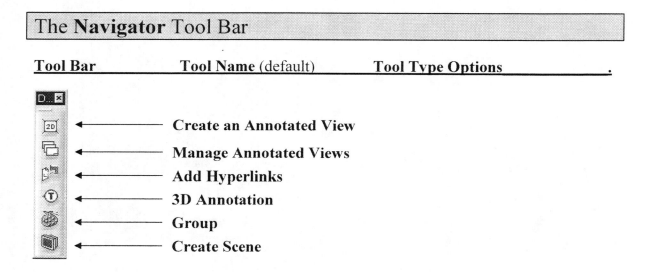

Tool Bar	Tool Name (default)	Tool Type Options
	Create an Annotated View	
	Manage Annotated Views	
	Add Hyperlinks	
	3D Annotation	
	Group	
	Create Scene	

The **Generic Animation** Tool Bar

Tool Bar	Tool Name (default)	Tool Type Options
	Simulation	
	Compile Simulation	
	Replay	
	Clash Detection	**Clash Detection Off, Clash Detection On, Clash Detection Stop**
	Record Viewpoint Animation	

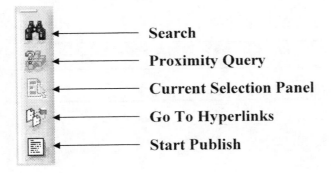

The **Data Navigation** Tool Bar

Tool Bar	Tool Name (default)	Tool Type Options
	Search	
	Proximity Query	
	Current Selection Panel	
	Go To Hyperlinks	
	Start Publish	

The **Viewing** Tool Bar

Tool Bar   Tool Name (default)   Tool Type Options   .

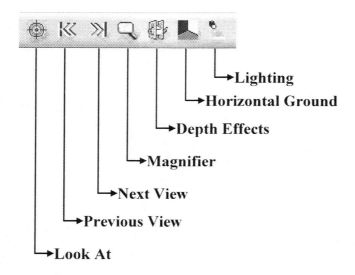

→ Lighting

→ Horizontal Ground

→ Depth Effects

→ Magnifier

→ Next View

→ Previous View

→ Look At

The **View** Tool Bar

Tool Bar   Tool Name (default)   Tool Type Options   .

→ **Fly Mode icon converts tool bar to this** ──┐

→ **Examine Mode icon returns menu to above**

The **Move** Tool Bar

Tool Bar   **Tool Name** (default)   **Tool Type Options**

◄——————— **Translation or Rotation**

◄——————— **Snap**

Steps To Downloading The SuperMilelage.Zip File

1   Downloading The File from the SDC Website

Before you can begin using the **DMU Navigator**, you must first download the zipped file (**SuperMileage.zip**) from the SDC Publications website to your hard drive. Create a directory called "download" in your **Temp** directory on your hard drive (**i.e. - C:\Temp\Download**). Use this directory for your download location. Now access the SDC website: **http://www.schroff.com/sdcpublications/pb_catia5_6.htm.** Click on the link labeled **Super Mileage** to start the download process to your download directory that you created (**C:\Temp\Download**). Note: The zipped file is 2 megabytes in size and therefore will take time to download.

2   Unzip The SuperMileage.zip File To Your Working Directory

Once you have successfully downloaded the **SuperMileage.zip** file to your download directory, you must then extract the **CATProduct** and **CATPart** files in order to use the **DMU Navigator**. Extract the files to the **Temp** directory and at the conclusion of the process, a directory called **SuperMileage** will be created in the **Temp** directory (**i.e. - C:\Temp\SuperMileage**).

Steps To Navigating The Assembly Using The DMU Navigator Work Bench

1   Entering the DMU Navigator Work Bench

In Lessons 1 and 6 you were taught two different methods of selecting a particular work bench. In this lesson you will be inserting an entire assembly as an **Existing Component** into the **DMU Navigator**. Follow the steps below to activate the **DMU Navigator Work Bench.**

    1.1   Prior to inserting an **Existing Component (SuperMileage.CATProduct)** into the **DMU Navigator**, the first step is to enter the **DMU Navigator Work Bench**. To do this, select the **Start** pull down menu from the top of the screen as shown in Figure 9.2.

    1.2   From the **Start** pull down menu, select the **Digital Mockup** option (Figure 9.2).

    1.3   From the **Digital Mockup** menu, select the **DMU Navigator** option. This will bring you into the **DMU Navigator Work Bench**.

NOTE: The name at the top of the **Specification Tree** is "**Product 1.**" You might have noticed that this applied to the **Assembly Design Work Bench** in Lesson 6.

Figure 9.2

2   Inserting Objects Into The DMU Navigator Work Bench

In Lesson 6 you learned how to insert detail parts to make an assembly. Although you can insert detail parts into a **DMU Navigator** session, during this lesson you will insert an entire assembly (**CATProduct**) as an **Existing Component** into the **DMU Navigator**. Follow the steps below to bring the **"SuperMileage.CATProduct"** assembly file into the **DMU Navigator Work Bench**. The following steps explain how this is done.

    2.1   The top of the **Specification Tree** must be selected before objects can be inserted into the **DMU Navigator Work Bench**. The top of the **Specification Tree** is labeled as "**Product1.**"

    2.2   Use your right mouse button to activate the menu, then scroll down and select the **Existing Component** icon (Figure 9.3).

Figure 9.3

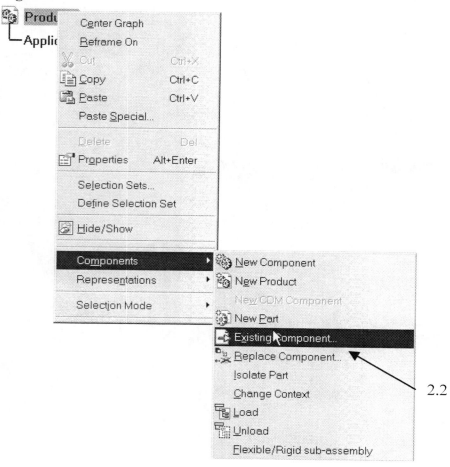

    2.3   The **Insert an Existing Component** window will appear (Figure 9.4).

Figure 9.4

2.4   In the **Insert An Existing Component** (Figure 9.4) window, find the
       file named "**SuperMileage.CATProduct.**" Select the **Open** button.
       The assembly should appear on the screen. If it does not, then select
       the **Fit All In** icon 🔲 and then select the **Iso** icon 🔲 from the **View**
       tool bar. Your screen should show the **SuperMileage** assembly
       similar to Figure 9.1.

3 Navigating Through The Assembly Using The Fly Mode

Up until this point you have been able to manipulate your part and/or assembly in the
Examine Mode. You have done so by using your mouse buttons to **Rotate**, **Pan** and
Zoom parts and assemblies. Now you will learn to fly freely through a digital
mockup of the **SuperMileage** assembly. You will use your mouse buttons to start the
Fly Mode, learn to use the mouse like a joystick, while controlling the speed with the
Page Up and **Page Down** keys on your keyboard (to the left of your numeric
keypad). The steps below will show you how to navigate using the **Fly Mode** from
the **Front View** of the assembly. Once inside the assembly, we will stop to use
several tools on the **Viewing** tool bar to give you a better perspective on how the
DMU Navigator can be used in the design review process. You will then repeat the
steps starting from the **Back View** to give you more experience in the **Fly Mode.**

3.1   First, turn off the **Specification Tree** to free up screen space by
       pressing the F3 key (Note: also use **View** – **Specifications** pop down).

3.2   Look at the assembly to verify that it is not one gray shaded mass, but
       has the materials files activated. If not, then select the **Applied
       Customized View Parameters** icon located in the **View** tool bar.
       Refer to 7.10.6 in the **CATIA Standard Menu and Tools** section in

the **Introduction** section of this book.

3.3   Select the **Sets The Fly Mode** icon ,which is located on the far
        left of the **View** tool bar. Look at the same location of the tool bar and
        you will see a new icon appear called the **Sets The Examine Mode**
        . Select this icon to take you out of the **Fly** Mode so we can make
        a small change to help in the visualization of the assembly.

3.4   Select the **Horizontal Ground** icon which will then display a
        black grid underneath the **SuperMileage** assembly (Figure 9.5)

Figure 9.5

3.5   Select the **Front View** icon ⊡ in the **View** tool bar. This will re-orient the assembly so you can move the **Horizontal Ground** closer to the bottom of the vehicle.

3.6   Place your cursor over the **Horizontal Ground** and move the ground plane closer to the bottom of the vehicle. Move the ground plane by holding down the left mouse button and moving your mouse (Figure 9.6).

Figure 9.6

place cursor (hand) on ground and move upward

3.7

3.8

3.6 move **Horizontal Ground** to here

3.7   Select the **Fit All In** icon ⊞ to position the vehicle and the **Horizontal Ground** in the middle of your window.

3.8   Select the **Sets The Fly Mode** icon and place your cursor on the **Horizontal Ground** and centered between the two wheels.

3.9   For the first **Fly Mode**, <u>DO NOT</u> move your mouse. While holding down the **Middle** mouse button, quickly tap the **Left** mouse button and continue to hold down the **Middle** button. Watch the vehicle fly over your head on the screen similar to Figure 9.7.

NOTE: A small white direction arrow and a circular target site appear on the **Horizontal Ground**. The large **Green Arrow** indicates direction controlled by the mouse and current speed. Speed can be controlled by quickly tapping the **Page Up** and **Page Down** keys.

Figure 9.7

forward
direction
arrow and
target site

Speed Control icons (or use **Page Up** and **Page Down** keys)

3.10   Select the **Fit All In** icon and then select the **Front** icon to position the vehicle and the **Horizontal Ground** in the middle of your window once again.

3.11.   Repeat the exact same process in Step 3.9, but when one half of the vehicle passes overhead, quickly tap the **Left** mouse button to reverse the direction. Watch the vehicle move back over your head. Try changing directions several times until you get the feel of the mouse.

3.12.   Select the **Fit All In** icon and then select the **Front** icon to position the vehicle and the **Horizontal Ground** in the middle of your window once again.

3.13.   Repeat the process as in Step 3.9, but this time you will move your mouse like a joystick to simulate left and right and up and down. Watch how the large **Green Arrow** changes shape in relation to the movement of the mouse.

3.14.   Select the **Fit All In** icon and then select the **Front** icon to position the vehicle and the **Horizontal Ground** in the middle of your window once again.

3.15   This time, place your cursor exactly in the middle of the front axle and then start the **Fly Mode**. Fly through the front of the vehicle and stop when your screen looks similar to **Figure 9.8**.

Figure 9.8

3.16   Select the **Lighting** icon 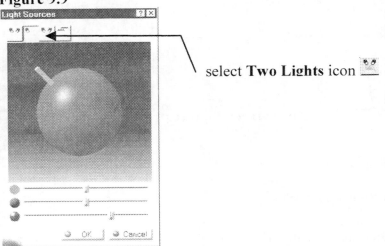 from the **Viewing** tool bar. This will open the **Lighting Sources** window.

3.17   The **Lighting Sources** window will appear on the screen (Figure 9.9). Select the **Two Lights** icon. Did you notice a lighting change?

Figure 9.9

select **Two Lights** icon

3.18   Close the **Lighting Sources** window and select the **Magnifier**
        icon from the **Viewing** tool bar.

3.19   The **Magnifier** window will appear on the screen. Position the
        window in the upper left hand corner as shown in Figure 9.9.1. Drag
        the **Green Square** over the shaft of the engine. This will put the shaft
        in the **Magnifier** window. You can grab one of the corners of square
        and drag it to enlarge its size.

Figure 9.9.1

resulting view of shaft

3.19 move **Green Square** over shaft

3.20   Select the **Measure Between** icon from the **Measure** tool bar.

3.21   The **Measure Between** window will appear on the screen (Figure 9.9.2).

Figure 9.9.2

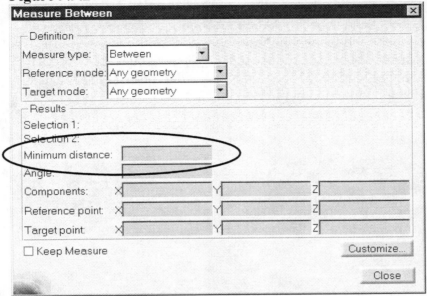

3.22   You will now measure the length of the shaft that sticks out from the engine. Take your cursor and select the circular geometry as show in Figure 9.9.3 and notice the results that appear in the **Magnifier** window. This same distance information appears in the **Minimum distance** area on the **Measure Between** window (Figure 9.9.2).

Figure 9.9.3

use your cursor to make two selections

3.23   Close the **Magnifier** and **Measure Between** windows.

3.24   Select the **Turning Head** icon from the **View** tool bar.
Place your cursor in the middle of the vertical tubing (refer back to
Figure 9.9.1) and hold down the **Left** mouse button. See if you can
rotate to your left using your mouse. Rotate until you can see the front
right wheel as shown in **Figure 9.9.4**. <u>Note</u>: if you release the **Left**
mouse button during the rotation, you need to reselect the **Turning
Head** icon in order to continue.

Figure 9.9.4

3.25   Turn off the **Horizontal Ground** and the select
the **Isometric View** and then the **Fit All In** icons. Click two times
on the **Zoom In** icon then place your cursor directly over the hole
of the front wheel and then click on your **Middle** mouse button to
center the wheel on your screen.

3.26 Place your cursor over the **Red dot** on the **Compass** and drag it over the outside of the front wheel as shown in Figure 9.9.5. Next, select the horizontal axis with your cursor and pull the wheel away from the body as shown in Figure 9.9.6. If you make a mistake, simply press **Ctrl Z** to undo the previous movement; then try again. Return the **Compass** to its default position, select **View** – **Reset Compass**.

Figure 9.9.5

Compass

Figure 9.9.6

3.27   Select the **Translation or Rotation** icon from the **Move** tool bar.
        Notice that the **Compass** moves from the upper right corner of the screen
        to the front wheel area of the vehicle. The positive X-axis direction runs
        from the back to the front of the vehicle. Enter **−750** in the **Offset X** area
        of the **Move** window as shown in Figure 9.9.7. Now, use your cursor and
        select the back cover of the vehicle and the **Apply** button will activate in
        the **Move** window. Click on the **Apply** button and watch the back cover
        move away as shown in Figure 9.9.8.

Figure 9.9.7

Figure 9.9.8

3.28   Finally, close the **Move** window and press **Ctrl Z** <u>two</u> times to
        return the back cover and the front wheel to their original locations.
        Congratulations on using the **DMU Navigator**.

Lesson 9 Summary

The **DMU Navigator Work Bench** is so much fun it is easy to forget what a powerful
analysis tool it is. This work bench brings the assembly to life. This lesson covers a
portion of what this work bench can do. Now that you have the basic skills to get around
in the **DMU Navigator Work Bench**, explore the power, and have fun doing it!

Lesson 9 Review

After completing this lesson you should be able to answer the questions and explain the concepts listed below:

1. How could the **DMU Navigator** be used in the product review process?
2. How many tool bars are available in the **DMU Navigator Work Bench**?
3. What type of file did you insert as an "**Existing Component**" during this lesson?
4. What file extension does CATIA V5 give to **DMU Navigator** files?
5. What option under the **Start** pull down menu gives you access to the **DMU Navigator Work Bench**?
6. What tool inserts a part or assembly file into the **DMU Navigator Work Bench**?
7. While navigating through an assembly in the **DMU Navigator**, what button do you press to reverse the direction?
8. What two keys do you use to increase and decrease the speed of your fly through?
9. How do you move the **Horizontal Ground** grid if it is activated?
10. What is the primary difference between using the **Fly Mode** versus the **Walk Mode**?
11. What tool can you activate, that will allow you to enlarge a component on the screen in a separate window?
12. What is the name of the window that appears on the screen when you select this icon?
13. What tool can you use to pull parts away from the assembly along an axis?

Lesson 9 Practice Exercises:

Now that you have navigated one assembly in CATIA V5, you can strengthen your newfound knowledge by completing the following practice exercises using **CATPart** and **CATProduct** files.

1. Insert the "**Catiaframe.CATPart**" as an **Existing Component** into a new **DMU Navigator** session. First, while in the **Fly Mode**, activate the **Horizontal Ground** and zigzag your way through the exterior surface of the frame. Secondly, attempt to fly through the interior of the frame tubing as though you were entering a tunnel.

Catiaframe.CATPart

Horizontal Ground

fly through here!

2. Bring in a part or an assembly file in IGES format (.igs) from another CAD software package into the **DMU Navigator** and use the **Fly Mode**.

    Suggested steps:

    2.1   Open a file in your other CAD software package and look for either **File Export** or **File Save As** to see if you can save or export your file in ***.igs** format. Remember where you save this file so you can retrieve it in CATIA V5.

    2.2   Open the *.igs file in CATIA V5 and wait for the file to be translated into CATIA V5, then click on **The Fit All In** icon ⊞ to make sure the object appears on the screen. Save the file as a **CATPart** file.

2.3   Apply a material to the surface of your part and activate the **Applies Customized View Parameters** to display the material you selected.

2.4   Now enter the **DMU Navigator** and use the **Fly Mode** with your translated part from another CAD software package.

3. Learn to use the **Walk Mode**.   The **Walk Mode** works like the **Fly Mode** except your object stays on the ground.

Suggested steps:

3.1   Bring the **SuperMileage.CATProduct** file into the **DMU Navigator**.

3.2   Select the **View** pull down menu and then pick **Navigation Mode** then **Walk**. Look at the bottom of your screen to see the **Walk Mode** icon appear in the **View** tool bar.

3.3   You can repeat the process in Section 3, "**Navigating Through The Assembly Using The Fly Mode**", using the **Walk Mode** icon wherever the **Fly Mode** icon appears. Try this and see if you notice a difference in the two modes.

4. (Optional) - Learn to use the **DMU Navigator** with a Data Projection system connected to a computer that has **CATIA V5** loaded on it.

Suggested steps:

3.1   Bring the **SuperMileage.CATProduct** file into the **DMU Navigator**.

3.2   Turn on the Data Projection system and project the **SuperMileage** file for a simulated design review session. Use the **Measure Between** and **Magnifier** windows to double check measurements of individual parts. Use the **Hide** function to hide various parts during the design review. Example: hide the back cover of the vehicle to expose the engine!

3.3   Use the **Turning Head** icon to look around the inside of the vehicle.

3.4   Place the **Compass** on the side (use the side with the shaft) of the engine and try to slide it off the mounting platform away from the frame.

Lesson 10   Rendering Work Bench

Introduction To The Rendering Work Bench

In order for you to complete this lesson, you will again use the **SuperMileage** files as you did in Lesson 9. Using this assembly within the **Rendering Work Bench** will allow you to better understand how create environments (see Figure 10.1), add a camera, and define lighting in order to produce a realistic rendering. You will also learn how to add image files and/or materials to the walls of the environment

Figure 10.1 SuperMileage Rendered in a Box Environment

Lesson 10 Objectives

This Lesson will show you how to do the following:

- Introduce you to the **Rendering Work Bench** tools
- How to enter the **Rendering Work Bench**
- How to load a model into the work bench
- How to create an **Environment**
- How to define a **Light**
- How to add and image to the walls
- How to create a **Camera** and a **Shooting**

Rendering Work Bench Tool Bars

There are three standard tool bars found in the **Rendering Work Bench**. The three tool bars are shown below. The individual tools found in each of the tool bars are labeled to the right of the tool icon. This chapter will attempt to cover every tool found in the **Rendering Work Bench**.

The **Scene Editor** Tool Bar

Tool Bar	Tool Name (default)	Tool Type Options

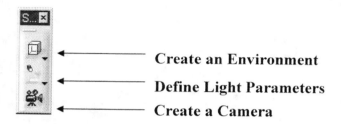

                             Create an Environment

                             Define Light Parameters

                             Create a Camera

The **Animation** Tool Bar

Tool Bar	Tool Name (default)	Tool Type Options

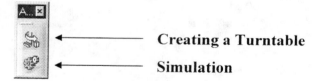

                             Creating a Turntable

                             Simulation

The **Render** Tool Bar

Tool Bar	Tool Name (default)	Tool Type Options

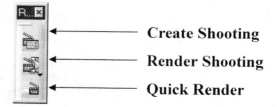

                             Create Shooting

                             Render Shooting

                             Quick Render

Bringing The Assembly Into The Rendering Work Bench

1   Entering The Rendering Work Bench

This lesson will follow the same process used in Lesson 9 for inserting a component. You will be inserting an entire assembly as an existing component into the **Rendering Work Bench**. Follow the steps below to activate the **"Rendering Work Bench."**

1.1   Prior to inserting an existing component (**SuperMileage.CATProduct**) into the **Rendering Work Bench** the first thing to do is enter the **Rendering Work Bench**. To do this, select the **Start** pull down menu from the top of the screen as shown in Figure 10.2.

1.2   From the **Start** pull down menu, select the **Infrastructure** option (Figure 10.2).

1.3   From the **Infrastructure** menu, select the **Rendering** option. This will bring you into the **Rendering Work Bench**.

NOTE: The name at the top of the **Specification Tree** is "**Product 1**". You might have noticed that this applied to the **Assembly Design Work Bench** in Lesson 6 and the **DMU Navigator Work Bench** in Lesson 9.

Figure 10.2

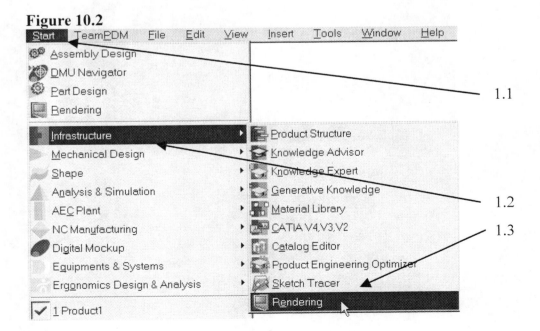

2   Loading Models Into The Rendering Work Bench

In Lesson 6 you learned how to insert detail parts to make an assembly and in Lesson 9 you brought the same assembly into the **DMU Navigator Work Bench**. You can insert individual part files, sub-assemblies and final assemblies into a **Rendering Work Bench** session. For this lesson your learning activity will focus on an entire assembly (**CATProduct**) brought in as an existing component into the **Rendering Work Bench**. Follow the steps below to bring the **"SuperMileage.CATProduct"** assembly file into the **Rendering Work Bench**. The following steps explain how this is done.

2.1   The top of the **Specification Tree** must be selected before objects can be inserted into the **Rendering Work Bench**. The top of the **Specification Tree** is labeled as "**Product1.**"

2.2   Use your right mouse button to activate the menu, then scroll down and select the **Existing Component** icon (Figure 10.3).

Figure 10.3

2.3   The **Insert an Existing Component** window will appear as shown in Figure 10.4.

Figure 10.4

2.4   In the **Insert An Existing Component** (Figure 10.4) window, find the file named "**SuperMileage.CATProduct**". Select the **Open** button. The assembly should appear on the screen. If it does not, then select the **Fit All In** icon ⊞ and then select the **Iso** icon ◙ from the **View** tool bar. Your screen should show the **SuperMileage** assembly similar to Lesson 9. The **Box Environment** will be added in the next phase of this lesson.

3   Creating An Environment

To better understand how to insert a camera and to apply light sources, you should first create an **Environment** around the object you are trying to render. There are three (3) types of **Environments; Box, Spherical** and **Cylindrical**. Figure 10.5 shows an example of each type of **Environment**. Follow the steps below to place the assembly in each of the three **Environments**.

Figure 10.5

       Box   **Spherical**   **Cylindrical**

3.1   Select the **Create Box Environment** icon in the **Scene Editor** tool bar.

3.2   Select the **Create Spherical Environment** icon in the same **Scene Editor** tool bar. If you have trouble locating it, remember to pick the black down arrow on the **Create Box Environment** icon!

3.3   Next, select the **Create Cylindrical Environment** icon

To see these three **Environments** within your **Specifications Tree**, you must expand the tree by clicking on **Applications** (+) and then on **Environment** (+). With the tree expanded, you need to return to a **Box Environment**. To do this, simply place your cursor over **Environment 1** in the **Specifications Tree**, click your right mouse button and scroll down and select **Environment Active**. Notice that this environment appears in yellow while the other two environments are gray. You will now use the **Box Environment** to experiment with managing walls, define lighting and materials within the environment, setting up a camera, and rendering a view.

3.4   Make sure you are in a perspective view from the pop down menu by selecting **View**, **Render Style**, and pick **Perspective View**.

3.5   With the **Supermileage** vehicle in the **Box Environment**, select the **Right View** icon and select the **Fit All In** icon. Pick the **Zoom In** icon three times to enlarge the view.

3.6   Next, expand the **Specifications Tree** to reveal the six walls of the **Environment 1** (Box) as shown in Figure 10.6. Click on the **Bottom** wall to make it active. It turns orange in color when active.

Figure 10. 6

3.7   Notice that the perimeter of the **Bottom Wall** is highlighted as shown
        in Figure 10.7. You can simply click on the **Bottom Wall** or any
        wall to activate it.

3.8   Now move your cursor over the **Bottom** area and look for
        a vertical arrow to appear.

Figure 10.7

                                3. 7   3.8

3.9   With your cursor over the **Bottom** wall, hold down the left mouse button and drag the **Bottom** upward until it almost touches the wheels of the vehicle.

3.10   Now select the **Isometric View** icon and then place your cursor over the **Bottom Wall** to continue moving the bottom closer to the wheels. Notice that if you get too close, the bottom of the wheels begin to disappear as shown in Figure 10.8. Position the **Bottom** wall so it is touching the wheels.

Figure 10.8

4　Defining A Light

Before we add a textured material and/or image to the walls of the **Box Environment**, you will create a **Spot Light** and position the light using the **Compass**.

4.1　Select the **Right View** icon and then the **Fit All In** icon.

4.2　Next, select the **Spot Light** icon ⬚ from the **Scene Editor** tool bar. Your screen should be similar to Figure 10.9.

Figure 10. 9

4.3　Use your cursor and grab the **Red Dot** at the bottom of the **Compass** and place it directly over the origin of the **Light** as shown in Figure 10.10.

Figure 10. 10

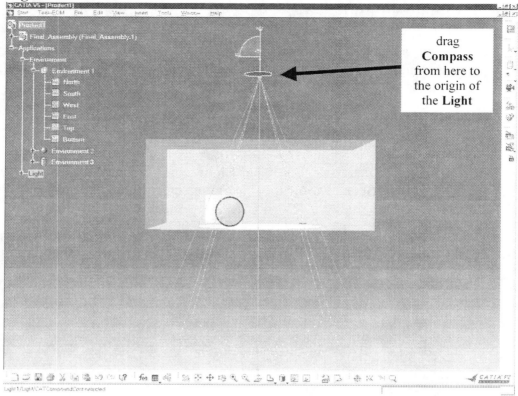

4.4   After placing the **Compass** on top of the **Spot Light**, click in
        Freespace and this **Lighting** symbol will appear above the
        environment under the **Compass**.

4.5   Change to the **Isometric View** and notice the **Light** projected the on
        the bottom of the environment. It <u>may not</u> be directly over the vehicle.

4.6   Use your cursor to click on the **Light** symbol to allow you to use the
        Compass (move one axis at-a-time: see **U** | **X** and **V** | **Y** on the bottom
        of the **Compass**) to position the light directly over the top of the
        vehicle as shown in Figure 10.11.

NOTE: When done positioning the **Light**, click on **Freespace** to get your
           Light symbol to appear and then use **View**, **Reset Compass** from
           the pop down menu to return the **Compass** to its original location
           in the upper right corner.

Figure 10. 11 Activate Light and Move Using Compass

4.7   With the **Compass** removed from the **Light** symbol, now reselect the **Light** symbol and move your cursor half way down the cone of light until you see a curved arc with arrows at each end appear, as shown in Figure 10.12. Drag and enlarge the cone to saturate the entire box environment with light.

Figure 10. 12

Use the Curved Arrow to drag the cone of light in order to expand the coverage in the entire environment!

5 Adding Images To The Walls

5.0   In order to see materials and images within a rendered environment, you will need to activate the **Applies Customized View Parameters** icon.

5.1   Select the **Apply Materials** icon and pick the **Other** tab. Look for the **DS Star** icon and drag this image onto three walls (**North, South,** and **West**), then select and drag the **Chessboard** image onto the **Bottom**. Close the **Library** window when done.

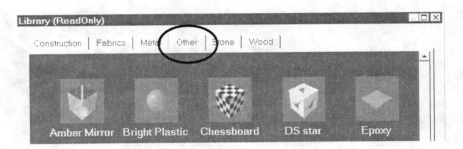

5.2 Now place your cursor over the **Bottom** wall and use your right mouse button to get the "**Contextual Menu**". Scroll down to <u>either</u> **Properties** or **Bottom object/Definition**. This will open the **Bottom Properties** window. Select the **Texture** tab and then click on the **Fit All in Wall** box. The **Chessboard** image should now become more visible on the bottom.

NOTE: <u>Repeat this process</u> for the **North, South** and **West** walls to reveal the **DS Star** image. The box environment will look like Figure 10.14.

Figure 10. 13 Bottom Properties

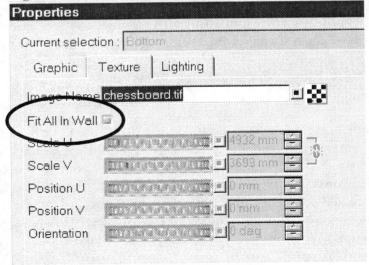

Figure 10. 14 Environment After Images Fit Walls

6   **Create A Camera And A Shooting**

You now have the **Supermileage** vehicle in a **Box Environment** with a light source. Before **Rendering**, we will add a **Camera** and create a **Shooting**, which allows you to select rendering parameters such as; which light sources to include, the environment of your choice, camera or current view. Lets begin by adding a **Camera**.

6.1   With the vehicle positioned similar to Figure 10.14, use your cursor to select the **Camera** icon from the **Scene Editor Tool Bar**. A large orange colored rectangle will appear around the perimeter of your screen and the **Specifications Tree** will now show the **Camera**. Expand the **Camera** (+) in the tree and then use your right mouse button to activate the **Contextual Menu** as shown in Figure 10.15, then select **Properties**. Once in the **Properties** window, select the **Lens** tab to see the **Camera** view of what is to be rendered.

Figure 10.15 Camera Properties And Lens View

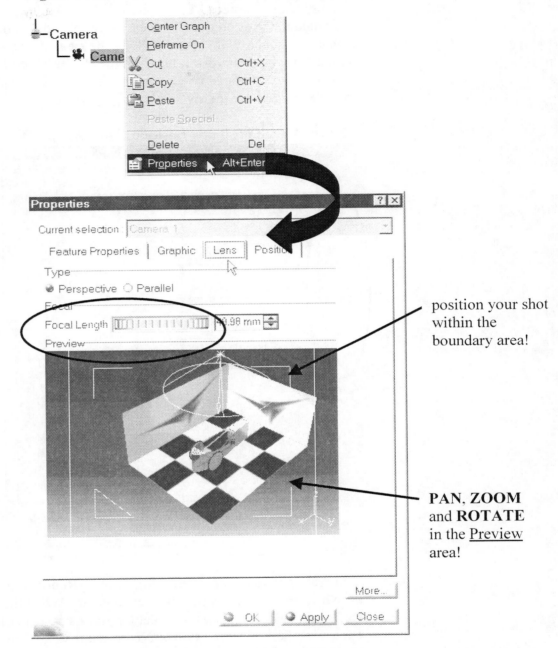

6.2 You can now adjust the view to be rendered within the **Preview** area of the **Properties** window using several methods. First, you can spin the dial using your mouse to adjust the **Focal Length** as shown above, or you can simply treat the **Preview** area like a regular CATIA screen and use the mouse to **PAN, ZOOM** and **ROTATE** the view to achieve the desired result.

6.3   Fine adjustments can be made if you select the **Position** tab. You
        can tweak one axis (X,Y,Z) at-a-time for either the **Origin** or the
        Target of the **Camera**. If you use this function, be sure to
        reference the axes on the **Compass** as your guide! You can make
        a change on an axis and then click on the **Lens** tab to see the result.
        You can go back-and-forth between the **Position** and **Lens** tabs
        until you are satisfied. Once you have the shot you want, click **OK**
        in the **Properties** window and <u>SAVE your file</u>.

Figure 10.16 Fine Tune Position Using X,Y,Z Dials

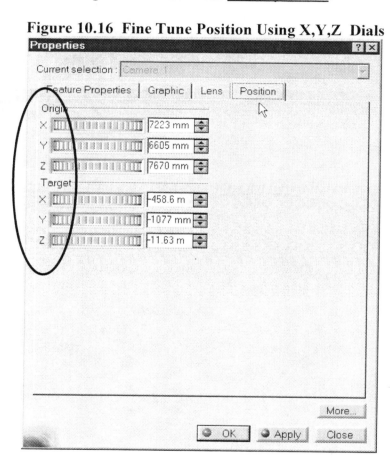

6.4   You are ready to create a **Shooting** prior to **Rendering**, so select
        the **Shooting** icon from the **Render** tool bar. When the **Shooting
        Definition** window appears, select **Camera 1** instead of **Current
        View** and then select the **Output** to be **On disk** as shown in Figure
        10.17. You could change the **Directory** and the **Frame** (file) if
        you so choose. After this, take a look at the **Quality** tab as seen in
        Figure 10.18. You can turn on/off textures and shadows, control
        the image output size and increase/decrease the geometry size used
        to calculate the model. Pick the **OK** button and **SAVE YOUR
        FILE** . . . <u>Note</u>: **Shooting 1** is added to the tree.

Figure 10.17 Shooting Definition - Frame Tab Parameters

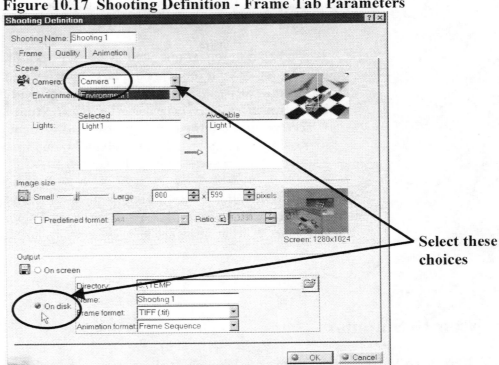

Select these choices

Figure 10.18 Shooting Definition - Quality Tab Parameters

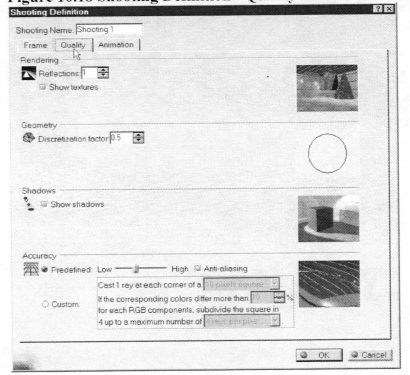

6.5   **You're ready to Render!** Use your mouse and select the **Render Shooting** icon from the **Render** tool bar.

NOTE: If you begin to render and your system crashes (due to the lack of memory or your model is too large), then you may need to reboot the software and change the **Properties** of **Shooting 1** in the **Specifications Tree** using the **Contextual Menu**. If the **Discretization Factor** (see Figure 10.18) is set at 0.5, try increasing to a higher number such as 3.0 and then **Render**. Each time you make a change, be sure to SAVE!

6.6   When the **Rendering** process is complete and the image appears, look for your saved image file. You can refer to Figure 10.17 to remind yourself what directory and file format you used.

Lesson 10 Summary

The Rendering Work Bench is a fun work bench, it allows you to complete your design. You will need to practice again-and-again the process of setting up your rendering the way you want it and to modify your current settings in the **Specification Tree**. You may not get it right the first time, and that's o.k. **So practice, practice, practice!**

Lesson 10 Review

After completing this lesson you should be able to answer the questions and explain the concepts listed below:

1. How many **Environments** are available in the **Scene Editor** tool bar?
2. How many tool bars are available in the **Rendering Work Bench**?
3. What other **Work Bench** prior to this lesson uses the same process for inserting an **Existing Component**?
4. What are the three types of **Lighting** available in the **Scene Editor** tool bar?
5. What option under the **Start** pull down menu gives you access to the **Rendering Work Bench**?
6. After **Rendering** an object, you can save the image in a variety of formats. One example of a format is known as a .tiff file. What are the three (3) formats available to you?

Lesson 10 Practice Exercises:

Now that you have **Rendered** one assembly in CATIA V5, you can strengthen your newfound knowledge by completing the following practice exercises; the first one using a **CATPart** file.

1. Insert the "**Engine.CATPart**" as an **Existing Component** into a new **Rendering** session. First, activate the **Apply Customized View Parameters** icon so the engine appears as though it were made of aluminum. Try an **Environment** <u>other than</u> **Box**.

2. Insert an assembly or part model <u>from another CAD software package</u> into a new **Rendering** session as an **Existing Component**. Be sure to look at all of the file types available (Pro/Engineer, Solidworks etc.). Try to apply a material too!

NOTES:

Workbook/CATIA V5 Terms And Definitions

The terms and definitions below are not your regular dictionary definitions. The definitions are based on how they are used in this workbook. The workbook definitions are included to help lessons to clearly communicate the meaning to the reader.

Blue Compass: A CATIA V5 tool used in the **Drafting Work Bench** to orient the orthographic layout of a part.

Boolean: Solids that share space.

CATDrawing: This is CATIA V5's file extension for files created in the **Drafting Work Bench**. The different file types (extensions) that CATIA V5 creates can be and are linked together. A **CATDrawing** is usually linked to a **CATPart** file. The purpose of the link is that the **CATDrawing** uses the part definition stored in the **CATPart** file to create the different views stored in the **CATDrawing** file.

CATIA V5: Computer Aided Three-Dimensional Interactive Application, Version 5. CATIA V5 is a product of Dassault Systemes and marketed by IBM.

CATPart: This is a CATIA V5 file extension. CATPart files are created in the **Sketcher** and **Part Design Work Benches**. This workbook at times refers to the part and/or file as a **CATPart**. The different file types (extensions) that CATIA V5 creates can be and are linked together.

CATProduct: This is CATIA V5's file extension for files created in the **Assembly Design Work Bench**. The different file types (extensions) that CATIA V5 creates can be and are linked together. Usually several parts stored in the **CATPart** files are used to create an assembly, stored in the **CATProduct** file.

Compass: A tool CATIA V5 uses to help move and/or manipulate the orientation of CATIA V5 parts. The location of the compass is by default the top right of the working screen. The compass looks similar to a sail.

Constraints: A method of parameterizing a profile sketch, part entity or assembly. The parameter determines the relationship of one entity to another entity, or a particular property of just one entity. A constraint looks and acts much like two and/or three-dimensional dimension.

Entity: Any kind of single, two or three-dimensional CATIA V5 creation. Entity is sometimes used interchangeably with element, geometry and/or component.

Extrude: Using the profile or periphery created in the **Sketcher Work Bench**, you pull the shape in the third dimension, and you make the flat, two-dimensional part, three-dimensional. This is accomplished in the **Part Design Work Bench** using the **Pad** tool. Lesson 1 and 2 talk about extruding the part or profile sketch, but they are referring to the **Pad** tool.

File: This is what the CATIA V5 creation is save in. The type of file CATIA V5 creates depends on the workbench it was created in. There are **CATPart** files, **CATDrawing** files and **CATProduct** files. CATIA V5 has more types of files, but this workbook only covers the three listed. CATIA V5 refers to a file as a document.

Geometry: Any kind of single or multiple, two or three-dimensional CATIA V5 creation. Geometry is sometimes used interchangeably with the word "element" and/or "entity".

Highlight: Highlighting an element is moving the mouse onto an element, selecting the left mouse button so the element is turned the default color, red. The element must be selected to highlight, so the word "select" is sometimes used interchangeably with highlight.

Icon: Represents the tool. The icon will have the same name as the tool but it is only a representation of the tool.

L Shaped Extrusion: The name of a specific part you create in Lesson 1. It is also referred to and includes its file extension, "**L Shaped Extrusion.CATPart**". The " **L Shaped Extrusion**" is sometimes referred to as the "part", during the particular lesson.

Normal: Perpendicular, 90 degrees to the reference element. Not parallel.

Part: This workbook uses the word "part" as a very general term meaning any kind of engineered entity. Part is at times interchanged with the words solid, object or wireframe. It is sometimes interchanged with the type of file it is such as a **CATPart**. It is sometimes interchanged with a specific part such as the "**L Shaped Extrusion.CATPart**".

Periphery: The outside edge and/or surface of a part. Periphery is at times used interchangeably with the word profile.

Plane: A graphical entity CATIA V5 uses to represent a defined two-dimensional slice of the CATIA V5 three-dimensional working space.

Profile: The profile is the cross sectional outline of a part. Profile is at times used interchangeably with the word periphery.

Prompt Zone: The bottom left of the CATIA V5 screen that has changing text, depending on the tool being used. You select a particular tool and CATIA V5 will prompt you on what selection and/or input is required.

Select: Moving your mouse button over the entity and clicking the left mouse button. This is sometimes used interchangeably with the word highlight.

Sketch: A two dimensional drawing consisting of lines, points, arcs ect. A sketch is usually created in the **Sketcher Work Bench** and/or the **Drafting Work Bench**.

Sketcher: Short reference for **Sketcher Work Bench**.

Solid: This word is sometimes interchanged with part. It is sometimes interchanged with the type of file, such as a **CATPart**. It is sometimes interchanged with a specific part such as the "**L Shaped Extrusion.CATPart**". A solid will not be interchanged with surface and/or wireframe.

Surface: A CATIA entity that describes a boundary in space but has no thickness. A surface can be stretched over a wireframe or extracted from a solid. A surface can look very similar to a solid. A surface can be shaded and enclosed to create a solid.

Tool: The operation that accomplishes a particular process, such as **Pad**. Tool is used as an action word in this workbook. The tool will have the same name as the icon that represents it.

Tool Bar: A designated bar containing one or more individual tools. The tool bar will be labeled according to the functions of the tools it contains.

T Shaped Extrusion: The name of a specific part you create in Lesson 2. It is also called out with its file extension, "**T Shaped Extrusion.CATPart**". The "**T Shaped Extrusion**" is sometimes referred to as the "part" during the particular lesson.

Wireframe: A combination of three-dimensional Open Body elements. Usually consists of points, lines and arcs. A wireframe cannot be shaded. The workbook will capitalize and bold the word wireframe when it is referencing a tool and/or a specific wireframe.

Work Bench: A specific part of the CATIA V5 software that is designed to accomplish a particular task. It has it's own screen layout, its own default tools and tool bars and files extension (document). For example the profile sketches are created in the **Sketcher Work Bench**. The specific screen and tool bar set up is specific to creating sketches. Usually the workbench name signifies what its particular task is.